# JUDICIAL REVIEW IN MEXICO
*A Study of the* Amparo *Suit*

LATIN AMERICAN MONOGRAPHS, NO. 22
INSTITUTE OF LATIN AMERICAN STUDIES
THE UNIVERSITY OF TEXAS AT AUSTIN

# Judicial Review in Mexico

## A Study of the *Amparo* Suit

*by*
RICHARD D. BAKER

*Published for the*
INSTITUTE OF LATIN AMERICAN STUDIES
BY THE UNIVERSITY OF TEXAS PRESS, AUSTIN AND LONDON

KGF2730
.B35
1971

International Standard Book Number 0-292-70105-5
Library of Congress Catalog Card Number 72-157411
© 1971 by Richard D. Baker
All rights reserved
Type set by G&S Typesetters, Austin
Printed by Capital Printing Company, Austin
Bound by Universal Bookbindery, Inc., San Antonio

*To my parents*
Dorothy and Leonard Baker

# Contents

# Preface

THE ATTAINMENT of constitutional government represents one of the most precarious triumphs of the modern state. The idea that political power and the manner of its exercise can and should be limited—subject to standard and rule in the interest of the individual—is assuredly not new. But the employment for this purpose of written constitutions, which rely for their validity upon no supernatural or extrahuman sanctions in religion or natural law, is a recent historical development. To argue that the achievement is a precarious one hardly requires documentation in an era which has witnessed unremitting conflict between the rule of law and the rule of will.

The essential concept of constitutionalism is to limit governmental power by a predetermined rule superior to all other enactments and legal precepts, and to confine governmental policy and action within regular and predictable channels. It follows that this idea cannot be made effective without a procedure for applying the constitution in specific cases, that is to say, for defending the constitution against outright violation and ill-founded interpretation of its provisions. To draft a viable constitution is a complex task, but this difficulty is outweighed by the problem of translating its terms into effective government and policy. The question of who is to have the final word about the meaning of the constitution has received two broadly different answers: either interpretation by a political agency, one of the regular branches of government or one especially created for the purpose, or interpretation by the judiciary, in some instances by a court created specifically for this purpose. It is recognized, of course, that no judicial agency can be the sole or, in the long run, the most important source of constitutional interpretation, development, and change. Ultimately a constitution must mean not what a court says it means but what the political forces active in the community demand that it mean. The experience of the United States demonstrates that an instrument of constitutional defense may act as a spur as well as a brake. Nonetheless constitutional defenses are essentially holding actions intended to perpetuate the spirit, if not always the letter, of the founders' intent. Consequently, effective constitutional defense serves as an instrument of conservatism, and its success can be estimated by the extent to which the principles of constitutionalism affect the inevitably changing substance of policy.

The development of constitutionalism in Latin America has encountered virtually insuperable obstacles; the persistent curse of Latin American government has been the alternation of instability and despotism. Constitutions have been written in abundance, but their common failing has been a radical inconsistency between their precepts and the real political forces they propose to organize and control. As a result, the constitution has only too frequently served as a mantle of invisibility masking the rapacity of a tyrannical officialdom.

Until recent times, Mexico has been in no way an exception to this rule of force interspersed with periods of civil war and anarchy: the short-lived empire of Iturbide, the long, confused reign of Santa Anna, the empire of Maximilian, the revolutionary and unsettling reform period of Juárez, the "scientific" regime of Porfirio Díaz. None of these offered a propitious soil for the growth of constitutionalism. Since the adoption of the Constitution of 1917, particularly after Plutarco Elías Calles' loss of influence over the presidency, Mexican political institutions, though lamentably deficient in many of the requisites of democracy, have demonstrated a stability and liberalism which give grounds for hope for the future of constitutionalism in that country.

After several decades of experimentation with a variety of devices that would defend the constitution, the Mexican constituent convention of 1856–1857, adopted the *juicio de amparo* ("the suit of protection"), an action based upon Alexis de Tocqueville's description of judicial review as practiced in the United States. Despite this and other foreign antecedents, *amparo* enjoys the advantage of being, in many respects, indigenously Mexican. *Amparo*, which was readopted in articles 103 and 107 of the Constitution of 1917, is an autonomous suit, summary in procedure. Its primary aim is to defend private persons against the violation, by unconstitutional laws or other arbitrary or illegal acts performed by public authorities, of the rights enumerated in the first twenty-nine articles of the Constitution. *Amparo* resembles several institutions in Anglo-American law, specifically the writs of habeas corpus, mandamus, error, and injunction. Since the suit is concerned exclusively with constitutional questions, it provides an explicit constitutional sanction for the practice of a form of judicial review. With the passage of time, the *amparo* jurisdiction has come to provide approximately 90 percent of the Supreme Court's transactions. This is in no way indicative, however, of the number of significant constitutional questions actually decided by the federal judiciary. Very few *amparo* suits touch upon matters of other than technical legal interest.

The *amparo* suit has been adopted in a limited form, usually as a type of habeas corpus, by several countries outside Mexico, among them El Salvador, Honduras, Guatemala, and Spain in the Republican Constitution of 1931. Mexican diplomatic delegations have also succeeded in implanting *amparo*, or provisions based upon it, in international conventions. The American Declaration of the Rights and Duties of Man, produced at the Interamerican Conference in Bogotá in 1948, contains a version of it, as does article VIII of the Universal Declaration of Human Rights drafted by the General Assembly of the United Nations in the same year. Finally, the Mexican *amparo* action has provided the basis for the procedural provisions of the European Convention for the Protection of Human Rights, signed in Rome in 1950.

The chapters that follow are not intended to provide a complete history of Mexico's constitutional experience or of its judiciary. The intent is to determine, primarily through analysis of cases, established precedents, and relevant statutes, the adequacy of *amparo* and various subsidiary institutions for the function of constitutional defense both in legal theory and in practice. These materials have been supplemented by study of the principal commentaries on *amparo*, by interviews with attorneys prominent in the field and members of the Supreme Court, and by discussion with and observation of the work of the secretarial staff of the Court. Since *amparo* is little known in the United States, more procedural material is included than would otherwise be necessary. This study must be considered preliminary rather than definitive, because of the vast amount of judicial materials available for study and the extensive application of *amparo*, which have necessitated a sampling procedure in research.

I am indebted to many people and institutions that have helped to make my research possible. Among the latter, my thanks are due particularly to the Southern Fellowships Fund, Inc., for a year's research grant, to the staff of the Hispanic Section of the Law Library of the Library of Congress, and to the secretarial staff of the Mexican Supreme Court.

In addition I wish to acknowledge my indebtedness to the late Professor W. W. Pierson and to Professor Federico G. Gil of the University of North Carolina for their advice and assistance in the direction of the research and their critical comments on the manuscript; Mrs. Helen L. Clagett, director of the Hispanic Section of the Law Library of the Library of Congress; Licenciado Antonio Martínez Báez, whose criticism of the manuscript was invaluable; Licenciados Raúl Carrancá y Trujillo, Ignacio Burgoa, Arturo Serrano Robles, and F. Jorge Gaxiola, all of whom were most generous with their time and advice during my research in Mexico; and to Supreme Court Ministers Felipe Tena Ramírez and Agapito Pozo. I am, of course, entirely responsible for errors of fact and interpretation that may have been committed.

# JUDICIAL REVIEW IN MEXICO
*A Study of the* Amparo *Suit*

## Chapter I

# The Origins of Constitutional Defense in Mexico

IN A STUDY of the first half century of its independence, Mexico confronts the student of its political institutions with a welter of constitutions, constitutional projects, and manifestos proclaimed in justification of every manner of revolution, civil war, and coup d'état. After the long experience of royal absolutism and with a population largely illiterate and impoverished, this was a society intrinsically incapable of setting out steadfastly upon the path of constitutional government. It could only plan and aspire and, through the impetus imparted by its abler and more devoted public men, gradually establish institutions adequate to its own peculiar circumstances. The process has been difficult and the effort still not completely successful.

Given the violence and instability of the period, we must look for an emerging theory of constitutional defense rather than for its practical achievement. The first endeavors are ambiguous and uncertain, but as we proceed from the day of Hidalgo to the reestablishment in 1865 of the Constitution of 1857, there is an evolution in the sophistication of the means proposed and adopted. With the creation of the *juicio de amparo* (*"amparo* suit"), although far from perfect as an instrument of inclusive constitutional defense, an institution finally appears capable of taking root in Mexican soil and developing to whatever extent the changing exigencies of society and politics permit.[1]

*Early Constitutions and Constitutional Proposals*

Surveying the confusing panorama of the Mexican independence movements, it is difficult to settle upon a point at which to pick up the thread of constitutional development. The first constitution officially promulgated in Mexico was the Spanish Cádiz Constitution of 1812, in effect though incompletely during the years 1812–1814 and 1820–1821.[2] The independence movements of Hidalgo and Morelos produced a constitutional project, the *Elementos Constitucionales de Rayón,* circa 1811, and the more finished Constitution of Apatzingán in 1814. The first of these, the work of Hidalgo's successor, Ignacio López Rayón, was little more than a collection of constitutional ideas and contained nothing pertinent to constitutional defense.[3] The Constitution of Apatzingán was a more polished effort and included some rudimentary provisions for its own maintenance, apparently derived from the Cádiz Constitution. Article 237 prohibited any amendment until a constituent convention could be convened and a permanent constitution drafted; in the meantime it authorized any citizen to protest against constitutional violations that he might observe. The manner in which this was to be done, the persons or governmental bodies before whom such objections were to be laid, and the action to be taken in such cases were not specified.[4] The constitutionality of legislation, and presumably its expediency, was subjected to a further and more practical control through the authority given the executive and the Supreme Court to express their opposition to legislation pending before the Congress.

---

[1] Since *amparo* has no satisfactory equivalent in legal English, the Spanish term will be retained.

[2] Felipe Tena Ramírez, *Leyes fundamentals de México, 1808–1957,* p. 59.

[3] Ibid., pp. 23–26.

[4] Ibid., p. 57.

The details of this procedure were not given, but since a second passage was specified for such cases it was evidently a veto power.[5] The Cádiz Constitution of 1812 was famous in its day as a repository of liberal principles, although to the modern reader its radicalism will not seem extravagant. Despite its other virtues, it offers us few mechanisms of defense. In articles 372 and 373 it provided that the Cortes, the legislative body, should, at the beginning of each session, consider any representations made about constitutional violations, provide the appropriate remedy, and enforce the proper penalties upon the person or persons responsible. The king could also be notified concerning constitutional infractions.[6] These provisions are similar to, and possibly derived from, the procedures of the medieval Cortes of Aragón, which was also obliged to give its first consideration to resolving and redressing grievances arising from the violation of *fueros*.[7]

Following the declaration of independence in 1821, Mexico was first organized politically under the *Bases Constitucionales* of 24 February 1822. This very brief document asserted the constituent convention's claim to possess and exercise full sovereign powers both for constituent and ordinary legislative purposes.[8] The *Bases* was not a constitution but a declaration of the intent to make one.

The *Bases* was soon followed by the *Reglamento Provisional Político del Imperio Mexicano*, promulgated in February 1823.[9] Although, as the title indicates, this was not considered a definitive constitution, it was a more complete and systematic document. The problem of defense was ignored, however, and the powers of the courts, even in the field of ordinary statutory interpretation, were limited. In the terms of section VIII of article 79, any questions about interpretation of laws that arose in the lower courts were to be transmitted to the Supreme Court and by the latter to the emperor, who would, in turn, consult the

---

[5] Ibid., articles 128, 129, pp. 44–45.

[6] Ibid., p. 103.

[7] Salvador Minguijón y Adrián, *Historia del derecho español*, p. 265. The term *fuero* has a variety of meanings, but here it refers to a body of laws or charter of privileges.

[8] Tena Ramírez, *Leyes fundamentales*, p. 124.

[9] Ibid., p. 122.

legislative power about its intent. Whether the Supreme Court was to avail itself of this procedure for resolving its own uncertainties was not made clear.[10]

## The Federal Constitution of 1824

The fall of Iturbide's empire, in 1823, again presented the problem of political organization. For the time, at least, the monarchical party was defeated, and political opinion divided on the issue of federalism versus centralism. With the former was associated the liberal thought of the day; with the latter the conservative tradition of the colony. The precarious result was a victory, in form, for the principle of federalism.

The new constituent assembly which met in November 1823, produced two charters, the *Acta Constitutiva de la Federación Mexicana*, which provided a temporary framework of government and assured adoption of the federal system, and, in 1824, the *Constitución Federal de los Estados Unidos Mexicanos*.[11] With the adoption of a federal organization, bringing in its train the problem of divided sovereignty, we find the first supremacy clauses explicitly written into a Mexican constitution. The supremacy clause in the *Acta Constitutiva* did not bind the state judiciaries but merely stated, in general terms, that the ratification of state constitutions would be delayed unil the completion of the general constitution in order to assure their conformity with its terms. There was, however, no indication of which persons or agencies would be responsible for determining this. The provisions of the Constitution of 1824 were more specific. They required the states to organize their governments in conformity with the general constitution and to observe and enforce within their territories the constitution, laws, and treaties of the federation, and empowered Congress to enact whatever enforcement legislation might be required. Of more interest is the succeeding clause which conferred upon the Congress an exclusive power to resolve any questions about the meaning of the constitution.[12]

---

[10] Ibid., p. 140.

[11] Ibid., p. 153.

[12] Ibid., pp. 158, 191, 193. The supremacy clause in the *Acta Constitutiva* is found

Although it is impossible to say whether the constituent convention intended to vest sovereignty in the Congress, this is the logical implication of this provision. In the light of the authority conferred upon the Congress any judicial control over constitutionality would appear superfluous. Nonetheless, article 137, section V, subsection 6, included within the jurisdiction of the Supreme Court cases dealing with infractions of the constitution and the laws of the union, subject to procedures to be established by statute.[13] These contrasting provisions are not necessarily incompatible in theory, but it is surprising to find them in the same constitution. The fact that the delegates to the constituent convention employed a translation of the United States Constitution as a guide in drafting their own might permit the inference that the inclusion of constitutional cases within the jurisdiction of the Supreme Court resulted from careless copying. The use of the phrase "infractions of the constitution," however, renders such a conclusion doubtful.[14] Taken by itself, this jurisdictional grant to the Supreme Court appears adequate to support the logical derivation of a system of judicial review. As it happened, the necessary enabling statute was never enacted, and the political conditions of the time were, in any event, far from favorable to such a development.[15]

The Constitution of 1824 remained in effect until 1835. It was the most influential of the early constitutions and remained a rallying point for both moderate and extreme liberals until the appearance of the Constitution of 1857.[16]

---

in article 24, that of the Constitution of 1824 in articles 161, sections I and III, 164, and 165.

[13] Ibid., p. 188.

[14] Ibid., p. 153. Tena Ramírez quotes Lorenzo de Zavala, president of the constituent convention, saying that a poor translation of the United States Constitution, printed in Puebla de los Angeles, circulated among the delegates and was used by them as a manual on how to write constitutions.

[15] Ignacio Burgoa, *El juicio de amparo*, p. 80.

[16] Felipe Tena Ramírez, *Derecho constitucional mexicano*, p. 493. In discussing these documents Tena Ramírez asserts that neither of them contained any provisions for their own defense. For the reasons given the author must disagree about the theoretical possibilities.

*The* Siete Leyes *of 1836*

In 1835 and 1836, the federal principle adopted in the Constitution of 1824 suffered an eclipse, and Mexico reverted in form, as it had remained in fact, to the centralism that had characterized its colonial existence. The Constitution of 1836, generally known as the *Siete Leyes*, provided the most exotic Mexican approach to the problem of constitutional defense by establishing the Supremo Poder Conservador ("supreme conserving power"). This odd institution, the most controversial of the proposals submitted to the convention, was envisioned as an arbiter that would constrain the three regular branches of government to strict adherence to the constitution. Despite the majesty of this conception, it was approved in the convention by only one vote.[17]

The Supremo Poder Conservador was made up of five members, serving staggered terms, elected by the Senate from lists of candidates previously selected by departmental electoral councils. On paper it was granted a fantastic range of powers over the procedures, policies, and personnel of government. In the general field of constitutional control it was authorized to nullify any legislation directly contravening an express constitutional provision—including acts of the executive—and any proceedings of the Supreme Court constituting usurpations of power. In the event of revolution, it was to reestablish the constitutional order, and constitutional amendments enacted by the Congress remained ineffective without its express sanction. This does not exhaust the catalogue of powers, which included such matters as suspending the Supreme Court under certain circumstances, suspending sessions of Congress, dismissing the ministry, and, perhaps most interesting of all, declaring the will of the nation when such information might be required. In none of these capacities, however, was the Poder Conservador authorized to proceed ex officio. In every case the request of one or more of the three branches of the government was required to set it in motion. To ensure a proper Olympian calm and impartiality in executing these functions, the Constitution stated that the Poder Conservador should be responsible "only to God and public opinion."[18] All

---

[17] Tena Ramírez, *Leyes fundamentales*, p. 202.
[18] Ibid., pp. 208–212, and article 12, pp. 210–211.

of its decisions were declared to be immediately obligatory and immune from question or objection. A failure to comply was high treason.[19]

To carry out these powers effectively in the absence of command over the armed forces—which the Poder Conservador did not have— would have necessitated not only a docile and law-abiding population but also a high order of integrity, impartiality, and political independence, for the successful exercise of great arbitrary power requires either force or faith or manifest justice. The Supremo Poder Conservador was inadequately supplied with these assets and was, in consequence, a resounding failure. During the five years of its existence, it was called upon to act only four times, and in none of these cases was a defense of constitutional provisions or principles directly at issue.[20] Despite its shortcomings, however, the Poder Conservador must be recognized as an excellent, if impractical, example of a political agency of constitutional defense, created primarily for this purpose and having otherwise no authority to operate in the ordinary business of government.[21] It also marked the first explicit recognition of the need for a workable means of enforcing constitutional limitations.

Judging from the prevalence of French culture among the Mexican educated class of that time and from their close family resemblance, the immediate ancestor of this rather preposterous institution was evidently the Sénat Conservateur, devised by the Abbé Sieyes for the French constitution of the year VIII.[22]

### The Proyecto de Reforma of 1840

By the middle of 1840, pressures for constitutional reform, originating chiefly among the federalists, resulted in the Chamber of Deputies appointing a special committee to study and recommend amendments to the Siete Leyes. The existing constitution prohibited amend-

---

19 Ibid., p. 211, article 15.
20 Tena Ramírez, Derecho constitucional, p. 494. On the operation of the Supremo Poder Conservador, F. Jorge Gaxiola states in León Guzmán y la Constitución de 57, p. 9, that it was never more than a compliant appendage of the executive.
21 Burgoa, El juicio de amparo, p. 58, asserts that the Supremo Poder Conservador was a true antecedent of the juicio de amparo, not in form, but in the essential purpose of constitutional defense.
22 Tena Ramírez, Derecho constitucional, p. 491.

ment until 1842, but the Supremo Poder Conservador, in November 1839, surrendered to public demand and decreed that the will of the nation permitted that this injunction be ignored.[23] The special committee included among its members José Fernando Ramírez, with whose individual report to the Chamber of Deputies we are chiefly concerned here.

The draft constitution, submitted by the committee majority, abolished the Supremo Poder Conservador but did not substitute anything in its place. The only provision which is relevant is contained in section XV of article 116, a reversion to the *Reglamento Provisional* of the Empire. This article obliged the Supreme Court to examine the doubts expressed by lower courts in interpreting laws and if, in its judgment, there were grounds for uncertainty, to transmit the law in question to the president for referral to the Congress.[24] According to the majority proposals, therefore, preserving the constitution rested with the self-restraint of the Congress and the executive.

The minority report (*voto particular*) submitted by José F. Ramírez did not hesitate to second the majority concerning the fate of the Supremo Poder Conservador. Ramírez objected to the extent of its powers and its total lack of responsibility. The inadequacies of this institution, however, did not distract him from the desirability of devising a method that would guarantee the enforcing of constitutional limitations. For this purpose he considered the forms of private litigation the most appropriate, and the judiciary, in consequence, the proper agency. Confessing that his proposal might seem strange at first glance, he recommended that the Supreme Court be empowered to determine the constitutionality of laws and executive acts; he asserted that this power of the Supreme Court of the United States, according to the report of a distinguished French author, went far to account for the peace and tranquility of that country.[25] The judiciary, he argued, is by its very nature set apart from the common stresses and temptations of public life, and because of this isolation possesses an impartiality that is in-

[23] Tena Ramírez, *Leyes fundamentales*, article 1, p. 244.
[24] Ibid., p. 276.
[25] The reference is to Alexis de Tocqueville, *Democracy in America*.

dispensable for the calm and just resolution of those great constitutional questions upon which the preservation of public peace and good order may largely depend. Members of Congress, ministers, the president himself, he added, are likely to be influenced in their public behavior by their private concerns or by those of their relatives and friends, and by the passions and caprices of politics. They are almost certain to evade constitutional limitations when these pressures are sufficiently strong. Although judges are not exempt from these influences, they are much less likely to be swayed by them because of that impartiality which is the ideal condition of their profession.[26] Specifically, he proposed that the Supreme Court should decide, by a trial utilizing the ordinary procedures of a lawsuit (*juicio contencioso*), the constitutionality of laws whenever the executive, the fourth part of the deputies and the third part of the departmental councils should challenge their validity. The same procedure was recommended for impeaching the constitutionality of executive acts by the Congress or the departmental councils. The procedures for trying such cases were to be prescribed by statute.[27]

Although the United States provided the model, which is evident from the references in the text of Ramírez' report, there was a decided departure from the original. The procedure prescribed is, to be sure, a suit; but it is a suit between official persons, a direct contest between two or more branches of the government in their official capacity. It is for this reason that Tena Ramírez asserts that this proposal simply intended transferring to the judiciary "the political functions possessed by the Poder Conservador."[28] Specifying the lawsuit form does not necessarily confer the real, legal characteristics of a suit. The points at issue in the suit suggested by Ramírez would have been the political relationships of the governmental branches and subdivisions, even in those cases in which the material effects of the law or executive act pertained only to private interests. The probable result in practice, assuming a willingness to employ the process, would have been an

26 Tena Ramírez, *Leyes fundamentales*, pp. 290, 297–298.
27 Ibid., pp. 301–302.
28 Tena Ramírez, *Derecho constitucional*, p. 494.

intragovernmental competition for power and prestige. It is unlikely that a court of law could survive for long in such a cross fire. The situation of a court is untenable enough in the United States system of judicial review, where the direct competition of powers is avoided by requiring juridically recognized private interests, material or otherwise, to initiate a suit. The constitutional issues involved may far transcend the private interests but legally and logically they are secondary consequences of these interests. Given the same situation, in the Ramírez' system the court might be called upon to declare that the president had usurped the powers of the legislature; whereas, under the United States system the judgment would release the complainant from having to comply with an administrative order on the grounds that it is unconstitutionally issued. The constitutional implications are the same, but the immediate issue is between the executive and the complainant rather than between the former and the legislative branch. That the private status of one or more of the parties may rest upon a legal fiction, or that a governmental agency, in its official capacity, is a party, does not alter the argument. Ultimately, of course, workability depends on the habitual readiness of both private parties and public agencies to submit the exercise of power to the formal channels of the law. Under the political conditions prevailing in Mexico at that time, Ramírez' system would have been no more unworkable than any other.

Despite these considerations, from this point on we find the idea of judicial control of constitutionality recurring more frequently and gradually gaining predominance.

## Manuel Crescencio Rejón and the Yucatán Constitution, 1840–1841

The paternity of the *amparo* action has been strenuously contested by Mexican legal scholars, with the preponderance of opinion at present favoring Mariano Otero, with whose contributions we will be concerned in examining the proposals of 1842, and the *Acta de Reformas* of 1847. There is no doubt, however, that Manuel Crescencio Rejón must be given credit for designing a judicial procedure of constitutional defense for the Yucatán State Constitution of 1841, and for naming this institution *amparo*.[29] That the *amparo* action, now exclusively associated with the federal judiciary, should first appear in a state constitution requires some explanation. During the period under consideration, the state of Yucatán not only was an adherent of the federal movement but also displayed a decided tendency to detach itself from the Mexican union altogether. In 1840, the legislature of 1834, which had been reinstated by a successful revolution, decreed the reestablishment of the state constitution of 1825, declared its continued adherence to the general constitution of 1824, and added that, until federal institutions were reestablished in the Republic, the State would remain separated from the union; its own government meanwhile assumed full powers.[30]

Impelled by the civil strife in the capital, Rejón found it advisable to retire for a time to his native state where he was called upon to head a committee charged with the task of drawing up a slate of amendments for the local constitution.[31] There were two other members of this committee, Pedro C. Pérez and Darío Escalante, but it is generally agreed that Rejón was largely, if not entirely, responsible for the content of the amendments presented to the legislature and the exposition of motives accompanying them.[32] Not only was he chairman of the

[29] Carlos A. Echánove Trujillo, "El juicio de amparo mexicano," *Revista de la facultad de derecho de México* 1 (January–June, 1951): 97–98.

[30] F. Jorge Gaxiola, "El amparo en un movimiento separatista," in *¿Una estatua para Rejón? Tres artículos sobre un mismo tema*, p. 9.

[31] Echánove Trujillo, "El juicio de amparo mexicano," p. 98.

[32] Isidro Antonio Montiel y Duarte, *Derecho público mexicano, compilación que contiene importantes documentos relativos a la independencia, la Constitución de Apatzingán, el Plan de Iguala, Tratados de Córdoba, la Acta de Independencia, cuestiones constitucionales tratadas por el Primer Congreso Constituyente, la Acta Constitutiva de los Estados Unidos Mexicanos, la Constitución de 1824, las Leyes Constitucionales de 1836, los Bases Orgánicas, la Acta de Reformas, la Constitución de 1857, y la discusión de estas constituciones*, III, 175. For the question of authorship see Echánove Trujillo, "El juicio de amparo mexicano" and *La obra jurídica de Manuel C. Rejón: Padre del amparo*, p. 3. Other comments are to be found in Gaxiola, *¿Una estátua para Rejón?*; Tena Ramírez, *Derecho constitucional*, pp. 495–497; Burgoa, *El juicio de amparo*, pp. 84–85. The phrase "exposition of motives" is a

committee, but the proposals are also in accordance with his known principles of political organization. One of the closest students of Rejón's career also affirms that the style of the project confirms his authorship.[33]

The draft was submitted for the consideration of the legislature in December 1840. In the exposition of motives, Rejón proposed to confer upon the Supreme Court the power to defend (*amparar*) individuals in the enjoyment of both their civil and political rights against the application of unconstitutional laws and decrees of the legislature and illegal actions of the executive. The original limitation, of applying constitutional defense to acts of the legislature, was altered in article 53 of the amendment proposals to include infractions of the constitution committed by the executive.[34] The extent of the powers Rejón wished to grant the Supreme Court is not completely clear either from the language of the exposition of motives or from the articles of the proposal itself. It seems, however, that he intended that the Court have jurisdiction to examine any legislation for unconstitutionality that might give grounds for an individual, private action at law. The most enlightening statement about this in the exposition stated "that the judges shall conform their decisions to the provisions of the fundamental code, disregarding such subsequent laws and decrees as may in any manner contravene its provisions."[35] Apparently then, it was intended that the Supreme Court exercise a general and inclusive power of constitutional defense, covering the organic sections as well as the bill of rights. As for the latter, the draft provided in article 63 that the judges of first instance have jurisdiction in cases involving the violation of the individual guarantees, listed, in nine sections, in article 62, except in cases where the violation was committed by a judicial official. In the latter case the superior of the court accused of the infraction was to

---

literal translation from the Spanish. It is a statement appended to a proposed statute or other legal draft explaining the necessity for such legislation and, normally, the manner in which the proposal is to function.

[33] Echánove Trujillo, "El juicio de amparo mexicano," pp. 98–99; idem, *La obra jurídica*, p. 3.

[34] Montiel y Duarte, *Derecho público mexicano*, III, 157–159, 172.

[35] Ibid., p. 158.

assume jurisdiction. In all cases the courts were to act only upon the motion of the injured party and exclusively for the purpose of making reparation for the injury suffered.[36] These, as will be seen, are essential characteristics of the present *amparo* action.

Although Rejón's purpose is clear, the intended operation is confused by a conflict of jurisdictions implied in articles 53 and 63. In the first of these, the Supreme Court was granted jurisdiction over constitutional and legal infractions committed by the legislature or the executive; in the second, the courts of first instance were to protect individuals in the enjoyment of their constitutional rights, but only the rights guaranteed in article 62. Is it assumed then that the Supreme Court was intended to take jurisdiction only in case of constitutional violations outside of the area covered by article 62; or were the Supreme Court and the courts of first instance intended to have concurrent jurisdiction over violations of the bill of individual guarantees?[37] The relevant articles also fail to make clear whether the Supreme Court was to have had appellate jurisdiction in cases initiated in the courts of first instance.

Rejón's argument for entrusting the judiciary with this great increase in its powers was approximately the same as that employed by José F. Ramírez; both were derived from Tocqueville's *Democracy in America*.[38] The following passage from Tocqueville, paraphrased in the exposition of motives, describes Rejón's understanding of the institution of judicial review and his expectations about its legal and practical results.

. . . as soon as a judge has refused to apply any given law in a case, that law immediately loses a portion of its moral force . . . The alternative is, that the people must alter the Constitution, or the legislature must repeal the law. The political power which the Americans have entrusted to their

---

[36] Ibid., pp. 172, 174.

[37] Ibid. Also, Tena Ramírez, *Derecho constitucional*, fn., p. 497, and Echánove Trujillo, "El juicio de amparo mexicano," pp. 101–102.

[38] Montiel y Duarte, *Derecho público mexicano*, III, pp. 157–158. The exposition of motives cites Tocqueville directly, and the substance of the argument, both about the suitability of the judiciary and the results to be expected, is a paraphrase of chapter six of *Democracy in America*.

courts of justice is therefore immense, but the evils of this power are considerably diminished by the impossibility of attacking the laws except through the courts of justice. If the judge had been empowered to contest the law on the ground of theoretical generalities, if he were able to take the initiative and to censure the legislator, he would play a prominent political part; and as the champion or the antagonist of a party, he would have brought the hostile passions of the nation into the conflict. But when a judge contests a law in an obscure debate on some particular case, the importance of his attack is concealed from public notice; his decision bears upon the interest of an individual, and the law is slighted only incidentally. Moreover, although it is censured, it is not abolished; its moral force may be diminished, but its authority is not taken away; and its final destruction can be accomplished only by the reiterated attacks of judicial functionaries.[39]

The result of an adverse decision on the constitutionality of a law, as described in this quotation and repeated by Rejón, is more consistent with the continental civil law system than with the common law system. In technical legal fact, a declaration of unconstitutionality by the United States Supreme Court produces no result beyond establishing res judicata in the case at hand; in practice it is usually the equivalent of repealing the offending statute. That the system, even under our rule of stare decisis, can work, as Tocqueville described it, is demonstrated, however, by the fact that the invalidation of segregation statutes has by no means terminated the practice of segregation. Rejón intended the former result rather than the latter, and, because of the lack of obligatory precedent in the civil law system of Mexico, the expectation was reasonable and justified. Apart from this divergence, the emulation of the United States was not as close as he apparently believed. Another conspicuous departure from the prototype was the proposal that the Constitution be defended by a separate and distinct suit concerned solely with the constitutional question, rather than following the United States practice, where this issue may be merely one

---

[39] From *Democracy in America*, by Alexis de Tocqueville, translated by Henry Reeve, and revised by Francis Bowen and Phillips Bradley. Copyright 1945 by Alfred A. Knopf, Inc., I, 102. Reprinted by permission of the publisher.

among many questions in litigation of any sort. This innovation also remains a characteristic feature of *amparo*.[40]

Following consideration by the Yucatán legislature, the amendment proposals were signed on 31 March 1841 and went into effect on 16 May. Both the draft proposals and the slightly altered final version voted by the legislature were printed in 1841.[41] The extent of circulation can only be speculated upon. It seems probable that Rejón's ideas on the subject of judicial review would have become generally known, considering the small size of the politically active community, his continued political importance, and the interest attaching to innovations in political thought, especially those relating to the desperate problem of stability.[42]

Rejón cannot be credited with establishing *amparo* as a federal institution, but there is no doubt that he deserves credit for introducing the idea into Mexican political thought in a well-developed and practical form. What then are the correspondences between the institution as conceived by Rejón and as it now exists? In summary these are (1) the selection of the judiciary as the agent of constitutional control; (2) the selection of a separate form of action, an independent suit, for the purpose of constitutional control; (3) the initiation of the action by the individual injured by an unconstitutional law or action; (4) the limitation of the suit to violations committed by public authorities; and (5) the limitation of the effect of the judgment to reparing the damage inflicted upon the injured party. Not all these features are as clearly delineated as this list might suggest, but the intent is clear. The major differences concern the federal aspects of *amparo,* which had no place in a state constitution, and the broad, and reasonably explicit, inclusion by Rejón of all parts of the constitution that may be subject to judicial action.

---

[40] Montiel y Duarte, *Derecho público mexicano,* III, 172, 174.

[41] Echánove Trujillo, "El juicio de amparo mexicano," p. 103.

[42] Echánove Trujillo, *La obra jurídica,* p. 16, states that the principal ideas contained in the proposals were also published in 1846 in a pamphlet entitled *Programa de la mayoría.*

*The Constituent Convention of 1842*

In 1842 Mexico turned again to the apparently insoluble problem of constructing a viable constitution. At the conclusion of its endeavors, the new constituent convention had to its credit three complete draft constitutions, none of which proved acceptable. Despite the ultimate futility of these labors, the drafts offer a number of interesting proposals for constitutional defense. The proposals submitted by the majority of the drafting committee contained a complicated mixture of the political and judicial approaches to the problem. Mariano Otero, with Rejón a contender for the title of father of *amparo*, was largely responsible for the minority plan, which also combined the political and judicial approaches. Its judicial provisions, however, more closely approximate the present *amparo* action than do those of the majority proposals.[43]

The majority proposals give the impression of carelessness in drafting, which results in a serious degree of ambiguity. Repeated readings leave one in doubt about whether the majority intended congressional legislation to be submitted to the test of constitutionality. If so, the responsibility was delegated to the Supreme Court, which was authorized, in article 112, section V, to hear cases involving infractions of the constitution in accordance with procedures to be established by statute. The only other explicit check on legislative discretion was the presidential veto. The extent and utility of the authority granted the Court is thrown into doubt, however, by article 114, which forbade it to hear cases involving the governmental or economic affairs of the nation or of the departments. Perhaps this was merely intended to exclude intragovernmental relations from judicial cognizance; but such a provision is susceptible to an interpretation that precludes the Court from dealing with any significant constitutional questions. In addition, the Court, along with those public officials directly responsible to the "Supreme Government," was empowered to suspend the execution of official orders on grounds of unconstitutionality or illegality. The de-

---

[43] Emilio Rabasa, *El juicio constitucional: orígenes, teoría, y extensión*, fn. 2, p. 233. This book is published in a double volume with the author's earlier work, *El artículo 14*. Also see, Tena Ramírez, *Leyes fundamentales*, p. 305.

partmental governors could also suspend orders inconsistent with the departmental constitutions, and the superior departmental tribunals could suspend orders emanating from the government or from the Supreme Court. The significance of the term "Supreme Government" is doubtful, but it seems to refer to the executive branch. It is also uncertain whether these suspensions were intended to be temporary or definitive; the former seems likely in the light of a further provision requiring that notice of suspension be given to the agency from which the order emanated and to the Senate.[44] Whatever the exact meaning of these provisions they seem to constitute an open invitation to administrative anarchy.

The division of powers, between the Congress as a whole and its two houses, also suffered from a lack of clarity. The national Congress was enjoined by article 79, section I, to annul departmental statutes in conflict with the Constitution or the general laws. Article 171, however, conferred upon the Senate an equivalent authority to determine the constitutional or legal status of local statutes, subject to the request of the departmental governors. According to article 171, it is permissible to conclude that both houses were required to take action ex officio. The Senate was also empowered to nullify acts of the executive when these violated either the general or departmental constitutions or the general laws. The Chamber of Deputies, in turn, received an exclusive authorization to annul acts of the Supreme Court, or of any of its chambers, but only in the event that these acts usurped powers or duties expressly assigned to the departmental courts or to other authorities.[45]

The minority proposals were somewhat simpler but more inclusive, although not free of ambiguity in the exact extent of powers and the demarcation of jurisdictions.

The state legislatures were granted general authority to determine the constitutionality of federal statutes. To initiate an examination, an allegation of unconstitutionality was to be laid before the Supreme

---

[44] Tena Ramírez, *Leyes fundamentales*, pp. 331–332, articles 173, 174, p. 339.

[45] Ibid., pp. 320, 335, 338. For the provisions on the obligations of departmental governors see article 148.

Court by three of the state legislatures, or by the president acting with the concurrence of his cabinet, or by eighteen members of the Chamber of Deputies, or by six senators. An allegation, from any of these sources, was transmitted by the Court to the state legislatures, which were, in turn, to decide simply whether the statute in question was constitutional. Whether the Court was expected, or even permitted, to express its own opinion on the question of constitutionality is not clear, but its role seems to have been viewed as exclusively administrative. Oddly enough, the draft did not specify the size of the majorities needed, either within a given legislature or among the entire number of legislatures.[46]

The constitutionality of state legislation, in conformity with the minority proposals, was subject to examination by the federal Congress, presumably acting on its own initiative. The extent of congressional powers upon the constitutionality of executive acts, state or federal, remained more uncertain. The Chamber of Deputies was explicitly authorized to suspend acts of the government under certain circumstances while deciding whether there were grounds for impeachment, but the constitutional implications of this are not clear. The Congress as a whole enjoyed a more general authority, which might be construed as relevant to this question, through its responsibility to preserve the constitutional order within the federation and to ensure that the states complied with their constitutional obligations.[47]

For the protection of the individual rights granted by the Constitution against infractions committed by the legislative or executive branches of the states, the minority report abandoned political instrumentalities and turned to the judiciary. This power was not extended, however, to violations committed by the federal Congress or executive, nor was the nature of the process to be used by the Court specified. This jurisdiction was limited exclusively to the Supreme Court, but the superior tribunals of the states were permitted to suspend the execution of the offending act or law at the time that the plea was received by the

---

[46] Ibid., article 8, section II, p. 368.

[47] Ibid., article 35, section II, and article 81, sections III and IV, pp. 357, 368–369.

Court. Violations committed by the courts themselves are nowhere mentioned in the constitutional draft; presumably, if these could be contested at all, it would have been through the ordinary process of appeal. The questionable factor here is the consistency of this jurisdiction with the general congressional capacity to annul state legislation on the grounds of constitutionality. It is logical to suppose that the two would have operated concurrently—the Supreme Court providing relief for the individual complainant, the Congress issuing declarations of universal applicability.[48]

The tendency to view civil rights as the sphere of judicial intervention was an anticipation of the *amparo* suit, as was also the provision for suspending the offending act or law. In other respects, however, the minority proposals were both too limited in scope and too uncertain in application to compare with the detailed presentation made by Rejón in 1840.

Neither of the draft constitutions met with the approval of the convention; therefore, a third, and final, project was elaborated and presented for discussion. This last and equally futile attempt to reconstitute the Mexican commonwealth was essentially a combination of the first two proposals. In the matter of constitutional defense the original majority recommendations were chiefly followed. The minority position prevailed, however, on civil rights and their judicial protection.[49]

### *The* Bases Orgánicas *of 1843*

The various proposals advanced in 1842 failed to meet the exigencies of the times, or more accurately, those of General Santa Anna; thus another constitution, the *Bases Orgánicas*, made its appearance in 1843. José Fernando Ramírez, whose contributions to the theory of judicial review were noted in dealing with the convention of 1840, was a member of this constituent assembly; since he did not succeed in moderating the unitary principles of political organization embraced

---

[48] Ibid., article 81, section I, p. 368.
[49] Ibid., articles 140, 141, 143, 144, 147, and 150, pp. 400–401. The latter article corresponds exactly to article 81, section I, of the minority report.

by its majority, he resigned and cannot be considered to have appreciably influenced the content of the new constitution. The *Bases* were promulgated in 1843 and remained more or less in force for a little over three years.[50]

The only provisions for constitutional defense were those set forth in article 66, section XVII, and article 142, section I. The former empowered the Congress to annul decrees of the departmental assemblies because of unconstitutionality or inconsistency with general legislation. The latter obligated the departmental governors to transmit to the Congress any acts of the assemblies that they deemed invalid for either of these reasons. The Constitution was not explicit on the point, but, failing the action of the governor, the Congress was presumably capable of acting upon its own initiative.[51]

## The Acta de Reformas *of 1847*

The *Acta de Reformas* of 1847 marks the first constitution to institute the *amparo* action on a national basis, with the essential legal characteristics it still displays. This achievement must be attributed to Mariano Otero, whose intransigent insistence upon the adoption of substantial amendments to the Constitution of 1824, despite the imminent arrival of General Winfield Scott's army, succeeded in swaying the majority to his position.

As the reference to the Constitution of 1824 indicates, the federalists had again come to the fore but were separated into contending moderate and extreme factions. The ubiquitous Santa Anna, having been rescued by the federalists from exile in Cuba, now adopted federalist principles. The Constitution of 1824 was exhumed, dusted off, and reestablished, on a temporary basis, as the fundamental law of the Republic, while a congress was convened to amend or replace the old constitution and to legislate meanwhile for the country. In addition to Otero, the drafting committee appointed by the Congress included one other person with whom we have been concerned, Manuel Crescencio Rejón, originator of the *amparo* provisions of the Yucatán

---

50 Ibid., pp. 403–404.
51 Ibid., pp. 415–428.

Constitution of 1840. In February 1847, a group of thirty-eight deputies moved to readopt the Constitution of 1824 in its entirety, postponing amendments until they could be proposed and ratified in the manner provided in the Constitution itself. The majority of the drafting committee agreed with this proposal and stated so in the majority report presented on 5 April 1847. Rejón interestingly enough, pleading the situation posed by the approach of the invading American troops, was included in this majority. The committee majority did insist, however, that the existing Congress undertake to make the necessary amendments as soon as the situation permitted, departing, consequently, from the amendment procedure prescribed in the 1824 Constitution.

Accompanying the majority report was Mariano Otero's celebrated dissenting report. On 16 April the Congress rejected the majority recommendations, and on the twenty-second began the discussion of Otero's proposals, which were chiefly accepted by the latter part of May.[52]

Otero's recommendations on *amparo* were laid down in article 19 of his dissenting report. Since this article contains the defining formula that still characterizes the scope and limits of the institution, it is worth quoting in full. "The tribunals of the Federation will protect (*ampararán*) any inhabitant of the Republic in the exercise of the rights granted to him by this Constitution and the constitutional laws, against any attack of the Legislative and Executive Powers, whether of the Federation or of the States, *limiting themselves to affording protection in the special case to which the complaint refers, without making any general declaration as to the law or act on which the complaint is based.*"[53]

Compared to the inclusive provisions of the Yucatán Constitution, the *amparo* projected by Otero is decidedly restricted in scope. Judicial cognizance of constitutional questions was limited exclusively to civil rights, and these rights were not explicitly defined in the Constitution itself. Instead, Otero provided that the rights of man, which he listed in general terms as liberty, security, property, and equality—rights to

[52] Ibid., pp. 439–443.

[53] Ibid., p. 471. These provisions constitute article 25 of the *Acta Constitutiva y de Reformas*, p. 475. Italics added.

be enjoyed by every resident of the republic without exception—were to be defined in detail and established legally by statute. This statute, however, was to enjoy the status of a "constitutional law," subject neither to alteration nor to repeal without a waiting period of six months between the presentation of the proposal and its debate. In the exposition of motives appended to his constitutional draft, Otero attached considerable importance to the superior status to be enjoyed by this legislation over other secondary laws. He justified the lack of detail in the constitution on the grounds that only a statute could be sufficiently explicit to adequately cover the rights that needed to be established and protected.[54] It should be noted that, contrary to the practice later instituted in the Constitution of 1857 but consistent with the proposals of 1842, violations of guarantees by the judiciary were not included within the scope of *amparo*. One can only assume that the ordinary course of appeal was to provide for this contingency. In prescribing the defense of statutory as well as constitutional rights, Otero, like Rejón before him, helped lay the foundations for one aspect of the control of legality that has increasingly characterized the modern practice of *amparo* but is only incidentally and indirectly related to the function of constitutional defense. It will be seen in more detail later that the control of legality—a function of *amparo*—really covers two dissimilar types of activity, both based on explicit constitutional guarantees; the examination of administrative orders to determine whether they are properly founded in law, and the examination of judicial decrees and arbitral awards to determine whether they are founded on a proper selection, application and interpretation of law. The latter is properly a variety of cassation and was obviously not included within the scope of the *amparo* action devised by Otero.

Despite the limitations noted, this proposal is a manifest improvement over that of the minority report of 1842, particularly in the precision of the defining formula and the extension of jurisdiction to federal as well as local authorities.

For the preservation of the federal system and the defense of the

---

[54] Ibid., articles 4 and 20, pp. 469, 471, and pp. 462–463. Also, Burgoa, *El juicio de amparo*, p. 139.

organic sections of the constitution, Otero reverted to the political modes of control introduced by previous constitutions and described in his own minority report in 1842. In the exposition of motives he asserted the necessity of granting the federal Congress the right to annul state laws that violated the general constitution or federal statutory law. On the other hand, for the protection of the states, the local legislatures were to be granted the power to annul unconstitutional federal legislation. "In this manner," he asserted, "each state is subjected to the union and *the states as a group will be the supreme arbiter of our differences and the true conservator of our institutions.*"[55] Considering that he commended the defense of civil rights to the judiciary, largely in accordance with Tocqueville's arguments on the desirability of avoiding direct clashes of governmental branches and subdivisions, it is difficult to see why the same arguments should not have applied to the general defense of the Constitution.[56]

Emilio Rabasa contends that Otero was unfamiliar with the American practice of judicial review, since otherwise he would hardly have adopted the political system of defense described here. He concludes that, on the constitutionality of laws not directly attacking civil rights, Otero saw only a question of politics whose remedy should likewise be political and thus could not properly be a subject for judicial inquiry. Had these provisions been reduced to practice, a conflict of jurisdictions between the Congress, or the state legislatures, and the Supreme Court would have arisen, since these legislative bodies were also competent to act on legislation affecting civil rights.[57] Having considered the concrete proposals of both Rejón and Otero, it is possible to draw some conclusions about their contributions to the development of *amparo*.[58]

[55] Ibid., p. 464.

[56] Ibid., pp. 464–465, 471, 474–475. The procedures for dealing with this type of constitutional violation are covered in articles 16, 17, and 18 of Otero's draft, corresponding to articles 22, 23, and 24 of the *Acta Constitutiva y de Reformas* as adopted. The procedure for dealing with unconstitutional acts of the federal Congress is taken directly from article 81, section II, of the minority report of 1842 and, as adopted, differs only in a minor matter of phrasing.

[57] Rabasa, *El juicio constitucional*, pp. 236–237.

[58] There is an extensive controversial literature on this subject in Mexico. Some

There is no denying Rejón's priority in time; but, because of the indebtedness of both men to Tocqueville for the basic idea of judicial defense of constitutionality, this does not deserve to be greatly emphasized. Rejón must, however, be credited with the preliminary adaptation of the idea to Mexican conditions and with foreshadowing some elements which have become characteristic of the *amparo* suit. His conception of its role within the constitutional system was also broader and more inclusive than was Otero's. Nonetheless, it is to Otero that the greater degree of credit properly belongs. With the opportunity of impressing his views upon the constitutional organization of the nation, Rejón, as we have seen, temporarily abandoned his own invention. The inclusion of *amparo* in the *Acta de Reformas* was a tribute to Otero's persistence. Of greater significance in the long run was Otero's creation of a precise juridical formulation within which *amparo* was capable of functioning and adapting to a political environment that has been, on the whole, unfavorable to the evolution of judicial power. It is probably true that he neither anticipated nor intended that *amparo* play any considerable part in general constitutional defense. That it has come to do so to a limited degree must be attributed partly to the apparent political innocuousness that Otero gave it, which permitted it to survive and take root. Between Rejón and Otero, the fairest conclusion is probably that expressed by Felipe Tena Ramírez, who said that "Otero's will was placed at the service of Rejón's thought."[59]

The implementing and regulatory statute prescribed by the *Acta de Reformas* was never enacted, although a bill was drafted and formally proposed in February 1852 by Lic. José Urbano Fonseca, the minister of justice. The final return to power of Santa Anna prevented action being taken on this measure.[60] Despite the failure to enact the regula-

---

of the more interesting comments are to be found in Burgoa, *El juicio de amparo*, pp. 84–89; Echánove Trujillo, "El juicio de amparo mexicano" and *La obra jurídica*; Gaxiola, *Mariano Otero, creador del jucio de amparo*, and *¿Una estátua para Rejón?*; Rabasa, *El juicio constitucional*, pp. 230–237; and Tena Ramírez, *Derecho constitucional*, p. 499.

[59] *Derecho constitucional*, p. 499.

[60] The exposition of motives and the text of the bill are reprinted in José María Lozano, *Tratado de los derechos del hombre: Estudio del derecho constitucional*

tory act, the *amparo* provisions of the *Acta de Reformas* were not without practical effect. A considerable number of complaints were filed, but these were chiefly rejected for lack of jurisdiction in the absence of the regulatory statute. Two cases are on record, however, of *amparos* granted by two district judges in San Luis Potosí and Saltillo in 1849.[61]

## The Legal Origins and Antecedents of Amparo

We have been concerned thus far with tracing the appearance of a number of systems of constitutional defense in the rapid succession of Mexican constitutions and constituent conventions. With the creation of the *amparo* suit, the solution of this constitutional problem, if there is one, was established. Following the reestablishment of the republican government in 1865, *amparo* began the vertiginous growth that has led it, at the present time, to its preeminent position among the federal legal forms of action; this growing importance has led Mexican publicists to devote much effort to discovering its origins and antecedents. Those who assert the antiquity of *amparo* have concentrated their search primarily on Roman, Spanish, colonial, French, and English legal institutions.

Since Mexico shares in the civil law tradition of continental Europe, a search for precedents in the Roman law is natural, although it has not proven notably fruitful. The only institution of the Roman law frequently cited as analogous to *amparo* is the praetorial interdict *de homine libero exhibendo*. This instrument provided for the temporary restoration of physical liberty to a person held under restraint by a private party, while the justification for the duress was tried by separate process. The only resemblance to *amparo* lies in the matter of personal liberty. The private status of the respondent in this action was wholly

---

patrio en lo relativo a los derechos del hombre, conforme a la Constitución de 1857 y a la ley orgánica de amparo de garantías de 20 de enero de 1869, pp. 425–427.

61 For details, including the text of one of these *amparos*, see Suprema Corte de Justicia, *Homenaje de la Suprema Corte de Justicia de la Nación, en nombre del poder judicial de la federación, al Código de 1857 y a sus autores, los ilustres constituyentes*, p. 151.

without parallel in *amparo*, where the complaint is always directed against a public authority.[62] Under these circumstances there is little reason to consider the Roman interdict as an antecedent of *amparo*, and there is no justification for citing it as a source.

The law of Spain, or more accurately, that of the kingdom of Aragón, offers more persuasive correlaries. The institutions commonly cited as precedents, or sources, for *amparo* are the *cuatro procesos forales*, and the court of Justicia Mayor. Oddly enough, the Cortes of Aragón, which could have supplied the inspiration for articles 372 and 373 of the Cádiz Constitution of 1812 and, consequently, for some of the subsequent political defenses of the constitution in Mexico, has apparently received little attention. The Cortes of Aragón, like the Spanish Cortes of 1812, was concerned at the beginning of each session with considering and redressing grievances inflicted by the king, by the royal authorities, by the estates on each other, or by the estates against the king, as well as other items of a political nature.[63] The resemblance to several systems we have examined is clear, but the relation is not necessarily causal.

The *procesos forales* and the Justicia Mayor are of greater interest for a study of judicial controls, although the rights they defended can hardly be considered constitutional in the modern sense. The term *procesos forales* can be translated as guaranteed procedures. *Foral* is an adjectival form of *fuero* meaning, here, a body of laws or charter of privileges granted by royal authority but binding upon it. Justicia Mayor can be translated as high court or chief judge, depending upon the gender of the article used with it, and the term is used with both references, that is, to the court and to the person who occupies the office. The origins of Justicia Mayor and the exact nature and extent of its powers at various periods are apparently matters of considerable uncertainty; it does not appear that the Justicia achieved a position of

---

[62] For more extensive comment on this subject, see Manuel Aguilar Arriaga, *El amparo de México y sus antecedentes nacionales y extranjeros*, pp. 15–17; Burgoa, *El juicio de amparo*, pp. 32–37; Rabasa, *El juicio constitucional*, fn. p. 186; and Ignacio L. Vallarta, *El juicio de amparo y el Writ of Habeas Corpus: Ensayo crítico-comparativo sobre esos recursos constitucionales*, pp. 427–430.

[63] Minguijón y Adrián, *Historia del derecho español*, p. 265.

independence or of authority until 1265, when, under the fifth law of the agreement of Egea, it was granted jurisdiction in all cases and controversies between the king and the nobility. Under the *Privilegio General* of 1283, the Justicia was granted jurisdiction over all litigation initiated or appealed before the throne. With the passage of time other functions were added, but the court still did not occupy a position of unusual authority until the Cortes of Zaragoza in 1348. This Cortes recognized the Justicia as the only court competent to hear actions directed against judges and other delinquent officials, with absolute powers of decision in each case; not even the king was empowered to intercede. All public officials were obliged to consult the Justicia about the proper interpretation of *fueros*, privileges, liberties, or uses of the realm, staying proceedings in the interim. In addition to its participation in the *procesos forales*, the Justicia served as a guardian of legality, intervening, on the motion of a party, in legal processes in order to determine whether the proper forms of law had been observed. The Justicia was also the final court of appeals from the lower courts within the royal domain.[64] Despite the extent of its powers, and the evident resemblance to the position of the Mexican federal judiciary as the guardian of civil rights, the Justicia cannot realistically be considered an early example of an institution of constitutional defense. Whatever else the Justicia was empowered to do, it could not veto the resolutions of the Cortes, which, in conjunction with the king, was legally sovereign. On the contrary the Justicia was strictly accountable to the Cortes.[65] The Justicia, and other legal institutions of Aragón, were excellent examples of the limitations to which medieval monarchy was subject; but it is not wise to press the analogy with modern principles of constitutionalism, nor to persist in seeing origins where only parallels exist.

The four *procesos forales* were *firma, manifestación, aprehensión,* and *inventario*. In the procedure of *firma*, the Justicia Mayor, and at times the judges of lower courts, issued, on the motion of the complainant, a stay of execution in order to remedy or prevent injury to

---

[64] Ibid., pp. 269–275.
[65] Aguilar Arriaga, *El amparo de México*, p. 25.

the complainant's person, goods, or rights, inflicted by judges or by private individuals. This order was based on the complainant's undertaking, apparently in the form of a signature, and a bond, to comply with the final decision in the case. The order was entirely provisional and was granted without consulting the opposing party. The procedure resembles both the incident of suspension in *amparo* and the Anglo-American writ of injunction. The procedure of *manifestación* existed in two forms, one of them similar to the Roman interdict of *de homine libero exhibendo*, the other designed to prevent torture or imprisonment inflicted by judges not possessing jurisdiction. This procedure could also be used to stop the execution of any criminal sentence because of notorious injustice or nullity of proceedings, and enjoyed such a privileged status that there was no place of detention from which the prisoner could not be extracted at its command. While the *manifestación* was in force, the Justicia held the accused in custody until the validity of his original incarceration could be determined. This procedure resembles the incident of suspension in penal *amparos* and the effects of the concession of *amparo* in some criminal cases. It also resembles the Anglo-American writ of habeas corpus. Of greater interest, given present practices in *amparo*, is that in applying this procedure the Justicia intervened by special process and outside the normal course of litigation in order to review the legality of the actions of lower courts. There is a definite resemblance here to *amparo*'s status as a special suit rather than a form of appeal, and to its function of legal, as distinguished from constitutional, control.

The remaining two procedures of *aprehensión* and *inventario* were concerned primarily with preserving the property at issue in civil suits; they show no significant resemblances to the procedures or purposes of *amparo*, except insofar as the judge in *amparo* is also under an obligation to preserve the substance of the suit until it can be settled.[66]

---

[66] Minguijón y Adrián, *Historia del derecho español*, pp. 299–302. Vallarta, *El juicio de amparo*, pp. 431–439, reprints the text of the *procesos forales* from the work of Juan Francisco la Ripa, *Segunda ilustración a los quatro procesos forales de Aragón: Orden de proceder en ellos según el estilo moderno, y reglas para decidir conforme a la naturaleza de cada uno.*

It is interesting to note that the protection granted the complainant in these actions was sometimes referred to as an *amparo*. This need not be taken seriously as an indication of a causal connection, however, since the legal use of the term, both then and now, is entirely consistent with the common usage.

It is not probable that the institutions of Aragón, despite the resemblances noted, influenced perceptibly the creation and subsequent evolution of the *amparo* suit. As a practical matter, they had been in abeyance for centuries. The tradition transmitted to the Spanish colonies was that of royal absolutism. Under these circumstances it is not likely that a knowledge of the ancient rights and privileges of medieval Aragón would have composed a large part of nineteenth-century Mexican education, legal or otherwise. Those who contend that the Aragonese institutions are the origin of *amparo* are obliged to demonstrate that the founders of the Mexican institution were familiar with them, and this remains to be done.[67]

[67] Among the leading advocates of a Spanish origin for *amparo* are Alfonso Noriega, Toribio Esquivel Obregón, Rodolfo Reyes, Gabriel García Rojas, and Ignacio L. Vallarta. Vallarta, *El juicio de amparo*, pp. 25–26, in discussing the *procesos forales*, says: "The *Privilegio General* granted by King Pedro III and raised to the status of a *fuero* in 1348, has, with reason, been compared with the Magna Charta of England; it enjoined respect for individual rights and, later, in other laws, was perfected to a degree exceeding in this point the English constitution itself." More recent Spanish influences have been cited by Fernando Yllanes Ramos, "El amparo. El mejor instrumento de defensa de los derechos individuales. Antecedents, experiencias y análisis comparativos del amparo mexicano," *El foro: Órgano de la barra mexicana*, 4th Series, nos. 8–10 (April–December, 1955): 63–90. He refers particularly to the powers of the *Audiencia* in the legislative and administrative aspects of the government of New Spain and quotes Book II, Title 15, of the *Recopilación de leyes de los Reinos de Indias*, that persons injured by the acts of the Viceroy or President could appeal to the *Audiencia* for redress. However, his general assertion that the *Audiencia* was supreme in the government of New Spain, perhaps a permissible inference from certain legal texts, is inconsistent with the usual historical views on this subject. Another practice from the colonial period sometimes cited as a source is that of *se acata pero no se cumple*. In this equivocal procedure, the recipient of a royal directive expressed his complete submission to its terms along with his refusal to carry it out in practice. On this point, see Burgoa, *El juicio de amparo*, p. 72. A strong case against Spanish origins is made by Aguilar Arriaga, *El amparo de México*. A more moderate position is taken by Burgoa, who accepts the Aragonese processes as analogues of *amparo* in some of its major phases; *El juicio de amparo*, pp. 42–46.

In judging the suggested origins of the *amparo* suit there are really two problems to be confronted: what is to be compared, and what did the founders of the Mexican *amparo* know of foreign precedents. For the first of these questions, it is reasonable to conclude that the objects of comparison are the forms, or structures, of legal institutions having similar purposes. To compare purposes alone may permit conclusions about similarity of aspirations of different legal communities but, as any developed legal system will provide some analogies for the purposes of *amparo*, this comparison alone cannot justify any inferences about a cause-and-effect relationship. Where similarity of purpose is accompanied by similarity of structure, a tentative conclusion in favor of a causal relation may be justifiable. If knowledge can also be demonstrated, the conclusion acquires about as much certainty as conclusions can possess in this basically uncertain field of study. On the basis of these supplementary criteria there still is little reason to assume any organic relationship between *amparo* and the institutions of Aragón.

Similar conclusions follow from the discussion of English and French influences. In the former there is considerable question that any of the persons associated with the creation of *amparo* were in the least familiar with the intricacies of common law. Similarity of purpose alone could lead to some comparisons. Only one of these, however, bears a structural similarity as well, namely, the writ of habeas corpus. In this instance, as in *amparo*, the procedure is independent and autonomous, and permits the judiciary to determine the legality of acts of public authority that are alleged to violate individual rights. Since *amparo* authorizes a general judicial control of constitutionality, the English experience is irrelevant; unless, perhaps, we can assume a Mexican familiarity with Dr. Bonham's case.[68] For judging influence of French legal institutions and practices, one is confronted with a paucity of comparable devices. In constitutional theory and the status and elaboration of civil rights, however, this influence is indisputable. This fact is demonstrated in Mariano Otero's dissenting report to the

---

[68] The most extensive comparison between *amparo* and English institutions, composing the major subject matter of the book, is by Vallarta, *El juicio de amparo y el Writ of Habeas Corpus*. A good, brief consideration can be found in Burgoa, *El juicio de amparo*, pp. 46–52.

constituent convention of 1847, which frequently supports its arguments on the authority of Rousseau, Sismondi de Sismondi, Tocqueville, Villemain, and Montesquieu. In one sense the influence of the United States' process of judicial review can be considered French when one remembers that Mexican knowledge of this institution was acquired through Tocqueville. In addition to this specious example, the most explicit instance of borrowing from the French remains the unfortunate Supremo Poder Conservador of the Constitution of 1836, an experiment as fruitless in Mexico as in its native land and at the opposite pole from *amparo*.[69]

We have seen that the three men most intimately associated with creating a judicial form of constitutional defense in Mexico were José Fernando Ramírez, Manuel Crescencio Rejón, and Mariano Otero. The evidence from their own choice of authorities in advocating the judiciary for this task indicates that the immediate source of *amparo* must be found in the American institution of judicial review transmitted to the Mexicans through Tocqueville's *Democracy in America*. The great structural dissimilarity between judicial review and *amparo* must be attributed to the intrinsic differences between the civil and common law systems, inadequate knowledge of the manner in which judicial review actually functioned, and the Mexican tendency to interpret the principle of separation of powers with a stringency inversely proportional to its workability. There is no evidence that the founders of *amparo* were familiar with, or at all concerned to adapt, the ancient and partially mythical institutions of Aragón, or that they derived any direct or indirect inspiration from the colonial institutions of New Spain. Their general ideas concerning constitutionalism, the purposes of government, and the rights of man were the heritage of the French Revolution and were the common intellectual property of the age. To search for more recondite sources would confuse casual similarity with cause.[70]

[69] Tena Ramírez, *Leyes fundamentales*, pp. 443–468. Also, Burgoa, *El juicio de amparo*, pp. 52–60.

[70] For an interesting commentary on the influence of Tocqueville, see Echánove Trujillo, "El juicio de amparo mexicano," pp. 94–96. For other comments, see Fe-

If we conclude that the United States provided the initial inspiration for creating a judicial procedure of constitutional defense, we must concede that domestic experience provided the motive and must have indicated the most appropriate means. Forty years of political violence, chiefly characterized by the arbitrary rule of caudillos, undoubtedly made the relative calm and peaceful deliberation of the judicial process singularly attractive; also, given the natural disillusion with the capacities for self-restraint of the executive and legislative branches and the failure of the Supremo Poder Conservador, the judiciary was the only means left untried.

## The Acta de Reformas *to the Revolution of Ayutla*

Before *amparo* could find permanent constitutional embodiment in the charter of 1857, Mexico was required to endure one more visitation of the ubiquitous and unprincipled Santa Anna, within whose scheme of personal government no system of constitutionalism could find accommodation. Recalled from exile in 1853 by the conservative party, he was authorized to govern for a year without a constitution while a new constituent convention would draft another instrument of government. Meanwhile Lucas Alamán, a conservative leader and head of the ministry, endeavored to clothe the nakedness of this dictatorship with a document entitled *Bases para la administración de la República hasta la Promulgación de la Constitución*, promulgated in April 1853. As one would expect under the conditions, the concept of constitutional defense finds no place in this declaration. The dictatorship continued until the victory of the revolution of Ayutla in 1855.[71]

The nation was temporarily organized under the *Estatuto Orgánico Provisional de la República Mexicana*, promulgated by President Ignacio Comonfort on 15 May 1856, while a new constitution was drafted which would be consistent with the principles of the Plan de Ayutla. The *Estatuto* contains a notable list of civil rights in fifty articles under

---

lipe Loria Pérez, *El amparo es una imitación que tuvo como fuente "la democracia en América" por Alexis de Tocqueville. Reforma que es necesaria para los casos de suspensión de oficio*, and Aguilar Arriaga, *El amparo de México*.

[71] Tena Ramírez, *Leyes fundamentales*, pp. 478–484.

the headings of "liberty," "security," "property," and "equality." In implementing these rights, and in the matter of constitutional defense in general, however, the Comonfort statute marked a retrogression from the principles established in the *Acta de Reformas*. The powers awarded the judiciary were confined within traditional limits and further restricted by a provision, borrowed from the majority report of 1842, prohibiting the Supreme Court from taking cognizance of any case dealing with the governmental or economic affairs of the nation or of the states. The impressive catalogue of rights rested essentially upon the benevolence of officialdom. Violations, by executive or judicial officials, were declared to constitute grounds for such punishment as the laws on official responsibility might indicate, but how, and by whom this responsibility was to be enforced was left in doubt. A more significant limitation, both upon rights and the principle of constitutionalism itself, was contained in the section dealing with the powers of the presidency. In article 82 the president was authorized to govern at his discretion when, in the judgment of his cabinet, the situation should demand it. The only explicit limits on this authority, aside from the prior approval of the cabinet, were a prohibition on the use of the death penalty and the imposition of punishments involving the lash, branding, declarations of infamy, and the confiscation of property.[72] The exposition of motives justified this liberal grant to the executive, although somewhat indirectly, as an accommodation to political reality; it was a power necessary for protecting the general interests of society against revolutionary movements. Persuasive arguments could be made to justify the constitutional recognition and formalization of executive supremacy, both in Mexico and elsewhere in Latin America, on the grounds that it is more profitable to attempt to regulate reality than to conceal it. The constitutions of 1857 and of 1917, however, did not confer discretionary powers upon the executive with such a lavish hand. The power to suspend guarantees and impose a state of siege is granted but under more extensive constitutional limitations.

---

[72] Ibid., articles 30–79, 82, 99, pp. 502–510, 512.

*The Constitution of 1857*

The *amparo* suit achieved its definitive constitutional form when it became part of the fundamental law of 1857; following the interval occupied by Maximilian's transient empire, it left the realm of legal theory for the concrete realities of the courtroom. Because of the importance of this achievement of the constituent convention of 1856–1857, the recommendations of its drafting committee and the debates that followed will be examined in detail.

*Amparo* is referred to as perhaps the most important reform recommended to the convention. The drafting committee confined its remarks, however, to applying the action to the maintenance of the federal system. Apparently the necessity of providing a judicial protection for civil rights was considered so self-evident as to need no explicit justification or explanation. Applying *amparo* to the regulation of federal-state relations was, however, a distinct departure from the political systems previously employed. The arguments advanced by the committee were essentially utilitarian. These arguments were based upon the success of judicial review in the United States and the dismal history of failure of the political systems of constitutional defense attempted in Mexico. They sought to demonstrate that the preservation of the constitutional order, which had not been attained by instituting direct confrontations of governmental branches and subdivisions, could be achieved indirectly by reducing the problem to the bounds of private interest, and submitting it to the processes of litigation. They assumed that breaches of the constitution would, in most instances, also produce injuries of a private nature. Given the appropriate legal instrument, laws and acts of authority so vitiated would be insensibly worn away and deprived of their moral and practical effects by a multitude of lawsuits. Since the contest would be between a private individual and the executing authority, the political status and prestige of the latter would not be called into question. In this manner it was hoped that constitutional issues would cease to be incitements to insurrection.[73]

[73] Francisco Zarco, *Historia del congreso extraordinario constituyente, 1856–1857,* pp. 323–324.

The committee's specific proposals, embodied in article 102 of the draft, provided that the *amparo* suit would be admissible in any of three situations: when laws or acts of any authority violated individual rights guaranteed by the Constitution; when laws or acts of the Federation violated or restricted the sovereignty of the states; or when acts of the states similarly infringed upon the authority of the Federation. The essential characteristics of the suit were then defined in accordance with Otero's formula. It was to be initiated only upon the petition of the injured party and lead to a judgment that would affect only private individuals; the effect of the judgment was to be limited to affording redress and protection in the special case to which the complaint referred, and the courts were forbidden to render decisions of general application concerning the validity of contested laws or acts. The committee draft also added two provisions which, in the judgment of later students of *amparo*, were inconsistent with the juridical nature of the action and a serious threat to its survival. The first of these provided for the federal and state courts to share jurisdictions under rules to be established by statute, and the second provided for trial of *amparo* cases before a jury.[74] Because of the concurrent jurisdictions exercised by state and federal courts in the United States it is difficult to perceive any serious objections to the first on purely legal grounds, assuming, of course, the possibility of appeal before the highest federal court. It could be alleged on grounds of logical symmetry that, since the federal constitution defined and guaranteed the rights to be defended, the federal judiciary would be the only appropriate agency for the task. Such formal considerations are not without influence in Mexican legal thought. The federal function assigned to *amparo* permits a more serious objection. To avoid that clash of governmental powers deplored by the committee and to establish confidence in the procedure, a high degree of judicial independence and integrity would be required. While the Mexican federal courts have not always displayed these qualities in the highest degree, the state courts have been notoriously subservient to local political pressures. To try the suit in these courts would consequently have tended to diminish its prestige with the

[74] Ibid., p. 341.

general public and would probably, in many cases, have tempted the authorities to employ it for political purposes.

An evaluation of the jury requirement presents more difficulty. From a purely practical point of view, however, the expediency of this provision is beyond question. Without it, *amparo* would probably have failed of approval on the convention floor.[75] To many, at that time, the jury seemed to be one of the trade secrets of British and American liberty, a device for instituting democratic participation in the judicial process and for checking any tendency toward arbitrary behavior on the part of the courts. The virtually hypnotic influence of the appeal to democratic principle prevented any exhaustive inquiry into the appropriateness of a democratic factor in the process of litigation, or the capacity of the Mexican people to perform such a function.[76] Regardless of the abstract merits, the jury was an exotic and unpromising innovation in the Mexican legal system. Previous and subsequent attempts to graft it to the main stem of Mexican procedure have been uniformly unsuccessful; to have constitutionally prescribed its use in *amparo* cases, frequently necessitating a highly technical interpretation of facts as well as law, would have seriously compromised the utility and survival of this suit.

In the convention debates, the jurisdictional and jury provisions received little attention, at least on their merits. During the three days devoted to the consideration of *amparo*, the question of concurrent state-federal jurisdictions was referred to only once and then for the sole purpose of objecting to the inclusion of the state courts. The jury provisions were considered only concerning the manner in which the jury should be constituted. The essential arguments of the opposition to *amparo* were expressed by Ignacio Ramírez, who considered it unworkable and inconsistent with democratic principle. Behind these objections it is possible to discern a conflict of opinion about the superior normative status of the Constitution. Ramírez saw the proposal as an attempt to impose a restraining supervision over the legis-

[75] Tena Ramírez, *Derecho constitucional*, p. 504.
[76] Zarco, *Historia del congreso constituyente*, pp. 989–998.

lative power. Whatever organization might be selected for this purpose, he felt, it could not function unless it possessed sufficient physical force to impose its will. If granted this authority it would necessarily arrogate to itself the prerogatives of the legislature, whereas, if not so empowered, that direct conflict of governmental powers which the committee sought to avoid would assuredly take place. In essence, Ramírez argued for the principle of legislative supremacy, rendered legitimate by its ultimate responsibility to the true sovereign, the people. The proper recourse against bad laws, he insisted, was an aroused and active public opinion expressed through the use of petition, the press, and, presumably, the ballot box. To confer upon the judiciary the power to check the Congress in the exercise of its proper function would be to transfer sovereignty to that agency and, in the process, to destroy responsibility. Other delegates denounced the project as a violation of the principle of separation of powers and, consequently, relying on the assertion of Montesquieu, destructive of liberty. The suggestion that *amparo* would permit the gradual, piecemeal derogation of unconstitutional statutes was derided as a juridical absurdity, a violation of the jurisprudential rule that only the authority that enacts has power to repeal.

The proponents of the *amparo* measure thought less of popular sovereignty and more of constitutional supremacy. They might well have replied, although Zarco's history gives no indication they did, that the principles of popular sovereignty and of responsibility were safeguarded by the amending procedure and that the major arguments of the opposition constituted, therefore, a non sequitur. Happily for the future of *amparo*, its friends were more concerned with practical politics than with logic. They accepted the arguments of their opponents in principle, and contended that both the responsibility of the courts and democratic principle were assured by the use of the jury. Oddly enough, no one took serious issue with this proposition. As for the effect of an *amparo* judgment, the proponents of the measure denied that the courts would infringe on the province of the legislative branch. The judgment handed down by the court would not constitute a partial revocation, but would merely state that in the case at hand a particular statute was inapplicable because of unconstitutionality. The legal status of the statute would remain unaffected until the legislature might think fit to defer to the opinion of the courts and repeal it.[77]

Upon the completion of debate, the committee reported a revision of their proposal, broken down into three articles, 100, 101, and 102. Somewhere in the process of revision the grant of jurisdiction to the state courts disappeared, but its absence apparently went unnoticed in the convention. The *amparo* provisions as then agreed upon, however, retained the jury requirement. The popularity of the jury was evidenced by the size of the vote: article 100 was approved by a margin of ten votes, article 101 by nine, and article 102, containing the jury provisions, by twenty-nine.[78] The disappearance of the jury from the completed version of the constitution, sworn by the convention on 5 February 1857, can be attributed, at least insofar as the immediate responsibility was concerned, to León Guzmán, sole member of the style committee. When originally elected by the convention, this committee had also included Melchor Ocampo and Joaquín Ruiz, but neither consented to serve, and Guzmán was authorized to proceed alone. He presented his draft to the convention on 28 January, where it was checked against the original by José María Mata, by the secretary of the convention and by two other secretarial employees, and was also read to the assembly. If anyone noticed the absence of the jury provisions he did not mention it. Guzmán later explained that this article had not been included with the material given him by the secretary; upon inquiry he had been told that the secretariat had conferred with the drafting committee and other delegates on this point, and all had agreed that the jury should be deleted as incompatible with other provisions of the *amparo* articles. Whether this explanation was made in good faith or not, Guzmán's right to remove an article formally approved by the convention is exceedingly doubtful, especially since he did not call the omission to the attention of the convention.[79] However

77 Ibid., pp. 989–996.

78 Ibid., pp. 996–998.

79 F. Jorge Gaxiola, *León Guzman y la Constitución de 57*, pp. 13–14. Also, Rabasa, *El juicio constitucional*, p. 238; Tena Ramírez, *Derecho constitucional*, pp. 504–505; and Vallarta, *El juicio de amparo*, pp. 462, 468–469.

one wishes to judge the moral justification for Guzmán's action, the disappearance of the jury provision removed the last of the anomalous factors the convention had attempted to impose upon *amparo* procedure, and subsequent generations have been grateful for the result, if they have not always approved the cause.

The sources from which the convention drew in drafting the *amparo* articles are clear, although not always adequately acknowledged. The text of article 102 was taken literally from the formula advanced by Otero in 1847. He must be credited consequently with establishing the legal form and scope of the action. Neither in the drafting committee's report nor in the convention debates, however, was this contribution recognized. On the contrary, all references were to the experience of the United States, primarily as reported by Tocqueville. Because of the unquestioned acceptance of the Otero formula, it is impossible to say whether the convention understood the differing consequences derived from judicial review and from *amparo*. The point is of little significance, however, considering that the purpose was to gradually and partially revoke unconstitutional acts. Perhaps the committee's seeming ingratitude to Otero derived from its predominant concern with preserving federalism and its concept of civil rights.[80]

In addition to *amparo*, article 126 of the Constitution suggested a further basis for a type of judicial review in the state courts. This article, evidently copied from the supremacy clause of the United States Constitution, provided that the Constitution, the laws passed in pursuance thereof, and federal treaties should be the supreme law of the entire union, and that the judges in each state should be bound thereby in preference to any contrary provisions in the constitutions or laws of their states. This provision, and the comparable one in the Constitution of 1917, gave rise to considerable differences of opinion about the degree to which it actually empowered the state courts to

[80] Zarco, *Historia del congreso constituyente*, pp. 315–324, 990. On the question of influences, see also Mario de la Cueva, "El constitucionalismo mexicano," in *El constitucionalismo a mediados del siglo XIX*, II, 1316–1317; Echánove Trujillo, "El juicio de amparo mexicano," p. 110; Rabasa, *El juicio constitucional*, p. 237, and *El artículo 14*, p. 86; and Tena Ramírez, *Derecho constitucional*, p. 502.

invalidate state legislation, with the majority holding that no such authorization was really intended. In practice, the state courts have rarely attempted to attack state legislation on this ground.[81]

With the establishment of *amparo* in the Constitution of 1857, political devices of constitutional defense were finally abandoned. The actual implementation of *amparo*, however, was delayed by the Three Years' War, the French intervention, and, during 1864–1867, the empire of Maximilian. The empire produced a temporary constitutional document entitled *Estatuto Provisional del Imperio Mexicano*, but this charter contained little that could be construed as pertinent to constitutional defense. The courts were specifically prohibited from suspending the execution of laws or administrative rulings; only a type of *residencia*, that is supervision by imperial inspectors, was provided for the control and redress of grievances.[82]

## The Legislative Evolution of Amparo

From the promulgation of the Constitution of 1857, to the Mexican Revolution in 1910, *amparo* was regulated under the provisions of five statutory codes enacted in 1861, 1869, 1882, 1897, and 1909. As one would expect, these successive codes were marked by increasing length and procedural complexity.

Because of the virtual annulment of the federal sections of article 101 of the Constitution by later judicial interpretation, perhaps the most interesting aspect of the law of 1861 was its clear indication that the personal injury required for bringing suit under these sections did not need to involve a violation of individual guarantees. Article 21 further bolstered the federal aspects of the action by providing that a judge, ordered to execute some command of the federal authorities, which in his opinion violated the reserved powers of the state, could sue for *amparo* before the appropriate federal district court. No provisions of this sort are to be found in any subsequent *amparo* legislation. The 1861 code also foreshadowed, in article 4, the incident of suspension of the act complained of, *amparo*'s equivalent of the tem-

[81] Tena Ramírez, *Leyes fundamentales*, p. 627. This subject is given further consideration in chapter three.

[82] Ibid., articles 18, 22, 23, pp. 672–673.

porary injunction, and provided for a maximum of two appeals, the first before the federal circuit courts and the second, before the Supreme Court; the latter was admissible only if the circuit courts altered or revoked the decision in first instance.[83]

In the law of 1869, the provisions about the content of the complaint in cases that involved federal-state usurpations of powers, although consistent with the law of 1861, were much briefer and essentially similar to those used in subsequent *amparo* legislation. From the text of the statute, therefore, it is not possible to determine whether the Congress intended that the complainant should also allege a violation of individual guarantees in those cases. The participation of the circuit courts in appeals was removed in this code, and the Supreme Court was required to review all district court decisions in *amparo*. This requirement was retained in the subsequent legislation, through the law of 1909. The provisions for suspending the act complained of were defined in some detail and, in article 8, *amparo* against judicial decisions, presumably those of a civil nature only, was prohibited. This latter provision did not survive long in the courts and was clearly opposed to the letter and the intent of article 101 of the Constitution, which established the admissibility of the suit against unconstitutional acts of any authority.[84]

The organic act, enacted in 1882, provided for the first time for employing state courts as auxiliaries in *amparo* in cases where a federal district judge was not immediately available. The local courts were limited, however, as is still the case, to receiving the complaint, granting temporary suspensions in urgent cases, and carrying out other preliminary procedures. They were not permitted under any circumstances to hand down a final decision on the case. Article 6 removed the unworkable prohibition on *amparo* against acts of the judiciary, and article 8 introduced the use of the telegraph for filing the complaint in urgent cases. Further advances were made in the procedural rules regulating suspension, and the courts were, for the first time, specifically

---

[83] Manuel Dublan et al., *Legislación mexicana o colección completa de las disposiciones legislativas expedidas desde la independencia de la república*, IX, 328–330.
[84] Ibid., X, 521–525.

authorized to correct defective complaints, but only to correct errors in designating the guarantees violated. Article 34, which foreshadows the appearance of obligatory precedent in the Mexican legal system, specified that the courts, in interpreting constitutional texts, should attend to the sense given them in the decisions of the Supreme Court and in the doctrines elaborated by legal writers.[85] This was perhaps the most interesting innovation of all.

The *amparo* legislation enacted in 1897 formed a part of the *Código de Procedimientos Civiles Federales* of that year. The new code excluded all reference to precedent and added little that was substantially new, except for introducing a remedy for third parties injured by excess in the execution of a judgment, these persons being permitted to apply to the Supreme Court for redress. In other respects the law of 1897 was chiefly notable for elaborating the reasons for inadmissibility of the *amparo* suit and the grounds for dismissing cases in progress.[86]

The last *amparo* law enacted under the authority of the Constitution of 1857 appeared in 1909 as part of the *Código Federal de Procedimientos Civiles*. The new law contained several innovations including a detailed procedure for establishment by the Supreme Court of obligatory precedent. Considering the Mexican civil law tradition and the lack, at that time, of any explicit constitutional basis for such a development, the validity of these provisions is doubtful. As far as establishing obligatory precedent can be construed as a legislative act, instituting this procedure could be, and was, considered a violation of the principle of separation of powers. The other innovations consisted of designating the responsible authority as a full party to the action and the injunction that all *amparos* against judicial decisions of a civil nature should be tried *stricti juris*. The new law also broadened considerably the area of defense open to injured third parties, who were defined as the opposing party in a civil action and the party entitled to civil restitution in a criminal action.[87]

---

[85] Ibid., XVI, 394–403.
[86] Ibid., XXVIII, 255–265.
[87] Ibid., XL, 699–721.

The constitutional provisions relating to *amparo* were amended only once during the life of the Constitution of 1857, in November 1908. The amendment was an addition to article 102, designed to limit the abuse of *amparo* against judicial decisions in civil actions: it was decreed that recourse could be had to *amparo* in these cases only after the definitive judgment had been handed down and where the law provided no other recourse or form of appeal by which the judgment could be revoked.[88]

On the evidence of the organic legislation and the few statistics available, *amparo* had become by 1910 an established, thriving, and vital part of the Mexican legal system, although much of this growth must be attributed to its use as a last chance appeal of decisions in civil actions. When the next constituent convention met in 1916, the continuance of *amparo* was no longer in question.[89]

[88] Tena Ramírez, *Leyes fundamentales*, p. 717.

[89] Isidro Rojas and Francisco Pascual García, *El amparo y sus reformas*, p. 60, give the number of *amparos* tried in 1869 as 123, and 2108 in 1880; for the quarterly periods of June–August and September–November 1901, there were 957 and 727, respectively. The number remaining to be settled in the December–February quarter, 1901–1902 is given as 924.

*Chapter 2*

# The Organization of *Amparo*
# under the Constitution of 1917

$$\frown\frown\frown\frown\frown$$

Bᴇᴛᴡᴇᴇɴ ᴛʜᴇ ꜰᴀʟʟ of the Díaz regime in
1910 and the inauguration of the new constitutional order in 1917, the
Mexican political scene, washed by the tides of a great revolution, did
not offer a very propitious environment for the further development and
practice of judicial review, or for any other form of constitutional defense less persuasive than trial by arms. The political program of the
revolution, summarized in the slogan "effective suffrage and no reelection," was essentially traditional in its aspirations and called for no significant alterations in the formal organization of the state. The various
revolutionary plans and proclamations scarcely touched upon the constitutional form and legal attributes of *amparo*. To judge by subsequent
events in the constituent convention of 1916–1917, the continuance
of this institution was so unhesitatingly accepted that it provoked no
comment.[1] The essence of the revolution, and its true title to the name,
lay in its social demands. In its innovations in agriculture and labor,

[1] Felipe Tena Ramírez, *Leyes fundamentales de México, 1808–1957*, pp. 731,
740–741.

the Constitution of 1917, while retaining the traditional organization of the state, turned its back on the liberal individualism of the nineteenth century and introduced the concept of the welfare state. The presence in the Constitution of rights which can be enjoyed only as the consequence of positive governmental action, especially when some of these rights are in conflict with traditional legal principles, has created both theoretical and practical difficulties in the application of *amparo*. The legislative history of the institution under the present constitution has been marked, consequently, not only by further procedural elaboration but also by attempts to adapt or evade the consequences of these new rights.

## The Constituent Convention of 1916–1917

During the period 1913 to 1916, the Constitution of 1857 remained officially in abeyance. Venustiano Carranza, the leader of the Constitutionalist forces, struggled to suppress the factions led by Pancho Villa in the north and by Emiliano Zapata in the south. The defeat of Villa and the virtual reduction of Zapata in 1916 presented the problem of renewing the constitutional order. The available alternatives were either to restore the Constitution in its existing form subject to later amendment, or to convoke a new constituent convention. Carranza chose the latter. By this time a number of the major social and political aspirations of the revolution had been given legal form by executive decree: the free municipality and divorce laws in 1914, the labor, agrarian, and civil code reform laws in 1915. It was Carranza's opinion that the social reforms, since they did not affect the organization and working relations of the governmental divisions, did not need to be incorporated in the text of the constitution; rather, they fell within the existing scope of the legislative authority. He felt, however, that the political innovations required constitutional sanction. These options were stated both in the text of the constitutional draft that Carranza presented to the convention and in the limitations that the convocation decree of September 1916 imposed upon that body. The latter directed the convention to occupy itself solely with the draft constitution submitted to it and allotted the brief period of two months for completing the task. According to the dictates of the convocation decree, therefore, the convention of 1916–1917 was not in full possession of those sovereign powers customarily associated with the constituent function. The convention, politically encouraged by Alvaro Obregón, the conqueror of Villa, was unwilling to entrust the consummation of the revolution entirely to the mercies of future legislatures; it ignored, therefore, the first of these commands and wrote into articles 27 and 123 the aspirations for agrarian and labor reform, which constituted the ideological essence of the long revolutionary struggle.[2]

In the matter of *amparo*, the convention displayed no such desire to depart from the spirit or letter of Carranza's recommendations and adopted the text of articles 106 and 107 (103 and 107 of the Constitution) with only minor alterations in phrasing. The exposition of motives appended to the draft did not question the readoption of *amparo* although it was highly unflattering in its appraisal of its operation under the previous constitution. The inadequacies of the suit were attributed more to political factors, which tend to subordinate the judiciary to the executive, than to any intrinsic deficiency in the institution itself. It was contended that the system of judicial appointments resulted in a judiciary subservient to the president. It was further observed that the Supreme Court's development of a jurisdiction that extended *amparo* to the review of judicial decisions in civil cases— based on the guarantee in article 14 of the 1857 Constitution of exact application of laws—permitted the Court to exercise a supervision over even the most trivial acts of state authorities; this extension destroyed both the independence of the states and the proper expedition of litigation. Despite the general harshness of this judgment, Carranza concluded that the development of such jurisdiction was a response to a genuine necessity, produced by the servility of the local courts in their relations with political officials. As a matter of justice and political wisdom, it would have to be readopted; it would be subject, however, to appropriate safeguards, limiting it to cases of obvious need and prescribing simplified and more expeditious procedures.[3] In accordance with this opinion, article 107 of the draft was devoted primarily to a detailed, essentially legislative, regulation of procedures and jurisdic-

---

[2] Ibid., pp. 809–813.
[3] Ibid., pp. 746, 750–751.

tions in civil and penal *amparo*. It may be noted that Carranza's strictures on the behavior of the judiciary under the Constitution of 1857 met with more effective response from the convention than from himself. Article 94 of the draft provided for a four-year term of office for Supreme Court ministers, presumably to run concurrently with the presidential term, which would hardly have served to make the Court less dependent upon the executive. The convention responded by introducing the principle of life tenure subject to good behavior.[4]

As proposed by Carranza and adopted by the convention, article 103 and the opening statement and section I of article 107 reenacted, in effect, articles 101 and 102 of the previous constitution. The remaining eleven sections of article 107 defined the general procedural and jurisdictional rules within which the suit was to function, subject to later and more detailed statutory regulation. Of these eleven sections, II through IX were devoted to procedures and jurisdiction in *amparo* against civil and penal judgments, and in *amparos* requested against nonjudicial acts or judicial acts executed outside the course of a suit, involving third parties, or inflicting procedural injuries impossible to remedy in the final decision. The remaining sections dealt with official responsibility in enforcing sentences and suspending orders and, in section XII, with a rather lengthy regulation of article 19 of the Constitution. This latter section was not relevant to *amparo*. Compared to previous *amparo* legislation, the major innovation was contained in sections VIII and IX, which introduced the jurisdictional divisions of direct and indirect *amparo*. In the former, violations committed in the definitive judgment rendered in a civil or penal case, as well as certain procedural violations affecting the nature of that judgment, were to be tried in a single instance directly before the Supreme Court. In indirect *amparo*, the following violations were to be tried by the district courts subject to review by the Supreme Court: (1) acts of all but judicial officials; (2) acts of judicial officials that took place outside the suit or after its conclusion, or acts that occurred during the trial that were

---

[4] Ibid., pp. 787, 790, 915. It may be noted here that in Mexico the judges of the Supreme Court are called ministers (*ministros*); those of the circuit courts, magistrates (*magistrados*); and those of the district courts, judges (*jueces*).

irreparable or involved persons not parties to the suit.[5] As expressed by the convention's study committee, the principal reason for adopting this proposal was the hope of speeding the process of litigation by simplifying various procedural steps and abolishing the appeal stage in the instances noted.[6] The general principle of the division depended on the criticalness of the situation: the most pressing cases were relegated to the district courts, since they were more readily accessible. It has also been suggested, although the published debates have nothing explicit to say on the point, that the convention desired to make *amparo* fully adequate as a substitute for the complex and time consuming remedy of cassation.[7]

Furthermore, the committee assured the convention, perhaps fearing that the constitutional statement was not sufficiently definite, that the admissibility of the *amparo* suit against violations of rights committed by administrative authorities remained completely valid.[8]

Two members of the committee, Heriberto Jara and Hilario Medina, filed a dissenting report, which contained virtually the only reasoned opposition expressed against the *amparo* proposals. They disregarded the previous history of *amparo* against judicial decisions and the necessary implication of article 103, which empowered the federal courts to hear cases arising from violations committed by any authority. Their contention was that, by establishing this jurisdiction, in article 107, the independence of the state judiciaries would be completely destroyed. They asserted that the proper arrangement for a federally organized state was to be found in article 106 of the Constitution of 1824, which had prescribed a complete separation between the federal and state judiciaries. It can hardly be denied that *amparo* is conducive to central-

[5] Ibid, pp. 922–924.

[6] *Cámara de Diputados, Diario de los debates del Congreso Constituyente*, Fernando Romero García, II, 500.

[7] Efrain Peniche López, *El amparo de México y su doctrina*, pp. 30–31 .The author points out that the rules concerning civil *amparo* in article 107 are not only similar to, but in some cases almost literally copied from, the procedures of cassation specified in the *Código de procedimientos civiles del Distrito y Territorios Federales* of 1884.

[8] Cámara de Diputados, *Diario de los debates*, II, 500.

izing the administration of justice, since it permits recourse to the highest tribunal in almost every case that the parties deem sufficiently important to justify the expense. Nonetheless, arguments based upon the sanctity of states' rights were certain not to win the sympathy of delegates who were all too familiar with the political subserviency of state courts. More significant, the objection was essentially irrelevant because the convention had already accepted article 103 and article 14. The terms of the latter article necessarily implied the practice of this form of *amparo* if its guarantee of legality in judicial procedure was to be rendered effective.[9]

During the course of debate, the Jara-Medina thesis was contested with the argument that the guarantee of legality in article 14 could not reasonably be considered an exception to the rule of federal jurisdiction, because article 14 provided that the individual guarantees contained in the Constitution apply indiscriminately to all the inhabitants of the republic, and article 103 consigned the protection of these guarantees to the federal courts. The alternatives were either to provide a constitutional regulation of this guarantee or to leave the matter to future legislative action. To delete the relevant portions of article 107 would not deprive the federal courts of this jurisdiction in any event. More generally, the advocates of article 107 argued that the sovereignty and independence of the states were not really at issue because this sovereignty could not be considered complete in any case if the Federation were to subsist, and because the judgments handed down by the local courts would not, in strict legal fact, be altered by *amparo* which only revoked those effects that constituted violations of the Constitution. It is only just to conclude that this last point seems more subtle than accurate. In the practice of *amparo* against judicial decisions under the previous constitution, it was alleged that the real abuse was that every procedural step taken by a judge had been subject to attack, which caused an indefinite delay in resolving litigation. By limiting the *amparo* action to definitive judgments, except for a few urgent and explicitly prescribed procedural situations, it was argued that this abuse could no longer continue. On the basis of this brief

9 Ibid., pp. 502–503.

and not very searching discussion, article 107 was approved substantially as presented.[10]

## *The* Amparo *Law of 1919*

The first *amparo* legislation under the new constitution was not promulgated until late in 1919, although it had been submitted to the Senate in August 1917. The law, officially entitled the *Ley Reglamentaria de los Artículos 103 y 104 de la Constitución Federal*, continued in force until January 1936. This legislation provided a detailed regulation of the direct and indirect forms of *amparo* introduced in article 107, defined the conditions of inadmissibility when procedural remedies other than *amparo* remained unused, and designated injured third persons as parties to the suit. In other respects, the law of 1919 added little of novelty in regulating *amparo* except for the rather ambiguous contents of article 6, which states that "official artificial persons may request it [*amparo*], when acting in the character of juridical entities, by means of the officials designated by the respective laws."[11] Judging by the wording of the article and by subsequent judicial interpretation, it was apparently intended that official persons have access to *amparo* only when acting in their private capacity as subjects of the civil law, but never in their official capacity as authorities executing functions granted in public law.[12]

If the *amparo* portions of the law provided little change, this cannot be said about the inclusion within the same statute of the altogether different remedy of *súplica*. This appeal procedure, essentially a form of cassation, differed fundamentally from *amparo* in its legal characteristics; it was neither an autonomous, independent suit nor, judging by its source in article 104 of the Constitution, was it properly applicable to constitutional questions. Under articles 131 and 132 of the law, *súplica* permitted bringing for review before the Supreme Court defin-

[10] Ibid., pp. 587–592.

[11] Estados Unidos Mexicanos, *Diario oficial, órgano del gobierno constitucional de los Estados Unidos Mexicanos*, XIII, no. 44, 710 (cited hereafter as *Diario oficial*).

[12] Suprema Corte de Justicia, *Jurisprudencia de la Suprema Corte de Justicia en los fallos pronunciados en los años de 1917 a 1954, apéndice al semanario judicial de la federación*, Thesis 450, III, 867–868.

itive decisions that had been handed down in second instance by either federal or state courts in cases that involved applying and executing federal laws and treaties. In such cases, which also involve the violation of individual guarantees or the invasion of sovereignties, as delineated by article 103 of the Constitution, either *amparo* or *súplica* could be employed, apparently at the election of the parties. If the reference to federal laws and treaties can be taken as excluding, by omission, the Constitution itself, it then appears that *súplica* was not intended to apply to cases where the only federal question was a strictly constitutional one. The precise situation arising from a controversy that included differences in applying and executing federal laws or treaties and violations of individual guarantees remained altogether uncertain. To employ *súplica* in these cases would have involved either reading into article 104 a greater range of jurisdiction than it appeared to authorize, or foregoing the constitutional question, since choosing one of these procedures excluded legally and logically the use of the other. Aside from the uncertainty about the manner or possibility of resolving constitutional issues, the jurisdictional scope of *súplica* exceeded that of *amparo*; it conferred on the Supreme Court the same powers of review in a given case as those that had been possessed by the court of second instance. The judgment in *súplica* extended, in the case of procedural error, to nullifying the error and returning the case to the court of second instance for retrial, and, in the event of error in the final decision, to revoking or appropriately modifying that decision.[13]

In the exposition of motives, the introduction of *súplica* was justified not only because it conformed to the command contained in article 104 of the Constitution, but also because it corrected a deficiency in the scope of *amparo*. The latter suit, it was asserted, did not serve to determine the proper interpretation of federal laws and treaties when applied by the state and local courts since its judgment could not directly modify decisions of these courts.[14] Presumably this erroneous and legalistic conclusion was deduced from the technical limitation of the *amparo* judgment: to the granting or withholding of protection against

13 Estados Unidos Mexicanos, *Diario oficial*, XIII, no. 46, 775.

14 Cámara de Senadores, *Diario de los debates de la Cámara de Senadores del Congreso de los Estados Unidos Mexicanos*, I, 12.

a certain act or acts alleged to constitute violations of the Constitution. In *amparos* granted against judicial decisions, however, such protection can, when necessary to achieve its purpose, have all the practical effects of decisions of the Supreme Court in *súplica*, while the guarantee of legality contained in article 14 ensures that no judicial decision, state or federal, is immune from such review. Furthermore, the interpretations formulated by the Supreme Court in *amparo* were neither more nor less effective than those in *súplica* in establishing uniform criteria among federal, state, and local courts. As a practical matter, most cases considered sufficiently important by the parties are subjected to Supreme Court review, producing, in consequence, whatever degree of uniformity the Court sees fit to maintain in its own decisions. More generally, the 1919 law provided that *jurisprudencia* be established in both forms of action.[15] Aside then from the possibility of more inclusive review of the relevant law, at least in civil cases—permitted by the equivalence of jurisdiction possessed by the Supreme Court and the courts of second instance in *súplica,* and by applying *amparo* to constitutional questions—the purposes of these actions as instruments of appeal overlapped to a degree, making the former superfluous. Between the two of them, there were few suits that the Supreme Court would not eventually have been required to review. Primarily for the reasons cited, the remedy of *súplica* disappeared with the amendment of article 104 of the Constitution in 1934.[16]

### The Judicial Amendments of 1928

Although no alterations were made in either the legislation or in the constitutional provisions directly pertaining to *amparo*, the judicial amendments ratified in 1928 had a considerable effect on procedure

[15] Estados Unidos Mexicanos, *Diario oficial*, XIII, no. 47, articles 147–150, p. 790. In Mexican law the term *jurisprudencia* has the technical meaning of obligatory precedent, which can, in turn, be established only in accordance with procedures specifically prescribed by statute. The term "precedent" will be used only when referring to court decisions having persuasive but not obligatory force. The establishment, content, and significance of *jurisprudencia* is examined in detail in chapter nine.

[16] Cámara de Diputados, *Constitución política de los Estados Unidos Mexicanos con sus adiciones y reformas*, p. 194.

in the Supreme Court and could be interpreted as damaging to its independence. These amendments have, in consequence, an important, though indirect, relevance to our subject. They were presented by Alvaro Obregón as president-elect, shortly before his assassination. The presentation of legislative proposals, including constitutional amendments, by presidents-elect has been a common practice in Mexico.

From the procedural point of view, the most important of these amendments was that of article 94, which enlarged the membership of the Court from eleven to sixteen, struck out the requirement that all decisions be taken *en banc*, and provided that the Court should function, as provided by statute, either *en banc* or in three chambers of five members each. Although not expressed in the text of the amendment, each of the three chambers was to have a different field of jurisdiction: penal, civil, or administrative law. The division of the Court was justified, in the exposition of motives, as a valid recognition of two essentially distinct functions presumably performed by it: namely that of reviewing the decisions of lower courts, and that of acting as one of the three coordinate branches of government. The more practical explanation, however, lay in the constantly increasing volume of cases, chiefly *amparos*, and the resultant necessity of devising more rapid procedures of adjudication.[17]

Of the other amendments, the most important were those modifying articles 96 and 111. In its original form, article 96 had provided that the members of the Supreme Court be elected by the national Congress with an extraordinary quorum of two-thirds of the members of each house and by absolute majority. The amendment prescribed appointment by the president with the approval of the Senate. If one considers the traditional predominance of the executive in Mexican politics, it is probable that this innovation was more formal than real. The amendment of article 111 consisted of an addition to the original text, which appended to the standard impeachment procedure a second, less complicated method of removing federal judges from office. This procedure, initiated by the president before the Chamber of Deputies,

17 Cámara de Diputados, *Diario de los debates de la Cámara de Diputados del Congreso de los Estados Unidos Mexicanos.* XXXII Legislatura, II, 5–6.

required only an absolute majority vote of both houses, acting upon an accusation of bad conduct, and dispensed with the necessity of a trial. The tenor of the remarks made on this subject in the exposition of motives leads one to conclude that the device was intended primarily to improve the quality of the personnel in the common courts of the Federal District and territories.[18] Given a pliant legislature, however—and no other kind is to be expected in Mexico—it is evident that the president was placed in a position to exert a great deal of influence over the entire judiciary.

### The Status of Amparo During the Cárdenas Administration

The Cárdenas administration is famous—some would say notorious—for the variety and importance of its accomplishments, innovations, and, perhaps, failures. Those relating directly and indirectly to *amparo* were not the least significant of these. Before embarking upon an examination of these developments, however, the amendment of article 27, in January 1934, must be noted. This amendment, section XIV of the article, deprived landowners, affected by resolutions that granted lands and waters to *ejidos*, of judicial recourse, including access to the *amparo* suit. The most immediate consequence of this provision was to render inoperative those provisions of article 27 that were designed to protect the small property owner and to assure legality of procedure in the land reform program.

While still president-elect, Cárdenas submitted to the Congress a series of amendment proposals relating to the judiciary. The most far-reaching of these, the amendment of article 94, was officially promulgated in December 1934. The membership of the Supreme Court was again enlarged, from sixteen to twenty-one, and a fourth chamber was created to handle appeals in labor *amparos*. This was in conformity with the recommendations contained in paragraph 108 of the Six-Year Plan formulated by the Second Ordinary Convention of the National Revolutionary Party. The interest displayed in the more expeditious handling of labor cases reflected the rise of Mexican unionism and

[18] Ibid.

the labor policies to be followed during the course of the Cárdenas administration.

The second innovation in article 94 was more fundamental. Declaring repeatedly that he had no desire to deprive the judicial branch of any of its proper functions nor to lessen its independence in any way, Cárdenas proceeded to recommend the repeal of the life tenure provisions and to develop a theory of the relation between the administration and the judiciary that belied these protestations. The state, he asserted, is a unity, and power also is one and indivisible. The traditional division into legislative, executive, and judicial branches implies no fundamental distinction, therefore, but only a functional specialization. Consequently, the separation of powers cannot be taken to signify a real division but, on the contrary, should imply a close collaboration for achieving the ends sought by the state. The existence of life tenure in the judiciary was construed as being a serious obstacle to attaining this happy state of affairs, [it was] "an absurdity in a young, democratically organized country, striving to establish a new concept of distributive justice and in which the law of the future is coming to birth."[19] Such a concept of judicial tenure, he continued, was inconsistent with the revolutionary principle of limited terms without reelection and derogated from the sovereignty that properly resided in the people. The practice of the courts and their legal views, their exaggerated reverence for tradition and established precedent, was only too well known, whereas the administration of justice in the new Mexico properly necessitated the flexible, expedient, spontaneous approach of the Revolution. To achieve this response to the problems of adjudication a very special type of judge was required. He had to be a sincere adherent of the Revolution, a genuine lover of the proletarian masses, a man capable of perceiving the historical necessity behind the norms created by the Revolution and of executing them in a manner that assists in achieving the collective program of society. To retain in the government men of divergent opinions, of different ideological convictions, and lacking in discipline, would necessarily produce the failure of any policy, however well founded. In conformity

19 Ibid., XXXVI Legislatura, I, no. 11, p. 13.

with these principles, it was suggested, and approved, that federal judges should serve six-year terms, presumably to run concurrently with those of the presidents'.[20]

Perhaps the most notable feature of the Cárdenas thesis was its failure to recognize any distinction between the processes and purposes of adjudication and those of policy execution. Given this innovation—appointment by the president and the simplified procedure of removal, contained in article 111 since the amendments of 1928—there remained little legal foundation for an independent judicial judgment. By 1939 Cárdenas had acquired a Court amply possessed of that revolutionary flexibility which he deemed necessary to the exigencies of politics.[21]

As a follow-up to the constitutional amendments of 1934, a new judiciary act was enacted in 1935, which provided in detail for conducting labor *amparos*: it modified—probably unconstitutionally—the jurisdiction that was competent to hear cases deriving from the awards of the Conciliation and Arbitration commissions. Under the amendment of article 94, which established the Labor Chamber in the Supreme Court, cases of this type were to be heard by the Court only on appeal from the district courts. This arrangement was fully in conformity with the provisions of sections II through IX of article 107 of the Constitution, which established direct *amparo* for definitive judgments in civil and penal cases, defined the nature of a definitive judgment, and specified that *amparo* be initiated in all other circumstances before the district courts. The new judiciary act, however, provided that the Labor Chamber hear *amparos* against arbitration awards directly and thus established an equivalence between these administrative decrees and the decisions of judicial bodies. The stated purpose of the change was to shorten the process of litigation in favor

[20] Ibid., pp. 13–14.

[21] For a conspicuous example see Suprema Corte, *El Aguila, S. A., y coags.*, 62 *Semanario Judicial de la Federación* 3021 (1939), the leading petroleum expropriation case. Whatever the merits of the decision in this case, it cannot be denied that the Court departed radically from a long line of previous decisions of procedural and other requirements in expropriation.

Future references to the *Semanario Judicial* will be by initials *S. J.* This publication contains the official case reports of the Supreme Court.

of the laborer, who was, presumably, placed at a special disadvantage by the delay involved in the former procedure.

The exposition of motives discounted possible claims of unconstitutionality, saying that the arbitral awards handed down by the Conciliation and Arbitration commissions possessed the same final and unmodifiable character displayed by the definitive judicial judgment; that is, they established res judicata, and the process employed was the equivalent of a judicial trial. Objections founded on section IX of article 107, which granted jurisdiction to the district courts in cases arising from acts performed by other than judicial authorities, were rejected upon the authority of Supreme Court decisions asserting the right of the Court to settle jurisdictional conflicts between the lower courts and the labor authorities. This power was, in turn, based on article 106 of the Constitution, which authorized the Supreme Court to resolve jurisdictional controversies arising between federal courts, between federal and state courts, and between the courts of different states. Since the Constitution grants no authority to the Court for settling jurisdictional disputes between courts and administrative agencies, in the Court's opinion, the Conciliation and Arbitration commissions were, in effect, judicial tribunals despite their legal and organizational status as administrative bodies.[22] The Court, however, had never carried the conclusion this far. Until the judiciary act of 1935 was promulgated, labor *amparos* deriving from any source were initiated uniformly in the district courts and reviewed in the Supreme Court in strict conformity with the provisions of section IX of article 107.

By the end of 1935, the extensive statutory and constitutional changes effected in the federal judiciary, particularly in labor matters, had rendered the *amparo* Law of 1919 obsolete. In December 1935 the executive, therefore, submitted proposals for new legislation in this field. The new code was promulgated in January 1936 and, as amended in 1950, 1957, 1963, 1967, and 1968, remains in force. Except for the modifications introduced to conform with the changes in the judiciary, this legislation contained nothing significantly new

[22] Cámara de Diputados, *Debates de la Cámara de Diputados*. XXXVI Legislatura, II, no. 16, p. 20.

in the theory or practice of *amparo*. There is one interesting point, however: articles 161 and 162, which regulated in detail the requirement of section II of article 107 of the Constitution—that violations committed during the course of a trial must be protested at the time if they are to serve subsequently as grounds for an *amparo* suit—were not extended to cover this type of violation when committed in the process of granting an arbitral award. In view of the argument that equated these awards with definitive judgments, granting them the benefits of section II without the corresponding disadvantages was somewhat illogical and of dubious constitutionality. The exception was justified primarily on the grounds that such procedural technicalities would necessarily interfere with the policy of making *amparo* more accessible to the working class.[23]

## The Amendment Proposals of 1944

By 1944 it had become apparent that economic and population growth, in conjunction with the universal and mandatory appeals jurisdiction imposed upon the Supreme Court by the guarantees of legality contained in articles 14 and 16 of the Constitution, was gradually rendering it impossible for that tribunal to perform its proper function. At the end of 1943, the backlog of unsettled business of all kinds amounted to 19,009 items, of which 12,862 consisted of civil *amparos*.[24] Enlarging the Court and dividing it into chambers had evidently proven inadequate to solve the problem posed by the rising flood of litigation.

In response to this unworkable situation, President Manuel Avila Camacho in 1944 presented to the Congress a series of proposals designed to attack the evil at its source, namely, the saddling of the Supreme Court with the functions and responsibilities of a general court of cassation. Avila Comacho conceded that the admissibility of

---

[23] Ibid., no. 23, pp. 7–10.

[24] Suprema Corte, *Informe rendido a la Suprema Corte de Justicia de la Nación por su presidente el Señor Lic. D. Salvador Urbina al terminar el año de 1943, informe de la presidencia*, p. 13 (cited hereafter as *Informe* plus year).

*amparo* against civil judicial decisions could not, in justice, be abandoned nor any other general limitation be imposed upon the availability of the suit; he suggested that the only remaining solution lay in reassigning jurisdictions between the various federal tribunals. There were two methods suggested for accomplishing this purpose: amend the constitution to change the jurisdictional assignments contained in its text, or grant power to the Congress to regulate jurisdictions by statute. The president indicated his preference for the latter, while retaining in the Constitution jurisdictional safeguards for the Court in matters essential to its status as one of the three governmental powers. The guiding principle of the legislator in exercising these new powers should be to restrict the Supreme Court to matters of genuine constitutional or public importance, thus suppressing the existing rule by which the Court was constitutionally compelled to hear, either directly or on appeal, every *amparo* that came to trial. The basis of legislative distinction, consequently, was to be between *amparo* as control of constitutionality and *amparo* as control of legality. Thus the latter should be entrusted primarily to the lower courts for definitive solution. The phrase "control of legality" refers to the cassation function performed by *amparo*, that is, the review of final judicial decisions to determine whether secondary legislation has been properly selected, interpreted, and applied. It appears from this that the president discounted the fact that the control of legality, by virtue of the terms of articles 14 and 16, invariably and by definition poses a constitutional question as well as a statutory one. He admitted that in some situations the "control of legality" could be more important than that of constitutionality; rather than create a rigid hierarchy of exceptions, which would restrain the discretion of the legislative branch, he concluded that it would be preferable to adhere to the formal distinction between constitutional and statutory control. Specifically, the proposed text of article 107 gave jurisdiction to the Supreme Court in all *amparos* involving an allegation of unconstitutionality directed at either federal or local laws, direct violations of a constitutional provision, acts in violation of *jurisprudencia*, or acts seriously affecting the public interest. Concerning the second of these, it stated explicitly that no infraction of a statute could be considered a direct violation of the Constitution.[25]

Before considering certain more theoretical criticisms of the amendment proposals, one serious practical flaw should be noted: since the litigant had the freedom to allege the unconstitutionality of the laws that had been applied in deciding his suit, the congestion of the Supreme Court's docket would have been little diminished.

A more basic criticism is that the problem of securing a greater degree of uniformity in interpreting and applying law was not adequately resolved. By requiring Supreme Court jurisdiction in cases involving violations of *jurisprudencia* and acts gravely affecting the public interest, it was possibly intended that the Court exercise some discretion about what cases it would hear, but the phrasing of this provision was so ambiguous that it caused uncertainty on this point. The Congress, of course, would also have been free to confer a discretionary jurisdiction on the Court, but this would be unlikely considering the traditionally rigid assignment of jurisdiction by law in Mexican practice. The most serious doctrinal criticism, perhaps, lay in the contention that the distinction between statutory and constitutional control was fictitious and, in itself, a violation of the guarantees contained in articles 14 and 16 of the Constitution.

The presidential proposals were the object of immediate and vehement attack by the Supreme Court, essentially in terms of the criticisms considered above. The Court also declared that the authority proposed for the Congress would violate the principle of separation of powers and leave the judiciary at the mercy of the legislative branch. Referring to the practical problem posed by the backlog of unsettled cases, the Court added that the proposed modifications would serve merely to transfer the load without disposing of it effectively.[26] This battery of

[25] Manuel Rangel y Vásquez, *El control de la constitucionalidad de las leyes y el juicio de amparo de garantías en el estado federal; la defensa integral de la constitución*, pp. 480–487. This thesis reprints the complete text of the 1944 proposals and of the exposition of motives attached thereto. It has been used in lieu of the senate debates, which contain the original publication of the proposals, since these were not available.

[26] Suprema Corte, *El problema del rezago de juicios de amparo en materia civil*, pp. 63–77.

criticisms proved effective, and, although the Congress had already given its approval, the proposals were not submitted to the state legistures for ratification.[27]

## The Supreme Court Proposals of 1945

Not content with the negative role of critic, and confronted with the increasingly serious problem of undecided cases, the Court itself produced a series of amendment proposals in 1945. These recommendations were partly the result of studies dating from 1941. The suggestions drafted at that time by ministers Salvador Urbina and Gabino Fraga had, however, failed to secure the approval of the remainder of the Court. Unfortunately, the Urbina-Fraga draft was so marred by ambiguities that it presented insuperable difficulties in interpretation. Nonetheless, several of its provisions are sufficiently indicative of the remedies that the Court then considered sufficient that a brief examination of them is pertinent. Referring to *amparos* directed against civil judgments, it was suggested that section II of article 107 be rewritten in a manner that would limit the extent to which infractions of the law based on alleged contradictions between the terms of the judicial decision and the letter or judicial interpretation of the law could be claimed. The statement of this proposal is by no means clear. The intent might have been to exclude, in whole or in part, cases alleging violations of legality not clearly founded on the express terms of a statute. In the case of contested actions that were performed by other than judicial authorities, it was proposed that *amparo* be admissible only when no extrajudicial form of appeal was available. In *amparos* directed against administrative resolutions pronounced in procedures having the characteristics of a suit at law, admissibility would be subjected to the rules set forth in sections I and II. The Court apparently hoped that a significant number of litigants would be content to waive appeal and recommended, therefore, that direct *amparo* by the Supreme Court be abolished and that all cases be initiated before the district courts. Where the *amparo* was requested against an act, other than a de-

[27] Mariano Azuela, "Trayectoria y destino del juicio de amparo," *El Foro,* 4th series, nos. 4–6 (April–December 1954): 144.

finitive judgment or its equivalent in administrative or labor proceedings, the appeal was to lie before the circuit courts, with powers of final decision, aside from certain, ill-defined cases of more general public or legal interest; in these the Supreme Court would retain a discretionary power to subject the matter to a further review.[28] On the whole, it is not probable that these proposals, except possibly the last, would have made much difference in the volume of business coming before the Supreme Court.

The proposals submitted by the Supreme Court in 1945 were more limited in scope but more promising. The major recommendations were three: the addition to the Court of five supernumerary ministers to be organized, temporarily, in an auxiliary civil chamber; the relegation of appeals in civil *amparo* to the circuit courts; and authorization to dismiss civil *amparo* when there was procedural inactivity on the part of the complainant. In one form or another, all of these recommendations were incorporated in the amendments approved in 1950. In the exposition of motives, the Court asserted that the bulk of the case backlog consisted of civil *amparos* and that, over a period of ten years, 45 percent of these were appeals. Appeals in civil *amparo* arose only from the exceptions listed in section IX of article 107 and related, usually, to questions of minor importance; relegating them to the circuit courts, while it preserved the principle of appeal, would not deprive the Court of any significant jurisdiction. It was estimated that the addition of four new circuit courts to the six already in existence would suffice to handle these appeals without delaying the conduct of other business. In direct *amparos* of a civil nature, however, the Court was now unwilling to forego any of its existing jurisdiction. It argued that by removing appeals in civil *amparo*, the Civil Chamber would be able to handle the ordinary influx of direct *amparos*. The problem posed by the existing backlog of some eight thousand cases would thus be solved by creating a temporary auxiliary chamber. When these cases were cleared, the supernumerary ministers would revert to the status of substitutes filling temporary vacancies in the ranks of regular ministers. The risk of introducing a political element into the deliberations

[28] Suprema Corte, *El problema del rezago*, pp. 9–13.

of the Court by further enlarging its membership would therefore be avoided. The Court recognized that both the transfer of jurisdiction to the circuit courts and the creation of an auxiliary chamber would involve difficulties in establishment and uniformity of *jurisprudencia*. It discounted the risk by referring to the mass of precedents already available in questions that ordinarily arose in civil *amparo* appeals. It suggested, furthermore, that meetings between the various circuit court magistrates and directions from the high court itself would suffice to resolve differences and produce the necessary degree of consistency. Considering the legally prescribed procedure whereby *jurisprudencia* could be established only by the Supreme Court in the process of settling actual cases, there were two principal weaknesses in the new argument: it provided no method for modifying the obligatory precedents already established within the jurisdictional area that would be transferred to the circuit courts, and it did not satisfactorily solve the problem that would arise if the regular and auxiliary civil chambers established conflicting *jurisprudencia*. The provision authorizing dismissal because of "procedural inactivity" was justified partly by reference to previous uses of the device, both in *amparo* and in other types of suits, and by the consideration that if the complainant were not interested enough in resolving the case to take necessary steps, it could be safely assumed to have become moot.[29] Although the Court's presentation was sufficiently sound, with the possible exceptions noted, it would not be uncharitable to note a certain inconsistency between the proposals of 1945 and some of the criticisms leveled at the executive suggestions in 1944, particularly in the matter of reassigning jurisdictions on the basis of the relative constitutional significance of the issues involved.

## The Alemán Amendments, 1950–1951

Although the amendment proposals of 1944 and 1945 aired the problem of the case backlog and explored various avenues of solution, they had no practical, legislative, or constitutional results. The crisis continued to mount, until by the end of 1950 the items of unsettled

---

[29] Ibid., pp. 88–106.

business in the Supreme Court reached a total of 37,881. During the same period the number of items annually dispatched by the Court fell from 87 percent of the new material coming in in 1946, to 68 percent in 1950.[30] The reforms of 1928 and 1934, which divided the Court into chambers and enlarged its membership, had been palliatives only. If the Court were not to become, in effect, an instrument for the denial of justice, it was evident that some drastic changes would have to be made. The urgent necessity of solving this dilemma provided the primary motivation for the constitutional and statutory amendments adopted in 1950.

In introducing his proposals, President Alemán disclaimed any intention of seeking a solution that limited the availability of the *amparo* suit, in judicial or nonjudicial matters. Having ruled out this possibility, he adhered, in principle, to the suggestions made by the Court in 1945, and recommended three major innovations in organization and procedure. The first of these provided for establishing a system of collegial circuit tribunals, each consisting of three members, to assume part of the Supreme Court's jurisdiction in both direct and indirect *amparo*. The other two paralleled the earlier Court recommendations: they provided for the appointment of five supernumerary Supreme Court ministers to serve temporarily as an auxiliary chamber, and authorized the Court to dismiss cases on grounds of "procedural inactivity."

The principle involved in distributing jurisdiction between the Supreme Court and the collegial circuit tribunals rested upon the constitutional, legal, or public significance of the issues likely to be raised in various types of cases. The actual assignment of jurisdictions was, as always, rigidly defined in the Constitution, which left the high court no discretion in the matter. In direct *amparo*, the collegial circuit tribunals were to hear all cases directed against procedural violations committed during the course of the trial, as well as to take cognizance of *amparos* against the final judgments handed down in civil or penal cases of such a minor character that they offered no ordinary legal right of appeal. Jurisdiction was retained by the Supreme Court in

---

[30] Suprema Corte, *Informe, 1946, 1950,* Annex 10 in each case.

*amparos* directed against violations in the final judgment in civil and penal cases of greater moment, or against arbitral awards. For the not infrequent situation in which both types of violation are claimed, the new text of article 107 provided for a prior hearing by the appropriate collegial circuit tribunal of the procedural violations, with the Supreme Court taking jurisdiction with respect to the judgment only if the case were dismissed or *amparo* denied. Appeals from the collegial tribunals to the Supreme Court in direct *amparo* were restricted to cases in which the former declared a law unconstitutional or established a direct interpretation of a constitutional provision. Even in these cases, an appeal would not be admissible if the collegial tribunal's decision was based on *jurisprudencia*. The question of who, precisely, was to determine this has never been answered satisfactorily. In appeals in indirect *amparo*, the Supreme Court continued to enjoy exclusive jurisdiction in all cases that contested the constitutionality of a law or alleged an invasion of sovereignties as referred to in sections II and III of article 103 of the Constitution; furthermore, the Supreme Court retained sole jurisdiction in cases contesting the acts of federal administrative authorities and, in penal *amparos*, those alleging violations of article 22 of the Constitution. Appeals not falling under these headings were assigned to the collegial tribunals, whose decisions were to be final.

The creation of the collegial circuit tribunals, as courts of last resort, necessarily raised those problems concerning *jurisprudencia* that the Supreme Court had attempted to deal with in 1945. The adopted solution provided that the appropriate chamber of the Supreme Court settle contradictions arising between the collegial tribunals, while the contradictory decisions of the chambers themselves be resolved in a session of the full Court.

The modifications designed to dispose of the Court's case backlog, although the most immediately important, were by no means the only significant changes introduced. The existence and obligations of *jurisprudencia* received constitutional recognition and sanction for the first time, in sections IX and XIII of article 107. The exposition of motives, in justifying this inclusion, speaks of it as a source of law. It is rather unusual in a civil law country that judicial precedent is accorded this status, and the conclusion is certainly not universally accepted among

Mexican lawyers and jurists. Nonetheless, the presence of this principle in the Constitution lends additional strength, potentially at least, to the practice of judicial review since it overcomes somewhat the limitation that the effect of judgments be restricted to the parties in the special case at hand, which is otherwise fundamental in *amparo*. The power to correct defective complaints, previously limited to the Supreme Court acting in penal *amparos*, was extended both in subject matter and in the courts empowered to employ it. In referring to this development, the exposition of motives indicated that the Court's *jurisprudencia* had already sanctioned the practice of supplementing such complaints in indirect penal *amparo*, an indication of the Court's willingness, upon occasion, to overstep the bounds of strict interpretation in the interest of equity. In addition to this modification, however, section II of article 107 also authorized the courts to correct defective complaints in any case in which the act complained of was based on laws declared unconstitutional in *jurisprudencia* and, in labor *amparos*, when the benefit of this action redounded to the laborer. These amendments were indicative mainly of the general tendency to mitigate technical requirements wherever these were unduly restrictive in making *amparo* available to the less prosperous classes of litigants. The extension of the power to correct defective complaints to any case based on laws designated as unconstitutional by *jurisprudencia* indicates a heightened degree of respect for the Supreme Court's constitutional control function and, perhaps, a desire to achieve a greater generality of effect for such decisions. Finally, among the substantive achievements was that equivalence—for purposes of *amparo*—of arbitral awards and definitive judicial decisions was established constitutionally, thus solving the question of constitutionality raised by the judicial amendments of 1935.[31] The changes introduced by the amended version of article 107 were implemented by appropriate modifications in the Amparo Law and in the Organic Law of the Judicial Power. The new system went into effect in May 1951.[32]

---

[31] Cámara de Diputados, *Diario de los debates de la Cámara de Diputados*, XLI Legislatura, I, no. 18, pp. 7–12.

[32] *Nueva ley de amparo orgánica de los artículos 103 y 107 de la Constitución Federal*, and *Ley orgánica del poder judicial de la Federación*, pp. 315, 362 bis 9a.

During their first few years in effect, the 1950 amendments seemed to have accomplished their primary purpose of disposing of the residue of unsettled cases and placing the Supreme Court in a position to keep abreast of the influx of new business. By the end of 1953, the backlog of civil *amparos* had nearly disappeared, and the auxiliary chamber continued in existence until the end of 1955 to assist the Penal and Administrative chambers in clearing up their lesser stock of unfinished business. Dismissals for "procedural inactivity" also contributed substantially to solving the problem and, since this procedure was given permanent status in the amended Amparo Law, continued to be available as a device for restricting the growth of a new burden of undecided cases. The short period of six months, after which the action lapsed if the aggrieved party took no procedural steps, was, however, criticized severely as being excessively burdensome. Other aspects of the amendments also met with a great deal of adverse criticism, particularly the jurisdictional division between the Supreme Court and the collegial circuit tribunals in direct *amparo* when both procedural violations and violations in the final judgment were alleged. It was said that the collegial tribunals occasionally rejected an entire complaint of this type, as inadmissible, thus invading the jurisdiction of the Supreme Court, which was left with no procedure for taking cognizance of the allegations directed at the final judgment itself. A similar difficulty arose concerning the power to correct defective complaints in direct penal *amparos* directed solely against the final sentence. Even though the Supreme Court might, in such cases, recognize procedural violations sufficient to justify granting *amparo*, it was prevented, by the grant of jurisdiction to the collegial tribunals, from taking cognizance of them.[33] It was also argued by some that the collegial circuit tribunals violated the principle of judicial hierarchy and, for this and the other reasons noted, should be abolished.[34] On the whole, however, after some years of experience, most of the innovations introduced by the 1950 amendments seemed to have met with general approval.

[33] Azuela, "Trayectoria y destino del juicio de amparo," p. 147.

[34] Ignacio Burgoa, *Reformas a la ordenación positiva vigente del amparo, proyecto de modificaciones a la Constitución Federal, a la ley de amparo y a la ley orgánica del poder judicial de la federación*, pp. 23–28.

After the temporary abolition of the auxiliary chamber, effective in 1956, and the renewed growth in the volume of new business submitted annually to the Supreme Court, however, the old problem of an accumulating mass of undecided cases reappeared. A few figures suffice to indicate the trend. In 1950, the last year prior to the inauguration of the amendments, 12,288 new items of all varieties were filed with the Supreme Court. With the establishment of the collegial tribunals in 1951, this number fell to 8,927 and reached the low point of 6,544 in 1952. From that date, the total has risen steadily to reach and surpass the 1950 level. This trend can best be accounted for by the country's continuing rapid economic and population growth. The increasing number of administrative *amparos* would certainly bear this out.[35] The abolition of the auxiliary chamber had a serious effect on the Court's capacity to keep up with this increasing work load. In 1950, business of all types dispatched by the Court amounted to only 68 percent of the new cases and other material coming before it. During the years 1952, 1953, and 1954, the period of greatest activity for the auxiliary chamber, these percentages rose to 112, 185, and 160, respectively. By 1956 and 1957, the figure had declined to 88 percent.[36] As the volume of litigation continued to climb, it proved only a matter of time before the case backlog again presented as serious and refractory a problem as it did in 1950.

## The Amendments of 1958

As the preceding remarks have indicated, the various reforms of *amparo* have been either formulated with the assistance of the legal profession or subjected to effective criticism prior to passage.[37] The announcement in the press, on 18 December 1957, of projected *amparo* amendments presented the Mexican bar, however, with something very much like a *fait accompli*. A delay in passage was requested,

[35] Suprema Corte, *Informe, 1935* (Informe de la presidencia), p. 4.

[36] Ibid., (1950, 1951), Annex 10; (1952, 1953, 1956, 1957), Annex 11; (1954, 1955), Annex 12.

[37] On this point, see also Francisco Yllanes Ramos, "Reformas inconstitucionales al amparo," *Revista de la facultad de derecho de México* 7 (October–June 1957): 186–187 (cited hereafter as *Revista de la facultad*).

and a committee of distinguished attorneys, consisting of Licenciados Jesús Rodríguez Gómez, Antonio Pérez Verdía, Francisco Javier Gaxiola, Jr., Roberto Mantilla Molina, and Gustavo R. Velasco, was appointed to make representations before the Congress and interested administrative authorities. They said that the measures should not be enacted until the legal profession had had adequate time to study them and make recommendations. Despite these efforts, the new amendments to the Amparo Law and the Organic Law of the Judicial Power were enacted in the Senate on December 20, and in the Chamber of Deputies on the twenty-seventh, to take effect on the first of January 1958. During their progress through the Congress only two speakers openly opposed them, Senator Fausto Acosta Romo and Deputy Manuel Sierra Macedo.[38]

The essential alteration introduced by these amendments was contained in article 11, sections XII and XIII, of the Organic Law of the Judicial Power. It specified that the Supreme Court, sitting *en banc* rather than in chambers, hear all appeals from the district courts and the collegial circuit tribunals that questioned the constitutionality of a federal or state law, as well as all cases that alleged the invasion of sovereignties referred to in sections II and III of article 103 of the Constitution. Article 92 of the Amparo Law provided that, in the former of the above cases, the chambers, or the appropriate collegial tribunal, retain jurisdiction in infractions that pertained to interpreting or applying ordinary legislation. This provision, consequently, introduced a divided jurisdiction, whereby the Court, *en banc*, tried that portion of the case relating to the alleged unconstitutionality of the law, while the appropriate chamber, or collegial tribunal, retained responsibility for the remaining allegations contained in the complaint. Curiously enough, articles 24 through 27 of the Organic Law of the Judicial Power, which designated the jurisdictions to be assigned to the chambers, left to them the responsibility for reviewing the decisions of the collegial tribunals in cases in which the latter might establish the

38 Jesús Rodriguez Gómez, introductory statement in "Sorpresivas reformas a las leyes de amparo y orgánica del poder judicial federal y debate al respecto," *El Foro*, 4th series, no. 20–21 (January–June 1958): 157–158.

direct interpretation of a constitutional provision.[39] What would happen if the aforementioned constitutional interpretation resulted from a decision on the constitutionality of a law was not clarified. Presumably the full Court would have had to decide the latter question first.

People have invariably two reasons for their actions, a good one—for public display—and the real one. This appears to be the case with the 1957 amendments. The official justification expressed by the executive in submitting the amendments to the Congress centered around the alleged inappropriateness of subjecting legislation to the test of constitutionality before a Supreme Court chamber which had the power to decide the question by a mere three votes. Determining the constitutionality of laws was, it was said, the most important function exercised by the Court, and nothing short of the consideration of its full membership could do it adequate justice.[40] The real motivation, at least what a large part of the Mexican legal profession believed, was considerably more mundane. Lic. F. Jorge Gaxiola expressed the general opinion when he suggested that the principal reason was simply that the Administrative Chamber of the Supreme Court had invalidated enough federal and state fiscal legislation, along with various price control and other economic measures, to render itself obnoxious to the administrative authorities.[41] The practical results of the amendments bear out this opinion. There is no evidence that any prior study was made to determine the extent of the burden that would be thrown upon the full Court by this transfer of functions. It was necessarily evident however that an interminable delay in settling such cases would be the most immediate result. This was shown by the fact, according to then current estimates, that the Court had on hand two thousand cases alleging the unconstitutionality of laws, while, during the year of

[39] "Reformas al amparo contra leyes," *Revista de la facultad* 7 (October–December 1957): 159–162.

[40] Gabino Fraga, "Carta del Lic. Gabino Fraga," in "Sorpresivas reformas," *El Foro*, 4th series, nos. 20–21 (January–June 1958): 185.

[41] "Ponencia del Lic. F. Jorge Gaxiola relativa a las recientes reformas en materia de amparo," in "Sorpresiva reformas," *El Foro*, 4th series, nos. 20–21 (January–June 1958): 167. In interviews with a number of Mexican attorneys, two ministers of the Supreme Court, and various members of the Court staff, this same opinion was invariably expressed.

1958, it was able, acting *en banc*, to dispose of only eighteen such cases.[42] At this glacial rate, an *amparo* suit of this type would have to become an inheritable property if it were ever to see the day of decision, while the Court itself would come to resemble Dickens' Court of Chancery. Furthermore, it was predictable that the number of *amparos* directed against laws would increase, particularly in the civil, penal, and labor fields where they had been previously rare, as less scrupulous litigants discovered the potentialities for delay inherent in this form of allegation. Because of the organization and volume of business of the Court, no procedure available to it seemed capable of mitigating this unfortunate effect. The Court was required by article 9 of the Organic Law of the Judicial Power to meet *en banc* at least once a week, but no reorganization procedure could suffice to permit the transaction of an appreciably larger amount of business during this session. Additional *en banc* sessions could have been held, of course, but only by interfering seriously with the ordinary business of the chambers. The only practicable solution of the problem lay in repealing or modifying the amendments substantially.

The plausibility of the administration arguments in support of the amendments was further vitiated by the following fact: the decisions on constitutionality that they referred to were arrived at originally in the district courts, therefore by one judge rather than the three or more provided by the Supreme Court chambers, and might never be subjected to review. Although virtually every case of this nature would be appealed, a defect in the statement of the complaint could easily prevent the Court from taking cognizance of the constitutional question. Whatever practical significance this point may possess, the logic of its own argument should have led the administration either to confine these questions exclusively to the Supreme Court, or at least to provide a mandatory review of any such decision reached at the district court level.[43] It is also possible to see in the administration's exposition

42 Interview with Lic. F. Jorge Gaxiola, 13 December 1958.

43 Antonio Martínez Báez, "Versión relativa a las diversas intervenciones en la reunión de estudio de las leyes de amparo y orgánica del poder judicial federal," in "Sorpresivas reformas," *El Foro*, 4th series, nos. 20–21 (January–June 1958): 195–196; and interviews 14 and 23 October 1958.

of motives a violation in spirit of the Otero formula, which limited the scope of the *amparo* judgment to the specific case at hand. The transcendent importance attributed to a decision on the constitutionality of a law and the requirement that only the full Court might render such a judgment implies that the Court, in these cases, is acting primarily in its capacity as one of the three coordinate branches of the federal government, rather than exercising the conventionally limited and concrete function of a court of law defining the legal rights and obligations of definite parties engaged in controversy. In Mexico, where the decision assumes a certain generality of effect only when *jurisprudencia* is established, the distinction is by no means as dubious as it would be in the United States. Given the traditional contention of the Mexican legal profession that the chief virtue of *amparo* as an instrument of constitutional control is that it avoids direct confrontations between public powers, an implication to the contrary is incongruous.[44]

Experience has revealed several additional problems, probably resulting from the rapidity with which the amendments were formulated and enacted. From the administration's point of view the most serious problem is that the fiscal authorities are placed, by delay, in a position potentially as disadvantageous as that occupied by their counterparts in the suit. Considering that the district courts were authorized to grant suspension orders in tax and other fiscal cases, whereby the sums in question were held in deposit pending the final disposition of the case, the federal and state fiscal authorities were likely to be deprived indefinitely of certain and useful possession. It is, of course, more than likely that the government hoped, by this measure, to discourage recourse to *amparo* in situations involving small amounts of money.[45]

---

[44] Fraga, "Carta del Lic. Gabino Fraga," 185. For a consideration of constitutional objections to the amendments see Yllanes Ramos, "Reformas inconstitucionales al amparo," pp. 188–196. The contention is that the amendments violate articles 1, 13, 14, 16, and 107, section XIII, of the Constitution. The argument, however, is rather strained.

[45] Carlos Cortés Figueroa, "Sobre la administración de justicia federal," *Revista de la facultad* 7 (October–December 1957): 178.

The Court itself uncovered two interesting, and doubtless inadvertent, loopholes in the amended legislation. One of these related to jurisdiction when the allegation of unconstitutionality referred to a *reglamento* rather than to a statute, and the other to the situation that arises when the allegation is brought in direct rather than indirect *amparo*.[46] In the former case, it was decided, by the full Court, that jurisdiction remained with the appropriate chamber. This conclusion was based on a long-standing interpretation of the meaning of the word *ley* ("law") as employed in the Constitution; the Court ruled that although the *reglamento* may possess the characteristics of abstractness, generality, and obligatory application, by which it resembles a law, it departs from the constitutional significance of the term because of its administrative rather than legislative origin. If, in the sense of the Constitution, nothing can be a law that does not constitute a legislative enactment, it follows that a *reglamento* can never possess this character and cannot be construed to be included in the jurisdictional changes instituted by the amendments, since these referred only and exclusively to laws.[47] The logic is impeccable but the administration's probable intent vanishes between the terms of the syllogism. In the second decision referred to above, the Civil and Penal chambers concluded that, since the amendments spoke only of appeals in *amparo*, a question of the constitutionality of a law raised in direct *amparo* remained within the jurisdiction of the appropriate chamber.[48] The conclusion was entirely reasonable, given the phrasing of the amendments, but evidently inconsistent with their purpose. The Labor Chamber, however, held that when the constitutionality of a law was attacked in direct *amparo*, this question should be referred to the appropriate district court, in conformity with the provisions of articles 78 and 84, section I, subsection (a), of the Amparo Law, and article 27, sections II and III, of the Judiciary Law. In conformity with this opinion, the

[46] The term *reglamento* refers to an administrative rule, order, or regulation, issued on the authority of a statute and providing in necessary detail for its execution.

[47] Asociación Nacional de Funcionarios Judiciales, *Manuel Martínez Pérez*, 133 *Boletín de Información Judicial* 514, September 1958. Future references to the *Boletín* will be by the initials *BIJ*.

[48] Asociación, *Daniel Castillo Rogel*, 126 *BIJ* 150, February 1958.

Supreme Court could consider the constitutionality of the law only on appeal and *en banc*.

Because of the obvious difficulty in applying the 1958 amendments —if the Supreme Court were not to be paralyzed—the undisguised hostility of the legal profession, and the disadvantages likely to redound to the administration itself, it was generally expected that the new government of President Adolfo López Mateos, inaugurated in 1958, would recommend their repeal as a part of a general revision of the laws pertaining to *amparo*.[49] Despite periodic debate in and out of the Congress and the administration, however, major reforms were not enacted until 1967.

## The Amendments of 1963

The reforms promulgated in 1963 were designed to ease procedures and speed litigation in *amparos* involving the constitutional interests of *ejidos* and other rural collectives whether de jure or de facto. This reflected the special role of agrarian reform along collective lines in the mystique of the Mexican revolution. The principal changes introduced provided for correcting, by the courts ex officio, defective complaints that alleged the violation of collective agrarian rights; the reforms also abolished the statutory fixed periods of time between the date of the alleged violation of rights and the last date upon which this type of *amparo* suit must be initiated, prohibited dismissals for procedural inactivity on the part of the plaintiff, and vested responsibility in the courts, ex officio, for securing and introducing relevant evidence in this class of cases. The agrarian collective has, consequently, joined the category of privileged complainants, along with the worker in labor *amparos*. Although this has encountered little criticism and a good deal of praise within the legal profession, the amendments have been subject to strenuous objections on technical, procedural grounds.[50]

---

[49] This opinion was uniformly expressed by the judges and attorneys interviewed between October and December 1958.

[50] For a detailed discussion of *amparo* in agrarian matters, see Ignacio Burgoa, *El amparo en materia agraria*.

*The Amendments of 1967–1968*

As noted above, the expedients adopted in the 1950 amendments served only briefly to halt the accumulating backlog of unfinished business in the Supreme Court; on the other hand, the requirement, introduced in 1958, that questions concerning the constitutionality of laws be decided by the Court *en banc,* added an additional, and serious, element of delay. Consequently, the situation had again reached the proportions of a crisis by 1967. Despite this fact, the amendments to article 107 of the Constitution ratified in that year, and the corresponding amendments to the Amparo and Judiciary laws promulgated in 1968, contained nothing that would provide a permanent solution. The new legislation, like that of 1950, is intended almost exclusively to speed the course of litigation, and it endeavors to secure this result primarily through procedural tinkering and reallocating jurisdictions. Both the constitutional and the statutory modifications were scheduled to go into effect in October 1968.

Although a detailed analysis of the *amparo* legislation, including the most recent amendments, is given in subsequent chapters, certain aspects of the new legislation deserve brief consideration at this point. From a doctrinal point of view, and considering *amparo*'s effectiveness as a juridical mode of constitutional defense, the most important innovation is that which authorizes the collegial circuit tribunals to establish *jurisprudencia.* This marks a considerable extension of the willingness to recognize judicial decisions as a true source of law. On more practical grounds, however, and since stare decisis does not exist in the Mexican legal system as a general governing principle of jurisprudence, this change may have very undesirable consequences. One can foresee a chaos of inconsistent and contradictory interpretations of the same laws, all presumably equally authoritative; the result would be juridical anarchy. To avoid this, provision has been made for allegedly inconsistent jurisprudential theses to be brought to the attention of the appropriate Supreme Court chamber by any minister of the Court, by the attorney general, by the tribunals themselves, or by any party to one or more of the cases in which the *jurisprudencia* was established. It can be anticipated, since *amparo* constitutes the bulk of litigation before the Supreme Court and all the litigation before the collegial circuit tribunals, that this procedure will prove unwieldy, burdensome, time consuming, and therefore relatively ineffective.

The adverse effects of the 1958 amendment, which required the Supreme Court sitting *en banc* to determine the constitutionality of laws, have been partially offset at least. The amended law now provides that this, as well as other questions, shall be decided by the appropriate chambers in all cases in which the constitutionality of a contested law has already been determined in *jurisprudencia* established by the Court in its entirety.

Finally, the new legislation repeals those sections of the 1950 amendments which provided that in direct *amparo* against final judgments the collegial circuit tribunals take exclusive jurisdiction over procedural violations allegedly committed during the course of the trial, while the Supreme Court would retain exclusive jurisdiction over those portions of the same cases in which the judgment itself was claimed to violate individual guarantees. In conformity with the 1968 amendments, both the collegial circuit tribunals and the Supreme Court, when, according to the statutory determination of their respective jurisdictions, properly seized of such a case are to take cognizance of both classes of violations and to resolve the suit in its entirety. This should reduce substantially the time required to try direct *amparo* suits.[51]

[51] Unless otherwise indicated, references to and citations from the current versions of the Constitution, Amparo Law, Judiciary Law, and Federal Code of Civil Procedures are taken from Alberto Trueba Urbina and Jorge Trueba Barrera, *Neuva legislación de amparo: Doctrina, textos y jurisprudencia.*

## Chapter 3

# The Constitutional Foundations of Mexican Judicial Review: Auxiliary Constitutional Defenses

$\frown\frown\frown\frown\frown\frown$

IN THE UNITED STATES, in the absence of explicit constitutional authorization, the practice of judicial review was derived deductively from the concept of constitutional supremacy. It was justified further by the power conferred upon the federal courts to hear cases and controversies arising under the Constitution, by the special competence and qualifications presumably inhering in courts for interpreting the law, including the Constitution, and by the special obligations allegedly imposed by the judicial oath of office. Judicial review in Mexico presents both similarities and differences in derivation. Although the logical, deductive basis of the institution has received some attention and even practical acceptance, the Mexican federal courts base their practice of the function almost exclusively upon the explicit authorization contained in articles 103 and 107 of the Constitution of 1917—the *amparo* articles. Nonetheless, the scope of *amparo* is subject to significant legal limitations. In consequence, additional constitutional provisions have, upon rare occasions, been

called upon to lend both theoretical and practical support to a supplementary jurisdiction lying outside of the *amparo* framework and, in
some instances, exercised by courts not included in the federal judicial
power. These provisions are to be found in articles 97, 105, and 133
of the Constitution.

### Article 97: The Supreme Court as an Investigative Agency

The provisions of article 97 of the Constitution do not pertain directly to the practice of judicial review because they contemplate a
procedure that is not intrinsically judicial. They are, nonetheless, relevant to the more general subject of constitutional defense and the participation of judicial agencies in this function. Paragraph 3 of the
article in question provides that "it [the Supreme Court] shall appoint
one or more of its members, or some district judge or circuit magistrate, or designate one or more special commissioners, when deemed
advisable, or when the federal executive, or one of the chambers of
Congress, or the governor of a state so requests, solely to investigate
the conduct of any federal judge or magistrate, or any act or acts that
may be a violation of any individual guarantee, or electoral violations,
or any other crime punishable by federal law."[1]

The terms of the article clearly indicate that these investigations may
be initiated either by the Court itself, ex officio, or in response to a
formal request by one or more of the officials or agencies named. In
the latter case, the compliance of the Court would appear to be mandatory.[2] In other respects, particularly the investigatory procedures to
be employed, the extent of the powers to be conferred upon the in-
vestigator, and the handling, destination, and effect of the findings, the
intent is less clear. The use of the term "solely"—*únicamente* in the
original—may, perhaps, justify the conclusion that the investigation

[1] Pan American Union, *Constitution of the United Mexican States, 1917*, p. 45.
Translations from the present Mexican Constitution are based on this edition. Minor
alterations have been made where this was necessary for more literal conformity with
the original text. Translations are the author's where subsequent amendment has
completely or substantially altered the text.

[2] Suprema Corte de Justicia, *Fernando Zavala González, Informe rendido a la
Suprema Corte de Justicia de la Nación por su presidente, 1944* (Informe de la
presidencia), p. 142 (cited hereafter as *Informe* plus year).

should be exclusively informational in character, at least insofar as the powers and duties of the Supreme Court are concerned. Nonetheless, it is reasonable to assume that the Court, in the absence of specific provisions to the contrary, might make recommendations that it deems desirable, particularly since the conduct of judges and the violation of individual guarantees—both are intimately related to the functions and responsibilities of the Court—are included among the subjects to be investigated. In the matter of electoral violations, however, the intervention of the Court in an active manner would carry a dangerous suggestion of political involvement, inconsistent with its, ideally, neutral position.[3]

Neither the exposition of motives attached to the Carranza draft constitution, nor the convention debates in 1917, is particularly helpful in clarifying the precise intent of this section of article 97. The exposition of motives speaks of the intervention of the judiciary, without reference to the Supreme Court itself initiating investigations, saying, "the investigation should be not merely informative, in order to judge the necessity or inadmissibility of a legislative measure, but has a merely judicial character," and continues with the assertion that it should serve "solely to clarify the fact concerning which information is desired."[4] Despite the internal contradictions and obscure phraseology of this statement, it is fairly safe to conclude that Carranza perceived the role of the Court to be purely informative in the exercise of this function.

The convention debates contribute no additional information on the subject. The judiciary articles were submitted to the convention by its study committee on 17 January 1917, but were considered only in part. Attention was preempted by the violent differences of opinion aroused by the proposals on judicial appointments and tenure, so that other, and less exciting, provisions were adopted with little or no serious consideration.[5]

---

[3] Suprema Corte, *Informe, 1943* (Informe de la presidencia), pp. 45–47.

[4] Felipe Tena Ramírez, *Leyes fundamentales de México, 1808–1957*, p. 758.

[5] Cámara de Diputados, *Diario de los debates de la Cámara de Diputados del Congreso de los Estados Unidos Mexicanos*, II, 412, 506, 539–541, 543–545, 547–548, 555–558.

Whatever the original expectations, the officials and agencies authorized to call upon the Supreme Court for initiating and conducting
investigations have been loath to avail themselves of the opportunity,
and the Court itself has shown little enthusiasm for the task. Neither
the Congress nor any of the state governors has yet seen fit to request
such an investigation, and the president has done so only once—in
1927—in connection with an alleged electoral fraud in the state of
Guanajuato. In this instance, the Court appointed a circuit magistrate
to conduct the investigation but made no comments or recommendations of its own about the findings. On eighteen other occasions the
Court has been urged to exercise its powers under article 97, once by
one of its own members, and in the other seventeen instances by private
persons. Action has been taken in only four of these cases, and in three
of them, in 1918, 1920, and 1923, the Court arrived at no official
conclusions. Since 1927, the Court, with only one exception in 1946,
has followed a policy of nonintervention. The 1946 case is of some
interest since it is the only instance in which the Court took official
notice of, and formulated conclusions about, the results of the investigation. Even in this case, the conclusions consisted of nothing more
than a decision to transmit a copy of the investigating committee's report to the president and the governor of the state concerned.

The investigatory power received renewed attention in 1945, in a
new electoral law proposed to the Congress by President Manuel Avila
Camacho. In accordance with the terms of the executive proposal, a
federal commission of electoral supervision, including two representatives of the Supreme Court among its membership, was to be created.
It was suggested that if the judicial members or the commission itself
supplied evidence sufficient to justify a presumption of electoral fraud,
the Court could, at its discretion, initiate an investigation. Aside from
including representatives of the Court on the commission, the presidential proposals obviously imposed no obligations or powers beyond
those already existing in article 97. Despite this, the Congress refused
to adopt the suggestion and, in articles 113, 114, 115, and 116 of the
measure enacted, provided only that the president, or the congressional
chambers, could request such an investigation, with the results to be
communicated to the Congress and the executive for any action that

they might deem necessary. The only departure here from previous practice under article 97 was the specific directive that the results of the investigation be conveyed to the authorities requesting it.[6] The next electoral law, enacted in 1951, deleted even these references to article 97 and provided that the investigation of irregularities in the conduct of elections be undertaken by the attorney general.[7]

In commenting on this article, Supreme Court Minister Felipe Tena Ramírez stresses the undesirable results to be anticipated from any intervention by the Court in the matter of elections. Referring to the long history of fraudulent electoral practices in Mexico, he states that the Court could do little of value to correct the situation and would assuredly lose its neutral status and, along with it, its principal source of strength. Quoting Guizot, he concludes that "politics would have nothing to gain, while justice would have much to lose."[8]

If article 97 is ever to have any practical value, it seems appropriate that it should be in dealing with the violation of individual guarantees, an area in which the Court, after a century of experience with *amparo*, can legitimately claim a special expertise. Referring to this possibility, Tena Ramírez expresses the opinion that the investigatory power should not be wasted on matters amenable to consideration in *amparo*; it should, rather, be restricted to cases in which the violation is of such an extensive nature that it arouses general public alarm and evades the customary judicial remedies.[9]

Although, in theory, article 97 could be utilized as a subsidiary method of constitutional defense, its practical significance has been slight. It is possible that a situation such as that envisaged by Tena Ramírez may arise that will resurrect and justify this almost forgotten judicial power, but the practice of recent years indicates little likelihood of effective use in the future.

### Subsidiary Defenses of the Constitution—Article 105

Besides *amparo*, articles 105 and 133 of the Constitution have offered some possibilities for deducing additional authorizations for the

---

[6] Felipe Tena Ramírez, *Derecho constitucional mexicano*, pp. 554–557.

[7] Felipe López Rosado, *El régimen constitucional mexicano*, p. 622.

[8] Tena Ramírez, *Derecho constitucional*, pp. 557–558.     [9] Ibid., pp. 559–560.

practice of judicial review. It must be admitted, however, that practical applications have been comparatively few. Following are article 105 and those portions of article 104 which contribute to its interpretation:

Article 104.   The federal courts shall have jurisdiction over:

I. All controversies of a civil or criminal nature that arise from enforcing and applying federal laws or from international treaties entered into by the Mexican State. Whenever such controversies affect only the interests of private parties, the regular local judges and courts of the States, or of the Federal District and territories may also assume jurisdiction, at the election of the plaintiff . . .

.   .   .   .   .   .   .   .   .   .   .   .   .   .   .

III. Those in which the federation is a party.

IV. Those that arise between two or more states, or one state and the Federation, and those that arise between courts of the federal district and those of the Federation or a state.

.   .   .   .   .   .   .   .   .   .   .   .   .   .   .

Article 105.   The Supreme Court of Justice of the Nation has exclusive jurisdiction in all controversies that arise between two or more states, between the powers of one state concerning the constitutionality of their acts, and in disputes between the Federation and one or more states, as well as in those in which the Federation is a party where the law so provides.

It should be observed at the outset that article 104, unlike article III, section II, of the United States Constitution, does not confer upon the federal courts a jurisdiction over cases arising under the Constitution; on the contrary, it refers only to laws and treaties. As will be seen, the statement in article 133—that laws emanating from the Constitution and treaties made in accordance with it are the supreme law of the whole union—could be considered as offsetting this deficiency. In practice, however, the failure of article 104 to include the Constitution among the legal instruments to be applied by the federal courts, taken in conjunction with the specific constitutional jurisdiction conferred by articles 103, 105, and 107, has led to the conclusion that no such general power of judicial review, certainly, no explicit declarations on the unconstitutionality of statutes, can be founded directly upon it.

In Supreme Court interpretation, as well as in legislation by the executive and legislative branches, article 105 has been interpreted as authorizing the Court to hear cases involving conflicts of powers between the Federation and the states in which these governmental divisions are themselves the adverse parties. The conduct of such suits, in lieu of special regulation, follows the rules prescribed for private litigation in the Federal Code of Civil Procedures, and the judgment, unlike that in *amparo*, resolves both constitutional and statutory issues.[10]

The most unusual of the jurisdictional grants contained in article 105, that relating to cases arising "between the powers of one state concerning the constitutionality of their acts," presents no problems of intent, but it does open questions about the extent of the authority granted and about which constitution or constitutions are meant. If the plaintiff in such a case is to demonstrate the necessary standing to sue— he must have a personal interest at law alleged to have been infringed —it seems probable that the most usual basis for such suits would be a state constitution.[11] Pertinent case material is very sparse. A search of the published reports has, in fact, uncovered only four cases of this type, all of which were dismissed for lack of standing on the part of the plaintiffs. In concluding for dismissal, however, the Court established the general requirements for a valid suit under this provision of the article. It held that the "powers" referred to are those recognized as such by the federal and state authorities—that is, the legislative, executive, and judicial branches only. Furthermore, these "powers" must, in fact, exist as such, and the allegedly unconstitutional act must have been performed during the normal conduct of governmental functions. It follows that governmental entities other than the "powers" mentioned, and persons claiming a right to the possession of public office, are ineligible to sue, and, hence, that the validity of elections, appointments, or other titles to public office cannot form the subject matter of the suit.[12] In the absence of a case deciding the merits of

---

[10] Suprema Corte, *Informe, 1934*, pp. 9–10.

[11] This conclusion was generally supported in interviews but, given the scarcity of cases, it must rest mainly on the logic of the situation.

[12] Suprema Corte, *Controversia suscitada por el señor Lic. Manuel A. Chávez, representante de Arturo Tremari y otras personas, que se ostentan integrantes del*

such an issue, the nature and scope of judgments and the procedures available and appropriate for enforcement remain uncertain. Since no special regulatory legislation has been provided for any part of article 105, cases of the sort under consideration have been heard by the Court *en banc*, in conformity with the rules of the Federal Code of Civil Procedures.[13] In the procedural sense, the issues arising under this jurisdiction involve the characteristic features of justiciable questions, that is, genuine controversy about the legal rights and obligations of adverse parties. The subject matter in contention, however, is of necessity essentially political and not what a court would normally wish to or be expected to handle, at least with governmental entities as the opposing parties. Certainly, in a case of this nature, the Supreme Court is placed in the position of arbitrating a clash of governmental powers—precisely the situation the founders of *amparo* most wished to avoid. The scarcity of cases indicates, however, that the practical significance of this jurisdiction is extremely limited and can be expected to remain so. Because of the generally accepted views about the nominal character of Mexican federalism and because of the political preponderance of the state governors vis-à-vis the legislative and judicial branches, few such controversies can possibly arise, and any that do would almost certainly be resolved administratively or politically.

There are some differences of opinion among publicists which revolve primarily around the questions: Should a constitutional suit between the Federation and a State ever be admissible and, if so, should it be admissible when the constitutional violation alleged can be settled in *amparo*? Despite this, the meaning and intent of the remaining provisions of article 105 seem clear. The admissibility of constitutional suits (*controversias constitucionales*) directed by the Federation against

---

*Ayuntamiento de Papantla, Estado de Veracruz, contra la Legislatura de Veracruz,* and *Domingo Ramos y otras personas que se presentaron como integrantes del Ayuntamiento de Villa Cuauhtémoc contra la Legislatura de Veracruz* (joined), *Informe, 1936,* p. 127. Also see, Suprema Corte, *Controversia entre el Poder Ejecutivo y un grupo de personas que se presentaron en nombre de la Comisión Permanente del III Congreso del Estado de Jalisco, Informe,* 1931, p. 93, and idem, *Solicitud de los componentes del Ayuntamiento de Motul, Yucatán, Informe, 1935,* p. 107.

[13] Suprema Corte, *Informe, 1934,* pp. 9–10. Also, Tena Ramírez, *Derecho constitucional,* p. 517.

a state, or vice versa, has been explicitly recognized by the Supreme Court and is provided for by the Organic Law of the Judicial Power, the Organic Law of the Federal Public Ministry, and the Law of Fiscal Coordination between the Federation and the states. The Court has expressed:

If the Federation contends that a law enacted by a state has infringed upon the powers it possesses exclusively, while the state maintains the contrary, it is indisputable that the question constitutes a conflict of constitutional character, the resolution of which belongs to the Supreme Court of Justice in accordance with the dispositions of article 105 of the Constitution . . . The provisions of articles 103 and 107 of the Constitution refer to acts of federal or local authorities that restrict or encroach upon the powers assigned to one or the other when, as a result, an individual guarantee is violated, but when the latter circumstance does not exist and a state or the Federation considers that its sovereignty has been invaded, the *amparo* suit cannot serve to resolve the conflict between the two entities. In each case, in accordance with article 133 of the Constitution and consistent with the judicial theory of the judicial power, which assigns to the federal judiciary the essential function of interpreting the Constitution, the Supreme Court of Justice is the only authority competent to maintain the integrity of the federal Constitution, not by means of the *amparo* suit . . . but in accordance with the aforementioned article 105. The latter, as has been held in previous cases, would be an unmotivated and redundant repetition of article 103 if the *amparo* suit were considered the only means available for resolving this class of conflict. Furthermore, if this were not so, there would be no other means than armed force for settling disputes between the Federation and the States . . .[14]

Alluding to the limitations applicable to disputes admissible within this jurisdiction, the Court added, in a reference to article 76, sections V and VI, of the Constitution, that the federal Senate was to settle conflicts of a political character. Although not specifically listed by the Court, these conflicts would include all disputes about the validity of elections and the legitimacy of governments.

To sum up, article 105, with the exception of controversies between

---

[14] Suprema Corte, *Controversia constitucional entre la Federación y el Estado de Oaxaca*, supplement, S. J. 144 (1932).

the powers of one state, is essentially a special case of sections III and IV of article 104, only conferring upon the Supreme Court an exclusive jurisdiction in those cases, previously defined in the more general article, in which the status of the parties rules out the intervention of lesser tribunals. In exercising such jurisdiction, it is evident that constitutional questions may be raised and resolved. It is equally clear from the highly centralized character of the Mexican political system and its domination by the president and the quasi-official Partido Revolucionario Institucional that any genuinely significant constitutional question of this sort will be resolved by political means.

### Subsidiary Defenses of the Constitution—Article 133

The supremacy of the Constitution in the Mexican legal order is established explicitly in article 133, which, as amended in 1934, provides:

This Constitution, the laws of the Congress of the Union that emanate therefrom, and all treaties that have been made and shall be made in accordance therewith by the president of the Republic, with the approval of the Senate, shall be the supreme law of the whole Union. The judges of each state shall conform to the said Constitution, the laws, and treaties, in spite of any contradictory provisions that may appear in the constitution or laws of the states.

The limitations imposed upon the constituent powers of the states are further reinforced by the terms of article 41, which states that:

The people exercise their sovereignty through the powers of the Union in those cases within its jurisdiction, and through those of the states, in all that relates to their internal affairs, under the terms established by the present federal Constitution and the individual constitutions of the states; the latter shall in no event contravene the stipulations of the Federal Pact.

The Supreme Court has established in unmistakable terms that the constitutional supremacy declared in article 133 is binding upon both the federal and state judiciaries.[15] The clearest expression of this is to be found in *Sociedad Cotera Hermanos*, in which the Court held:

---

[15] Suprema Corte, *Jurisprudencia de la Suprema Corte de Justicia en los fallos, pronunciados en los años de 1917 a 1954*, thesis 268, II, 514.

In conformity with article 133 of the federal Constitution every judge in the Republic is obligated to subject his decisions to the provisions of that document regardless of anything to the contrary in the secondary legislation. This being the case, it would be illogical and unjuridical to assert that this obligation can be complied with if the judges do not possess the corresponding power to determine whether the laws applicable to the case are consistent with the supreme code of the Republic when this question forms part of the dispute. To accept the contrary opinion would impose an obligation upon the judges without granting them the necessary means for complying with it.[16]

It should be noted, however, that the Court has not always been so unequivocal. Although the above-cited case apparently represents the consensus, some of its decisions imply strongly that state courts, and federal courts trying cases other than *amparo*, should apply the Constitution in preference to an incompatible statute or state constitution only when this incompatibility has been previously established in *jurisprudencia*.[17] In practice, as distinguished from theory, it appears that state courts rarely arrive at decisions based on the directive contained in article 133. When allegations of unconstitutionality of this sort are made, the constitutional question is normally resolved in a subsequent *amparo* suit or, if the parties are official entities, in a constitutional suit (*controversia constitucional*) based on article 105.[18]

[16] Suprema Corte, 41 S. J. 644 (1934).

[17] See, for example, Suprema Corte, *Competencia entre el Juez de Primera Instancia de Pátzcuaro, Michoacán y el Juzgado de Distrito del mismo Estado, Informe, 1947* (Informe de la presidencia), p. 150; idem, *Núñez de Quintana Maria*, 45 S. J. 2042 (1935), and *Garza de Grauman Aurora*, 117 S. J. 85 (1953). Various doctrinal controversies exist about the legal nature of State court actions in these cases, but they seem to be distinctions with no practical consequences. State courts, under article 133, appear to have the same obligations imposed upon State courts in the United States by the federal Constitution's supremacy clause.

[18] Evidence about the actual practice of State courts is contained in Suprema Corte, *Jurisprudencia de la Suprema Corte*, thesis 593, IV, 1065–1066.

## Chapter 4

# The Constitutional Foundations of Mexican Judicial Review: The *Amparo* Articles

IT HAS BEEN SEEN in the preceding chapter that the subsidiary defenses of the Constitution provided by articles 97, 105, and 133 are of little practical importance. Aside from these limited cases, the practice of judicial review in Mexico is associated at present exclusively with the *amparo* suit. While later chapters will deal with the technical aspects of the action and with the results achieved in applying it, our present concern is with the meaning of the constitutional provisions that establish it. These provisions—article 103 and, in its immediately relevant portions, article 107—state the following:

Article 103.   The federal courts shall decide all controversies that arise:

I. From laws or acts of the authorities that violate individual guarantees;

II. From laws or acts of the federal authority restricting or encroaching on the sovereignty of the states, and

III. From laws or acts of state authorities that invade the sphere of federal authority.

Article 107. All controversies mentioned in Article 103 shall be subject to the legal forms and procedures prescribed by law in accordance with the following rules:

I. The *amparo* suit shall always be prosecuted at the instance of the injured party.

II. The judgment shall always be such that it affects only private individuals, being limited to affording them shelter and protection in the special case to which the complaint refers, without making any general declaration about the law or act on which the complaint is based.

.  .  .  .  .  .  .  .  .  .  .  .  .  .  .  .  .  .  .

XII. Violation of the guarantees set forth in article 16, in criminal matters, and in articles 19 and 20, may be protested before the superior of the court committing the violation, or before the appropriate district judge, and in either case the decision can be appealed in accordance with the terms prescribed in section VIII [providing for review by the Supreme Court or collegial circuit tribunal].

With the exception of the situation envisaged by section XII of article 107, it is to be noted that jurisdiction in *amparo* is entrusted entirely to the federal judiciary. The attempt to confer a concurrent jurisdiction on the state courts, in the constituent convention of 1856–1857, and the reasons for its failure have been discussed. It is reasonable to assume that the same motives operated in retaining a virtually exclusive federal jurisdiction in the present Constitution. The reason for the exception in the case of violations of the criminal sections of article 16 and articles 19 and 20, which also relate to criminal procedure, is that the provisions of these articles must be complied with promptly if they are to achieve their purpose. The grant of an extraordinary jurisdiction to local courts in such instances could prevent the delay occasionally involved in reaching the nearest federal district court. Neither section XII nor article 37 of the present Amparo Law, which relates to it, makes clear the process to be followed if these violations are contested before the immediate hierarchical superior of the court committing the infraction. Presumably the hearing is to be held in conformity with the provisions of the Amparo Law, but the statute does not explicitly provide for this, nor is it certain whether the case is to constitute a separate and independent suit or whether it is to be merely an exception taken on appeal. The Amparo Law of 1919, in regulating paragraph II of article IX—the equivalent of the present section XII—provided: "When the complainant claims the violation of these articles [16, 19, and 20] before the superior of the tribunal committing the infraction, the claim shall be tried and decided in accordance with the dispositions of the local legislatures, and against the judgment rendered the complainant may sue for *amparo* before the Supreme Court of Justice in conformity with the general rules."[1] During the life of this provision, obviously, such cases were not considered to be *amparos*. Article 37 of the present law, on the other hand, limits itself to repeating the provisions of section XII, which, in lieu of anything more specific, may sufficiently justify the inference that only *amparo* procedures may be used. The practical importance of this concurrent jurisdiction, which extends to the federal unitary circuit courts as well as to state and other local courts, is not very considerable. Access to the district courts is not usually too difficult: articles 38, 39, and 40 of the Amparo Law authorize any judicial official to extend temporary relief in certain specified emergency conditions, and the general distrust of the independence and capacity of the state judiciaries leads most litigants, in any event, to avail themselves of the services of the federal courts whenever possible.[2]

*Article 103—Section I*

As indicated in section I of article 103, the controversies to be decided by the federal courts in *amparo* must allege that specific constitutional guarantees have been violated, and this violation must derive from either a law or an act of an authority. Technically, the individual guarantees consist of the first twenty-nine articles of the Constitution, but the Supreme Court has held the following: "It is said that an act of authority violates the individual guarantees when, to the prejudice

[1] Estados Unidos Mexicanos, *Diario oficial*, XIII, no. 46, p. 771. The reference is to paragraph 3, article 90, of the law.

[2] This impression was derived primarily from information obtained in interviews conducted during the last three months of 1958, which included both practicing attorneys and members of the Supreme Court staff. Observations made on subsequent trips to Mexico suggest no reason to alter this opinion.

of a real or artificial person, it infringes any of the rights established in articles 2 through 28 of the federal Constitution, since article 1 contains a general declaration and article 29 establishes the procedure for suspending the individual guarantees."[3] Nevertheless, neither article 1 nor article 29 can be considered devoid of interest for *amparo*. Article 1 establishes the federal nature of the rights conferred by the general Constitution—that is, their status as limitations on all levels of government—and extends them to "every person," whether citizen or alien, except when otherwise specifically provided. It also guarantees that rights may not be suspended or restricted except in the cases and under the conditions specified in the Constitution itself. This latter guarantee refers mainly to article 29, but the Court has established that any other constitutional provision that may, upon occasion, restrict the individual guarantees will be given this restrictive effect, and no such application can be construed as constituting a violation for purposes of *amparo*.[4] For the scope and application of *amparo*, the most interesting questions raised by article 29 concern its inclusiveness. Since this point can be more advantageously considered with the other major limitations applicable to the *amparo* suit, its discussion will be undertaken in a later chapter.[5] Aside from articles 1 and 29, the content of the remaining guarantees can be classified according to a host of such traditional civil liberties as freedom of speech, press and assembly, rights in civil and criminal procedure, property rights and social rights. The latter are elaborated in article 3, which deals with education, in article 27, which defines the rights of property in land and mineral resources and establishes the principles for a program of agrarian reform, and in article 28, which prohibits monopolies and defines the government's responsibilities for suppressing them. They are all more concerned with the powers and active obligations of government than with limiting it. Consequently, they are difficult, if not impossible, to enforce by judicial process.[6] For the situation envisaged by section I of

[3] Suprema Corte de Justicia, *Rojas Guadalupe*, 106 S. J. 1355 (1950).

[4] Suprema Corte, *Yusim Nicolás A.*, 43 S. J. 519 (1934).

[5] See chapter five.

[6] The judicial problems posed by social rights are discussed by Ignacio Burgoa in *Las garantías individuales*. Note particularly the discussion on pp. 178–186 and 344–347.

article 103, the only portions of the Constitution that are, therefore, judically enforceable in *amparo* are the individual guarantees, and the practicability of enforcing some of these is questionable. As a result, the constitutional scope of the action depends on the extent to which these guarantees can be considered to incorporate other provisions of the Constitution. This is true not only of the organic sections but also of provisions, such as article 123, dealing with labor, which, although undoubtedly incorporating individual or social rights, are not included within the bill of individual guarantees. In short, in terms of the applicability of *amparo*, not all constitutional rights are created equal. Theoretical and practical attempts to expand the constitutional scope of the action have been based primarily on interpretations of the due process clauses in articles 14 and 16, a subject which will be examined in detail in the following chapter.

When an act or law violates an individual guarantee, article 103 requires further that the infraction be committed by an "authority." In the general public law of Mexico, an authority is understood to be "an organ of the State legally vested with the powers of decision and command necessary for imposing upon individuals either its own determinations or those that emanate from some other organ of the State."[7] For the purposes of *amparo* this definition has been expanded to include "all those persons who dispose of public power by virtue of either legal or de facto circumstances and who, consequently, find themselves in a position to perform acts of a public character."[8] It follows then, that an *amparo* suit is admissible even though the person who violates an individual guarantee is not the legitimate holder of the public office whose authority he exercises. It is also true, in accordance with the decision in the *Campos Otero* case, that the violative act need not be performed within the general range of the agency's or official's jurisdictional competence. To assume the contrary would remove from the cognizance of the courts one of the most serious, and prolific, sources of such constitutional violations. It is essential, however, that the power employed be public in nature; otherwise, the act, even

---

[7] Suprema Corte, *Campos Otero Julia*, 45 S. J. 5033 (1935).

[8] Suprema Corte, *Jurisprudencia de la Suprema Corte*, thesis 179, II, 360.

though performed by a legitimate holder of public office, must be construed as that of a private individual, and for infractions of this type *amparo* provides no remedy.[9] Not all governmental agencies and officials can be considered "authorities" in the terms of this definition, but only those which are, legally or otherwise, in a position to execute their own or the decisions of others by a coercive use of public power. As a result, those agencies whose functions are entirely of a staff or consultative nature are not "authorities" in the sense of article 103, and their acts cannot be attacked in *amparo*. It is equally true that not all the acts performed by a governmental agency that undeniably possesses the character of an "authority" are in this sense authoritative. Thus, when an official agency acts as a subject of private law, the validity of these acts is not subject to examination in *amparo*.[10]

Although section I provides, without distinction or exclusion, that the federal courts shall hear controversies arising from violations of individual guarantees by acts or laws of authorities, by no means are all such acts or laws subject to adjudication in *amparo*. The exceptions, which are either logically implied in articles 103 and 107 or which conform to their provisions, can be classified as acts that entail injuries for which *amparo* can provide no material redress, those that inflict no injury on the complainant, those against which a suit would involve a juridical absurdity or a violation of the rule of res judicata within the ambit of *amparo* itself, and those whose exclusion is temporary and designed to discourage excessive litigation or interference in the ordinary course of judicial procedure.

The first of these categories comprises those acts which the *amparo* law and *jurisprudencia* refer to as irreparably consummated, the classic example being an executed death sentence.[11] Since article 107 states that the purpose of the *amparo* suit is to protect and shelter the individual in the enjoyment of his constitutionally guaranteed rights, it

---

[9] Ibid., thesis 36, p. 97.

[10] *Baz Eduardo Jr., y coag.*, 68 S. J. 2404 (1941). Also see Burgoa, *El juicio de amparo*, fn., Suprema Corte, p. 162.

[11] Suprema Corte, *Jurisprudencia de la Suprema Corte*, thesis 32, II, 90. Also see article 73, sections IX and X, of the Amparo Law, which provide that this irreparability may be either material or juridical.

is evident that it would be wholly irrelevant in situations of this kind. Nonetheless, not every act that has been executed can be considered irreparable. The rule bars the suit only when it is materially or juridically impossible to return the injured party to the position occupied prior to the violation.

The second category of acts excluded from consideration in *amparo* embraces both those which inflict no injury recognized legally as such and those in which the injury, although it may exist, has not, in fact, been suffered by the complainant. The exclusion by the Court of acts that have not yet occurred but are merely anticipated can be included under the first of these headings. The justification in this case is clear, since there would be little point in extending the protection of the courts against injuries that not only do not presently exist but may never be inflicted. Simple futurity, nonetheless, is not in itself a sufficient bar to the suit. If the execution of the act is imminent and certain, although not formally complete or in process, *amparo* is admissible.[12] The operative principle in such cases is certainty of execution. The Court has decided that an act cannot be considered as future—and hence of uncertain occurrence—if its execution will necessarily and immediately follow upon the fulfillment of predetermined conditions.[13] In further illustration of this conclusion, the Court has also held that acts that are themselves the necessary consequences of other acts against which *amparo* has been legitimately requested cannot be considered as future in the sense of the exclusion.[14]

Also falling within the second category of inadmissible cases are those against laws that, upon their promulgation, can cause no injury except through a subsequent act of execution, and against acts that do not affect the juridical interests of the complainant.[15] The subject of *amparo* against laws is considered at length in chapter VI. At this point it is sufficient to note that a law may be attacked in *amparo* either immediately after it is promulgated, when the mere fact of its

[12] Ibid., theses 44 and 45, pp. 110, 113. Also see Suprema Corte, *Rivera Río José*, 18 *S. J.* 1255 (1926), and *González Matamoros Fernando*, 26 *S. J.* 1928 (1929).

[13] Suprema Corte, *Verduzco de Igartúa Guadalupe*, 43 *S. J.* 2533 (1935).

[14] Suprema Corte, *Couttolenc Antonio, Suc. de.*, 19 *S. J.* 366 (1926).

[15] Article 73, sections V and VI, of the Amparo Law.

existence creates an injury, or following the first administrative or judicial application. In both cases, of course, the complainant alleges the unconstitutionality of the law. It is not the unconstitutionality, however, but the reality of the injury that determines the question of admissibility. The prohibition of suits against acts that do not affect the juridical interests of the complainant, on the other hand, distinguishes between the common and legal definitions of interest. It is not enough that an act of authority should bear some injurious relation to the wishes and expectations, or even the objective material concerns of the complainant, unless at the same time it contravenes an interest recognized as such by law.[16] A seizure of private property, for example, although undoubtedly injurious to the expectations of presumptive heirs, infringes upon none of their existing legal interests. In the same sense, when a man is imprisoned the material interests of his family may be severely prejudiced, but the injury thus inflicted is not actionable.

Even in situations in which the material reality of the injury is unquestioned, the *amparo* law and the *jurisprudencia* of the Court have established the inadmissibility of the suit when the complainant has expressly or tacitly consented to the act complained of (*acto reclamado*). Tacit consent is presumed when the complainant fails to initiate suit within the periods specified for this purpose by articles 21 and 22 of the Amparo Law.[17] The second paragraph of section XII, article 73, bars from this rule on tacit consent suits directed against the first application of laws susceptible to attack at the time of promulgation. This exception eases considerably the burden on litigants, who were compelled—before the 1950 amendments—to ascertain, or more accurately, to guess whether a new statute could be considered as inflicting an injury upon them immediately or only upon later execution. An

---

[16] See Burgoa, *El juicio de amparo*, pp. 382–384. The same author treats extensively all the legal grounds for inadmissibility in chapter thirteen, pp. 372–407. Also, Asociación Nacional de Funcionarios Judiciales, *Constructora S.I.P.R.E., S. A.*, 128 *BIJ* 220 (April 1958), and Suprema Corte, *Jurisprudencia de la Suprema Corte*, thesis 753, IV, 1376.

[17] Article 73, sections XI and XII, of the Amparo Law. Also see Suprema Corte, *Jurisprudencia de la Suprema Corte*, theses 29 and 30, II, 82, 86.

erroneous choice could either bar the action permanently or, at the very least, increase the cost of litigation. In the interests of equity, the Supreme Court has added to the exceptions on consent the rule that an act cannot be so considered if it imposes a corporal penalty or any of the cruel and unusual punishments specifically prohibited by article 22 of the Constitution.[18] Lastly, the 1963 amendments to the Amparo Law added a further exception for suits filed by *ejidos* or other agrarian communities.

The Amparo Law, again in conformity with the rulings of the Court, also bars the suit—on grounds of the nonexistence of an actionable injury—against the resolutions of electoral boards and decisions of the federal Congress and state legislatures about the elections of their members and other matters in which the Constitution grants them unrestricted discretion.[19]

In the third category, the Amparo Law establishes four grounds of inadmissibility. The first of these stipulates that the suit may not be admitted against an act of the Supreme Court itself.[20] Since the Court is undeniably an authority within the meaning of article 103, and, conceding the possibility that it may occasionally act in a manner that would inflict injuries upon private individuals, the exception might, at first glance, seem inconsistent with the unqualified reference to authorities in section I. A moment's reflection, however, is sufficient to demonstrate justification. To confer upon any other court the power to review acts of the Supreme Court, entirely aside from the special presumption of constitutionality conferred upon these courts because of the Court's status as supreme interpreter of the Constitution, would contradict the fact and violate the principle of its supremacy. Within the hiearchical pattern of judicial organization, it can never be considered valid, or logical, to empower a subordinate to exercise control over its own superior. Nor is it more reasonable to suppose that the Court should exercise a review over its own acts through the medium

---

[18] Suprema Corte, *Jurisprudencia de la Suprema Corte*, thesis 31, II, 89.

[19] Article 73, sections VII and VIII. A detailed discussion of the Mexican doctrine of political questions, of which these exclusions form only a part, is to be found in chapter five.

[20] Article 73, section I.

of *amparo*. Aside from the manifest impracticality of such a procedure, it would require the Court to be both judge and party. On the other hand, to confer such power on a nonjudicial agency would not only violate the principle of separation of powers but also the specific terms of article 103, wherein jurisdiction is conferred exclusively upon courts of law. The situation created by the adoption of any of these alternatives would constitute an obvious juridical absurdity.

In order to avoid a sort of legal perpetual motion, sections II, III, and IV of article 73 are designed to prevent the use of *amparo* against *amparo* decisions themselves and to prohibit the multiplication of suits by one claimant on the same set of facts. To this end, section II declares that *amparo* is inadmissible against decisions taken in an *amparo* suit or against the acts through which the judgment in such a suit is executed. The latter provision is capable of creating difficulties in practice, but article 95, section IV, of the Amparo Law provides the motion of complaint (*recurso de queja*) for cases of excessive or defective execution of the judgment, while any acts not related to the execution of the judgment, even though performed at the same time and by the same authority, would obviously give valid grounds for a separate *amparo* suit. Section III of article 73 prohibits the same complainant to initiate additional *amparos* directed against the same authorities and the same acts or laws that form the subject matter of a suit already in progress. The rule applies even though different constitutional violations are alleged. This situation must, of course, be distinguished from that in which a connection but not an identity exists between the suits. For the former case, article 57 of the Amparo Law stipulates that the actions be joined. Within the conditions of identity defined in article 73, section III, section IV prohibits the initiation of additional suits against acts or laws which have already been the subject of *amparo* judgments. It establishes, in short, the applicability of the rule of res judicata in *amparo*.

The fourth category, including sections XIII, XIV, and XV of article 73, establishes a temporary inadmissibility based on the rule that *amparo* should be employed only when all other remedies have been exhausted. Sections XIII and XIV provide, respectively, that *amparo* may not be admitted against the acts of either judicial or nonjudicial authorities when the law provides some other mode of defense whereby the act may be modified, revoked, or nullified. There are, however, exceptions to this rule in both cases. For obvious reasons of equity, section XIII dispenses with the necessity of utilizing other remedies when the act in question threatens life, deportation, or exile and in cases involving any of the punishments prohibited by article 22 of the Constitution. Section XV grants an exception when the requirements of the ordinary remedy for suspending the application of the act exceed in severity those required for a definitive suspension in *amparo*.[21] Section XIV, in turn, prohibits filing of an *amparo* suit while the courts are engaged in considering some other legal recourse or defense interposed by the complainant and that has the purpose of modifying, revoking, or nullifying the violative act. If the complainant has elected an ordinary remedy, as presupposed by this section, it is reasonable to assume that the exceptions established in sections XIII and XV would not apply here. The Supreme Court has upheld this conclusion in a jurisprudential thesis holding that the *amparo* suit is inadmissible when directed against a formal order of imprisonment against which an appeal is pending.[22] It is interesting to note that the complainant, in conforming with his obligations under these sections, must take care to avail himself only of those remedies which are themselves properly admissible. If he does not, the time consumed in considering and rejecting the inadmissible remedy does not interrupt the running of the term during which *amparo* may legally be sought. The assumption here, apparently, is that the complainant has, by such behavior, tacitly consented to the act.[23]

Finally, it should be observed that section XVIII of article 73 apparently introduces unlimited possibilities for creating additional rules of inadmissibility by its reference to cases that "may result from some disposition of the law." If taken literally, this would suggest that any legislative enactment, state as well as federal, could determine causes

---

[21] The definitive suspension in amparo is approximately equivalent to the temporary injunction in Anglo-American law. This subject is considered at greater length in chapter eight.

[22] Suprema Corte, *Jurisprudencia de la Suprema Corte*, thesis, 158, II, 339.

[23] Ibid., thesis 886, V, 1638.

of inadmissibility. Such a broad interpretation, however, is unaccepta-
ble on both constitutional and practical grounds. Article 103, as has
been seen, establishes the admissibility of *amparo* against the violation
of individual guarantees by the acts or laws of any authority, subject
only to the restrictions provided expressly by the Constitution itself or
implied by it. To permit a miscellaneous legislative definition of additional limitations would, in practical terms, allow state and federal authorities to ignore the requirements of any of the individual guarantees
that their legislative bodies might find inconvenient, and would be in
evident conflict with both the letter and intent of article 103.[24] Such
legislation would be, in effect, the equivalent of constitutional amendment. For these reasons, it is justifiable to conclude that the apparently
unrestricted authorization of section XVIII should be read rather as
referring exclusively to other grounds of inadmissibility that may be
contained elsewhere in the Amparo Law or the Constitution. An example is the prohibition imposed by section XIV of article 27 of the
latter. This conclusion receives additional support in *jurisprudencia*
holding that: "the *amparo* law, because it regulates articles 103 and
107 of the Constitution, is placed on a superior plane of authority with
respect to any other federal or local laws. Consequently, the Mexican
Petroleum Company [Petroléos Mexicanos] cannot claim exemption
from the obligation of giving bond in suspension, [by citing the
terms] of one of the emergency decrees, since the latter cannot repeal
any article of the *amparo* law.[25]

In the light of the above remarks, it can be concluded that any law
or act, not specifically or by implication excluded by the Constitution,
that inflicts an injury by violating one or more of the individual guarantees and that emanates from an authority acting in its official capacity
may be attacked in *amparo*. For clarification, it should also be pointed
out that when the act complained of is a judicial or administrative
application of a law alleged to be unconstitutional, the law itself and
not merely the act of execution or application must be attacked in the
complaint. If this were not done, the only grounds upon which the

[24] Burgoa, *El juicio de amparo*, p. 396, considers this subject at length and ar-
rives at a similar conclusion.
[25] Suprema Corte, *Jurisprudencia de la Suprema Corte*, thesis 778, IV, 1420–1421.

validity of the act of application could be judged would be those of conformity with the terms of the statute.[26]

## Article 103—Sections II and III

The interpretation of sections II and III of article 103 has caused a considerable amount of controversy on the questions of who may sue and what sort of constitutional infractions are required to support a valid complaint. The position of the Supreme Court, however, has been clearly established. The relevant *jurisprudencia* states:

The *amparo* suit was established by article 103 . . . not to safeguard the entire body of the Constitution but to protect the individual guarantees, and sections II and III of the aforementioned precept should be understood in the sense that a federal law, when it encroaches upon or restricts the sovereignty of the states, or a state law, when it invades the sphere of federal authority, can only be challenged in *amparo* when an individual complainant exists who alleges the violation of individual guarantees . . . as a result of such encroachments on, or restrictions of, sovereignty. If the constituent authority had wished to concede the right to request *amparo* as a protection against any violation of the Constitution, although not resulting in an injury to a private interest, it would clearly have done so, but this it did not do. Through the constitutions of 1857 and 1917, and the constitutional projects and acts of reform that preceded them, it is to be seen that the constituent authorities, familiar as they were with the various systems of control that may be employed for remedying violations of the Constitution, did not wish to vest in the federal judicial power all-inclusive powers for opposing every unconstitutional act by means of the *amparo* suit, but that they desired to establish this suit solely for the protection and enjoyment of the individual guarantees.[27]

It follows that, in the opinion of the Court, sections II and III are ruled by the provisions of section I. If the federation encroaches upon the powers reserved to the states, or vice versa, this act, although un-

[26] Chapter seven discusses some exceptions to this general rule under the title of "Correction of the Defective Complaint."

[27] Suprema Corte, *Jurisprudencia de la Suprema Corte*, thesis 111, II, 246. Also see idem, *Secretaría de Hacienda y Crédito Público*, and *Cía. Textil de Guadalajara, S. A.*, 70 S. J. 4718 (1940), and *Síndico del Ayuntamiento de Pátzcuaro*, 109 S. J. 488 (1951).

constitutional, can give rise to an *amparo* suit only in the event that it violates simultaneously one of the individual guarantees and, in the terms of article 107, inflicts an injury thereby on a private individual. The fundamental objection to this thesis, however, is that it renders sections II and III superfluous. It is therefore contrary to the usual canons of constitutional interpretation, whereby every provision, insofar as possible, must be construed as possessing some significance. If the violation of an individual guarantee is a necessary prerequisite for the admissibility of the suit, it is surely immaterial whether the same act also violates the constitutional distribution of powers between the federation and the states, since the suit is admissible, in such a case, under the provisions of section I. Nonetheless, it is difficult to suggest a more satisfactory interpretation. The commentaries on this subject have tended generally to deny the necessity of a violation of individual guarantees, as long as the invasion of jurisdictions results in a legally recognized injury to the material or juridical interests of a private party.[28] Both the wording of article 103 and the debates in the constituent convention of 1856–1857 support this conclusion. The form of the article suggests a clear differentiation between three separate grounds of admissibility, connected only by the requirement, contained in article 107, of injury to a private party. The intent of the framers on this point is nowhere explicitly stated, but the stress laid upon *amparo*'s federal function, in the debates and in the exposition of motives, as well as the form of the first draft of the article, support this interpretation by implication.[29] Nonetheless, even if it be granted that the violation of an individual guarantee is not a prerequisite for suit under sections II and III, nothing of practical value would be gained. Whatever the nature of the injury inflicted upon the complainant, the violation from which it results derives from a lack of jurisdiction on the part of the responsible authority. For this situation, article 16 of the

[28] See Emilio Rabasa, *El juicio constitucional: orígines, teoría, y extensión*, pp. 247–248; Miguel Lanz Duret, *Derecho constitucional mexicano y consideraciones sobre la realidad política de nuestro régimen*, p. 355; Burgoa, *El juicio de amparo*, p. 214; Romeo León Orantes, *El juicio de amparo*, p. 52.

[29] Francisco Zarco, *Historia del congreso constituyente, 1856–1857*, pp. 324, 990–996. Also see Felipe Buenrostro, *Historia del segundo congreso constitucional de la República Mexicana, que funcionó en los años 1861, 62 y 63*.

Constitution provides a sufficient prohibition, stating that "no one shall be molested in his person, family, domicile, papers, or possessions except by written order of the competent authority." Consequently, any act that violates either section II or section III, with a resulting personal injury, necessarily violates article 16 as well, and the suit may be based exclusively on the latter within the terms of section I. The scope of article 16 is, in fact, more extensive in this respect than that of sections II and III. The latter are restricted to situations in which the federation exercises a power belonging properly to the states or vice versa, whereas the prohibition in article 16 applies also to acts forbidden to both.

Because of the futility attending the above interpretations of sections II and III, Romeo León Orantes, in *El juicio de amparo*, argues that they should be interpreted as authorizing the admissibility of *amparo* suits initiated by the governments affected by such acts. In summary, he contends that the Supreme Court has restricted itself in this instance to a purely grammatical, and erroneous, interpretation, whereas proper juridical logic and the evidence of history justify the conclusion that the constituent conventions of 1856–1857 and 1916–1917 intended to define distinct types of constitutional violations by these provisions and to provide a workable and nonredundant remedy for their redress. Section I of article 107, in turn, identifies the complainant in these cases. Its reference to the "injured party" (*agraviado*) requires that the *amparo* suit be initiated by that person, or legally recognized moral entity, who, in fact, suffers the injurious consequences of the constitutional violation. Since the violations envisaged by sections II and III consist in the invasion by one government of the constitutionally assigned jurisdiction of another, it follows that the victim of such an act is the governmental entity itself and not a private individual, whose interests, although they may be incidentally affected, are protected by the provisions of section I. If this reasoning is accepted, logic demands that the remedy provided by these sections be extended to the affected governmental entity as the only party capable of benefiting from it. The major obstacle to this conclusion, and the source of the *jurisprudencia* cited above, is the statement in section II of article 107 that "the judgment [in *amparo*] shall always be such that it affects only private individuals . . ." (*individuos particulares*). León Orantes contends, however, that this expression, as well as the term "injured party" employed in section I of article 107, should be understood as a generic reference to all three of the situations covered in article 103. From this point of view, he holds that it should be defined as covering both the physical and moral persons of private law by the provisions of section I, and the moral persons of public law by the provisions of sections II and III.[30] This exercise in legal semantics, although convenient and indeed essential to the success of the argument, is in conflict with the dictionary, which defines *particular* as that which is private and personal as distinguished from that which is public and general. The appeal to history, in this instance, also lends more support to the position of the Court than to that of León Orantes. It will be recalled that in the debates of the 1856–1857 convention great stress was laid upon the fact that *amparo* would avoid direct clashes between governmental powers, substituting instead the politically innocuous interests of private persons. The defense of the federal system, it was said, would emerge as a secondary consequence of such litigation. To reconcile these arguments with the León Orantes thesis hardly seems possible.

In reply to the opinion advanced by León Orantes, Felipe Tena Ramírez has objected that the concession of *amparo* to the Federation or to a state would necessarily transgress the requirements of section II of article 107, which state that the *amparo* judgment may make no general declaration about the law or act on which the complaint is based nor extend beyond affording protection in the special case to which it refers. In support of this position, he points out that granting *amparo* to a state against the application of a federal law would, at the very least, benefit all the inhabitants of that state and would, consequently, amount to a judicial repeal of the law within that area. The case would be even more clear if *amparo* were granted to the Federation against a state law, since the judgment would then totally nullify that statute. Such results, he concludes, would constitute judicial intrusions into the jurisdictions of the other powers and would be contradictory to the limited and individualistic purposes of *amparo*.[31] The objection is well taken insofar as the spirit of the action is concerned but is less

30 León Orentes, *El juicio de amparo*, pp. 51–55.
31 Lanz Duret, *Derecho constitucional*, p. 520.

easily justifiable in strictly legal terms. The prohibition of general statements about the law or act with which the complaint deals must be understood to refer exclusively to the terms of the judgment and not to subsidiary and indirect effects that the judgment may have. In practice, the courts are not forbidden to attend to the general issue of the constitutionality of the law or act complained of, which they must do in order to reach a decision, but are constrained to limit the terms of the judgment itself to only those points that are required for defining the legal rights and obligations of the parties within the specific situation presented by the case.[32] From this standpoint, it appears that the generality of effect to which Tena Ramírez objects would not result directly from the form or content of the judgment itself but would derive from the nature of the act and the identity of the parties. A similar although more restricted effect can also arise under section I, when the complainant is a private moral person.[33]

Despite the various interpretations proposed in the hope of conferring some practical utility upon sections II and III, the position established in the Court's *jurisprudencia* compels the conclusion that these sections are of no present significance. Given the application of article 16 to those federal-state conflicts that produce private, personal injuries, and the interpretations of articles 105 and 133 advanced in the *Oaxaca* case, there seems to be no shortage of legal instruments for the judicial defense of federalism. If they have been seldom used, the cause is more properly to be sought in the weakness of Mexican federalism as a political institution than in the armory of the law.

### Article 107

Although the general provisions of article 107 have been considered at some length in the preceding pages, one further significant point remains to be explored. As has been seen, section I of article 107 provides that the *amparo* suit must always be initiated at the instance of the injured party, but does not indicate which real or moral persons

---

[32] Suprema Corte, *Caridad Cortés de Vázquez*, 111 S. J. 1507 (1952), and idem, *Manuel García Santillán*, 104 S. J. 1493 (1950).

[33] León Orantes, *El juicio de amparo*, pp. 58–60, presents a similar argument in rebuttal of the objections of Tena Ramírez.

may be capable of acquiring that character. Because *amparo* exists primarily as a means of enforcing the individual guarantees, which are, in turn, limitations on government in the interest of the governed, there is no difficulty in concluding that both real and moral private persons, as subjects of government, are included among the beneficiaries of the action. Any doubts which might arise about the capacity of a private moral person to possess individual guarantees and, hence, to sue in *amparo* are sufficiently removed by article 8 of the Amparo Law, which explicitly authorizes such suits. Difficulties do arise, however, about the provisions of article 9 of that law, which states that public moral persons may seek *amparo* "when the act or law against which they complain affects their patrimonial interests." These interests do not include the entirety of the possessions that are subject to administration, use, and control by the government but only those over which it exercises rights comparable to those established for private persons in the civil law of property—that is, things subject to a pecuniary valuation of which the government is, in the civil sense, the proprietor.[34] The distinction, of course, can be extremely difficult to draw in particular cases, but the general principle is sufficient for present purposes. Since neither the Amparo Law nor the Constitution identifies explicitly those entities which have the character of public moral persons, reference must be made to the Civil Code of the Federal District and Territories, which provides, in article 25, that the nation, the states, the municipalities, and other corporations of a public character have this status.[35] That these official entities should be permitted to avail themselves of *amparo*, even in the restricted sense of article 9, has an incongruous appearance in the light of the usual requirements of admissibility. In justification of this rule, the Supreme Court has established *jurisprudencia*, holding that:

the State . . . may appear under two different aspects in its relations with individuals: as a sovereign entity charged with the guardianship of the general welfare and acting through imperative commands of obligatory

---

[34] See Burgoa, *El juicio de amparo*, p. 268, for a discussion of this point. See also the case material and *jurisprudencia* cited below about particular aspects of the subject.

[35] Cited by Burgoa, *El juicio de amparo*, p. 268.

observance, and as a juridical entity, which, as the possessor in its own right of property indispensable to the exercise of its functions, must also necessarily enter into relations of a civil nature with other property owners . . . From the foregoing, it can be deduced that the state, as a moral person, capable of acquiring rights and of contracting obligations, is in a position to exercise all those remedies that the law concedes to civil persons for their defense, among them the *amparo* suit. As a sovereign entity, however, it can exercise none of these remedies without disavowing its own sovereignty . . . further, it is not possible to concede the extraordinary remedy of *amparo* to organs of the state against acts of the state itself manifested through other of its agencies, since this would establish a conflict of sovereign powers, whereas the *amparo* suit is concerned only with the complaint of a private individual directed against an abuse of power.[36]

By virtue of this duality of functions, it becomes possible to reconcile the concept of *amparo* as a device for protecting the governed from the unconstitutional impositions of government, with the admissibility of suits initiated by government itself. In its governmental aspects, the public moral person acts authoritatively; it imposes its will without the agreement or acquiescence of the persons affected. In its other aspect, however, the public moral person is itself a subject of private law; its relations with other persons, real and corporate, require a free meeting of minds and are of the nature of contract rather than command. In this latter guise, it is possible to view the public moral person as the beneficiary of individual guarantees and, hence, as the active party in an *amparo* suit. In further clarification of this distinction the Court has established *jurisprudencia*, holding that an *amparo* suit is inadmissible when initiated by a public moral person against a judicial decision resolving a case in which the government has defended the validity of an act of authority, such as the collection of a tax or fine.[37] The fact

[36] Suprema Corte, *Jurisprudencia de la Suprema Corte*, thesis 450, III, 867–868.

[37] Ibid., thesis 503, pp. 951–952. Since they have been included in the most recent compilation of *jurisprudencia*, both this thesis and number 450, cited above, should probably be considered as good law. Absent from this compilation and, consequently, presumably rescinded, is a more recently established and flatly contradictory thesis published as number 717 of the *Apéndice al tomo XCVII del semanario judicial de la federación* (1949) p. 1293. This ruling stated that: "From the dispositions of article 103, section I of the federal Constitution, and article 1, section I, of the Amparo Law, it is to be observed that for the *amparo* suit to be admissible

that the government has submitted its interests to the test of litigation does not, in accordance with this rule, divest it of its authoritative, or sovereign, status. The present validity of this thesis has been thrown into doubt, however, by more recent cases dealing with the power of eminent domain. In earlier cases of this type, it had been held that *amparo* sought by the Federal Public Ministry was inadmissible on the grounds that the government had acted "as a sovereign entity . . . and not as a juridical entity possessing personal property indispensable to the exercise of its functions . . ." and that the "act complained of does not affect its patrimonial interests."[38] In summary, the more recent decisions on the point hold that when the Public Ministry submits to the rulings of a court in cases of this kind, it exercises no act of sovereignty but places itself in a position equivalent to that occupied by any private person party to litigation. As a consequence of this, it is held that when the government subjects its powers to such self-limitation, it should enjoy all the legal remedies available to any other litigant, including the *amparo* suit. The existence of the patrimonial interests, required by article 9 of the Amparo Law, is, of course, also affirmed.[39] A similar conclusion had been reached previously by the Labor Chamber of the Supreme Court on the government's right to seek *amparo* against the awards of the Arbitration Tribunal in cases concerning

---

it is necessary that the person who initiates it be capable of enjoying such [individual] guarantees, and despite the fact that the Nation is a judicial entity it cannot be equated with the individual concerning the rights protected by the federal Constitution. [The Constitution] protects the fundamental rights of the individual against the arbitrary acts of the various organs of the public power and, with the object of maintaining those rights intact, instituted the *amparo* suit. In such conditions, the primordial object of the aforesaid suit would be weakened if one were to go to the extreme of equating the State with an individual entity susceptible of suffering the violation of these rights . . . Consequently, if the Nation initiates an amparo suit, it falls within the cause of inadmissibility envisaged in article 73, section XVIII, of the *amparo* law." See also Burgoa, *El juicio de amparo*, pp. 271–275, who, in a similar argument, says that the state and its agencies should never be permitted to employ *amparo*.

38 Suprema Corte, *Apéndice al tomo XCVII*, thesis 712, p. 1280.

39 Suprema Corte, *Agente del Ministerio Público Federal*, 85 S. J. 11 (1945). Also, idem, *Agente del Ministerio Público adscrito al Tribunal de 5° Circuito*, 92 S. J. 1726 (1947).

public employees. The relevant part of the *jurisprudencia* established on this subject states that "when the State does not make free use of its sovereignty but, limiting it, subjects the validity of its acts to the decisions of an agency empowered to judge them, it is equitable, logical, and just to conclude that it should enjoy the same remedies that are available to its colitigants . . . and thus, it is necessary to conclude that it may make use of both ordinary and extraordinary remedies equally with other parties."[40]

The existence of the requisite patrimonial interest, particularly vague in the labor cases, is evidently being judged, in these instances, by standards considerably at variance with those previously used here in defining the term. Of more significance is the ease with which these decisions could be generalized to authorize the use of *amparo* by public moral persons in any case in which the government has been a party to litigation. If this should occur, it would constitute a substantial departure from the traditional theory of *amparo* as an instrument for the defense of the individual against the abuses of government, and would contribute little to the scope of the jurisdiction within which the federal courts are enabled to practice judicial review.

[40] Suprema Corte, *Jurisprudencia de la Suprema Corte*, thesis 451, III, 875.

## Chapter 5

# The Constitutional Scope
# and Limits of Amparo

$\frown\frown\frown\frown$

F ROM AN EXAMINATION of the constitutional foundations of judicial review as practiced in Mexico, it has been indicated that the exercise of this function is confined almost exclusively to the *amparo* jurisdiction. This raises necessarily the question of the extent to which the action can be considered technically adequate to the exigencies of a general constitutional defense. In accordance with the criteria of admissibility established in article 103, only those constitutional articles that define the individual guarantees and those that relate to the distribution of powers between the Federation and the state fall within the protective sphere of *amparo*. The *jurisprudencia* of the Supreme Court has further limited the area of applicability, holding that "the *amparo* suit was established . . . not to safeguard the entire body of the Constitution but to protect the individual guarantees," a conclusion, which in practice, as noted previously, limits the application of the suit to cases involving alleged infractions of one or more of the first twenty-nine articles of the Constitution, and only those articles.[1] Because of these considerations, it is evident that any attempt to extend the protection of *amparo* to the remaining sections of the Constitution must depend upon the content and interpretation of the guarantees themselves. For this purpose, a number of ingenious constructions, chiefly of articles 14 and 16, have been advanced and adopted by the Supreme Court in varying degrees. Because of this development Ignacio Burgoa has been able to assert with some color of theoretical validity that the *amparo* suit is "the most perfect device for the defense of the Constitution . . ." and to contend that it has been expanded to afford a defense of *"the entire order established by the fundamental law."*[2] In the following pages these interpretations are examined, and an attempt is made, in the light of the case record, to ascertain the extent of their effective application by the courts as well as the limitations to which they are subject.

### The Contributions of Ignacio L. Vallarta

Don Ignacio L. Vallarta, by general consent the most notable Mexican jurist of the nineteenth century, served as president of the Supreme Court from May 1878 until November 1882. During this brief period he contributed substantially to the evolution of *amparo* as an effective instrument of constitutional control.[3] On such questions as the constitutional status of the extraordinary legislative powers traditionally delegated to the executive and the applicability of *amparo* to the defense of political rights, Vallarta's conclusions remain substantially in force to the present day. Concerning the constitutional scope of the action, his major contribution lay in the "concordance of articles" theory, which held that the meaning of the individual guarantees, and consequently the fact of their violation, should be determined in the light of other constitutional precepts that might serve to explain, modify, or expand them or to provide regulatory rules for applying them. Thus, in the *Amparo Tavares*, he wrote that

[1] Suprema Corte de Justicia, *Jurisprudencia de la Suprema Corte*, thesis 111, II, 246. As has been observed, only articles 2 through 28 are actually enforceable as guarantees.

[2] Ignacio Burgoa, *El juicio de amparo*, p. 138. Italics in the original.

[3] Moisés González Navarro, *Vallarta y su ambiente político-jurídico*, pp. 21–22.

in the case of the individual guarantees, it will frequently be necessary to refer to texts other than those that define them in order to decide with certainty whether one of them has been violated. Because of the intimate connection that exists between the articles containing the guarantees and others that, although they do not mention them, nonetheless presuppose them, explain them, or complement them; because of the undeniable correlation that exists between them, [the guarantees] cannot be considered in isolation without weakening them, without contradicting their spirit, without frequently rendering their application impossible . . . for example, in order to know if persons may be deprived of the property guaranteed by article 27, under the form of taxation, it would be necessary to consider article 31, which provides that [such] contributions be proportional and equitable; similarly, to determine whether the personal liberty defined in article 5 is violated by requiring the performance of public services, it would be necessary to [interpret] it in terms of the same article 31, which specifies certain limits on that liberty . . . [or] finally, in order to explain the competence (*competencia*) to which article 16 refers, it is necessary to examine article 50, which established the constitutional distribution of powers between the three branches of government . . . I believe that the aforesaid is sufficient to condemn the doctrine that prohibits the linking of constitutional articles, whether for purposes of mutual explanation or for the purpose of citing those not included in the section on individual guarantees, in order to fix the scope and extension of those that do grant guarantees . . . *Amparo* does not cover every class of constitutional infraction . . . The suit is admissible only in the cases defined in article 101 [103 of the present constitution], but it can be based on the concordance of the guarantees found in section I of the Constitution with articles not included under that heading.[4]

The expansive effect of this argument lies in the fact that, according to it, *amparo* is deemed admissible even when the constitutional violation alleged relates most immediately and directly to an article not included within the catalog of individual guarantees, but which may be construed as related to one or more of these guarantees in the manner stated. The reasoning is persuasive, although in practice, since nonpenal *amparos* are subject generally to the rule of *stricti juris*, it

4 Ignacio L. Vallarta, *Cuestiones constitucionales. Votos del C. Ignacio L. Vallarta, Presidente de la Suprema Corte de Justicia en los negocios más notables*, III, 145–149.

would place a considerable strain on the ingenuity of litigants. This, however, cannot serve as a criticism of the legal or logical validity of the theory.

The most serious and uncompromising objections to the concordance theory were advanced by Emilio Rabasa in his book *El juicio consti-tucional*. To summarize, Rabasa contended that the practice of relating the individual guarantees to other constitutional articles in the manner recommended by Vallarta accomplished either nothing or too much. Should a given law or act of authority violate a guarantee, the intro-duction into the suit of articles from other sections of the Constitution would be superfluous. If, on the other hand, the article violated was not one of those contained in the section on guarantees, the suit would be inadmissible under the terms of article 101 (103 of the present constitution). From this point of view, Vallarta's thesis becomes either legally and logically irrelevant or itself violative of article 101, de-pending upon the manner and extent of its application. In illustration of these conclusions, Rabasa referred at length to the *Amparo Rabasa*, decided in 1880, with a majority opinion written by Vallarta.[5] The case arose under a law of the state of Chiapas, which required lawyers to serve as legal advisors to state lay judges and inflicted penalties ranging from fines to disbarment for refusal to render such services. Payment, in accordance with the terms of the statute, was to be pro-vided from fees assessed on the parties to the litigation in which these advisory services were performed. The complainant, having refused to comply with the law, was fined; he then sued for *amparo*, alleging the violation of the guarantee against involuntary and unremunerated per-sonal services in article 5 of the 1857 Constitution. The statutory provisions for payment were dismissed since they, in turn, violated article 17, which prohibited the imposition of court costs. There was, however, no claim that article 17 had been, in fact, violated in this instance, since, obviously, the injury in that event would fall not upon the recipient of the illegal fees but upon the person required to pay them. Vallarta cited Zarco's history of the constituent convention as

[5] The complainant in this case is identified in the opinion as Don Emilio Rabasa, an attorney. I have been unable to discover if he was identical with the distinguished author of *El juicio constitucional*.

evidence of the intent of the framers and denied that the Chiapas statute directly violated article 5. He construed the intent of the article as prohibiting forced or gratuitous labor when exacted in the interest of a private person but not when required as a public service. Turning to the concordance theory, however, he held that the power to exact such services was limited in the form and the conditions of application by article 31 of the Constitution. Article 31 required that the obligation of the Mexican citizen to contribute to the cost of government be imposed in a proportional and equitable manner. He compared this rule on taxation with the burden imposed by the Chiapas statute on the twenty lawyers resident in that state, and concluded that the services in question were neither proportionally nor equitably imposed, and that they were, consequently, unconstitutional. Thus, in reasoning similar to that employed in evolving some aspects of the concept of substantive due process in the United States, Vallarta, in effect, held that article 5 incorporated the provisions of article 31, with the result that a violation of the latter constituted a violation of the former as well.[6] In criticizing this opinion and the theory that it illustrates, Rabasa presented a summary of the holdings at variance with the one given above. Briefly, he contended that Vallarta ruled out the applicability of article 5 altogether and based his decision on a concordance of the provisions of article 31 with those of article 17. If this interpretation is accurate, the contention that the opinion is unsound can hardly be avoided, since the former article was not an individual guarantee, and the latter neither formed a part of the pleadings nor, in the circumstances of the case, was it susceptible of being violated to the detriment of the complainant. At various points the opinion is admittedly obscure, but a careful analysis has convinced the present writer that Vallarta's references to article 17 were in the nature of *obiter dicta*. Insofar as the essence of Rabasa's objection is concerned, however, the correctness of his interpretation of particular opinions is immaterial. As a purely logical proposition, the criticism is unassailably simple and conclusive: if, as noted above, an individual guarantee has been violated, reference to other sections of the Consti-

---

[6] Vallarta, *Cuestiones constitucionales*, II, 306–322.

tution is unnecessary, whereas if no such violation exists, the suit is patently inadmissible.[7] If practical considerations, however, are substituted for the formal attractions of logic, the proposition is much less convincing. The fundamental issue posed by any *amparo* suit is the existence of the constitutional violation alleged by the complainant, and the resolution of this question must depend upon the meaning attributed to the guarantee affected. Since the phraseology of the individual guarantees is not free of ambiguity, determining their meaning is a matter of interpretation. Aside from the limitations imposed by the rule of *stricti juris*, where applicable, it is difficult to see, therefore, what valid objection could be made to the use of other constitutional precepts that might contribute to properly performing this conventional and inescapable judicial function. Nothing in Rabasa's works justifies the conclusion that he advocated a mechanical, or slot machine theory of the judicial function. On the contrary, in introducing his criticism of the *Amparo* Rabasa, he objected precisely to what he considered to be Vallarta's excessively rigid interpretation of article 5. This, taken in conjunction with his summation of the opinion in the case, indicates that Rabasa saw in the concordance thesis not a mere theory of interpretation. Rather he envisioned a device whereby the courts might grant *amparo*, in contravention of article 101, whenever a more or less plausible relation between a violated constitutional article and one or more of the individual guarantees could be shown, irrespective of whether the guarantee was included in the complaint or whether it really had been violated. If this was really Vallarta's intention, Rabasa's objections were well taken; but, for the reasons given above, this interpretation of the theory seems questionable. If the alternative view advanced here is correct, the Vallarta thesis would not only appear to be constitutionally valid but, in the manner of substantive due process in the United States, obviously capable of creating a considerable extension in the constitutional scope of the *amparo* action.[8]

---

[7] For the entirety of Rabasa's argument and his commentary on the Amparo Rabasa, see *El juicio constitucional orígines, teoría, y extensión*, pp. 252–253.

[8] Burgoa, *El juicio de amparo*, p. 205, accepts the validity of the concordance theory. For his general appraisal of Vallarta's contributions, see pp. 203–206.

With the development and partial acceptance of what might be called substantive interpretations of articles 14 and 16, upon which current expansions of the constitutional scope of *amparo* are mainly based, need for the concordance procedure and examples of its use have largely disappeared. It will be seen that these newer interpretations do not, after the fashion of the concordance theory, incorporate within the individual guarantees themselves provisions found elsewhere in the Constitution, but hold that articles 14 and 16 establish generic guarantees of legality susceptible to direct violation by almost any deviation from constitutionality. It is still necessary, of course, that various constitutional precepts be associated for purposes of interpretation, but the customary intent at present is to demonstrate a direct violation either of article 14 or 16 or, more frequently, of both. Although the broad interpretation of these articles incorporates logically all the results obtainable from the use of the concordance theory and seems to render it superfluous, the case reports continue to provide occasional examples of the older procedure.[9]

Although the concordance theory extended the constitutional scope of *amparo* considerably, Vallarta, as the quotation from the *Amparo Tavares* suggests, never acquiesced in the view that the action might properly be adapted to all constitutional violations that might cause disputes of a justiciable character. On the contrary, he adhered persistently, if not always with perfect consistency, to the limitations established in article 101 and to interpretations of the individual guarantees themselves that embraced only isolated provisions from the remaining sections of the Constitution. To supply this deficiency in the judicial instrumentalities of constitutional defense, he turned to article 97, which he believed to be the full equivalent, in the powers

[9] See, for example, Suprema Corte, *Yusim Nicolás A.*, 43 S. J. 519 (1934), which holds that when a constitutional precept limits the scope of an individual guarantee this limitation will be given judicial effect and cannot be construed as itself constituting an actionable violation of the guarantee; and *Díaz de Garza Consuelo*, 111 S. J. 1919 (1952), in which that section of article 27 which grants to the federal government the exclusive power to establish the legal characteristics defining private property is interpreted in the light of article 124, which establishes the general basis for the distribution of powers between the Federation and the States. Also, see *Pedroza Guadalupe y coags.*, 76 S. J. 2507 (1943).

conferred upon the judiciary, of article 3, section II, of the Constitution of the United States, and which he construed as incorporating a general power of judicial review. Thus, in the *Amparo Tavares,* he stated:

Rather than extend [*amparo*] to all constitutional infractions instead of limiting it to the three [situations] specified in article 101, I would accept, on the basis of the concordance of this article with article 97, the practice of hearing and judging these infractions, whenever falling within the sphere of judicial competence, in accordance with the ordinary procedures established by our legislation for matters not otherwise specifically regulated. Considering that these controversies, in the last analysis, deal with applying and enforcing *the first of the federal laws, the Constitution,* there are abundant reasons for validating that practice in the absence of an organic law disposing otherwise.[10]

As subsequent commentators have uniformly observed, Vallarta, by some odd aberration, failed either to observe or to attach importance to the fact that, whereas the United States Constitution explicitly confers jurisdiction in cases arising under the Constitution, article 97, the equivalent here of the present article 104, grants jurisdiction only in controversies arising from the application and enforcement of federal laws and treaties. Instead, as the citation from the *Amparo Tavares* indicates, he appears to have concluded that since the Constitution was both federal and a law it must fall within the meaning of the term "federal laws" in section I of article 97. The most concise and persuasive criticism of this position is that advanced by Emilio Rabasa, who, noting the differences between the United States and Mexican constitutions in this respect, observed "that the Constitution never refers to itself as a *law*; that article 126 [the supremacy clause] distinguishes it from federal law in a fundamental enumeration; and that if there are *federal* laws by virtue of the fact that they derive from the federal power, the Constitution, deriving from a superior power, is referred to as federal [only] because it creates and main-

---

[10] Italics added. Also see Vallarta, *El juicio de amparo,* p. 73, where he indicates a belief that the general power of judicial review, which he perceived in article 97, should properly be subjected to the regulation of a special organic law. As the above indicates, however, he was willing to proceed even in the absence of such legislation.

tains the federal system."[11] On this basis, Rabasa proceeded to draw a distinction between the purely judicial (or legal) jurisdiction conferred by article 97, and the constitutional (or political) jurisdiction granted by article 101, with only the latter justifying the judicial defense of the constitution itself. For the proper interpretation of article 97, Rabasa's views are uncontested, and no further attempts have been made to institute a general system of judicial review based on Vallarta's proposal.[12]

*Article 14—Expansion of* Amparo *via the Concept of "Laws"*

Despite disagreement about constitutionally valid procedure, Emilio Rabasa was no less determined than Vallarta to discover a means whereby the review powers of the judiciary might be extended to the entire Constitution. In support of this endeavor, he contended that the framers of the 1857 Constitution, although concerned particularly with safeguarding the individual guarantees, intended undoubtedly to create, through the agency of the *amparo* suit, a system of judicial review equivalent to that of the United States in its constitutional scope. "Their error," he stated, "if indeed it was one, consisted in believing that all the constitutional violations susceptible of a judicial remedy were included in the three sections of that article [101]."[13] Given, at the time Rabasa wrote, the judicial and legislative evolution of *amparo*, for which former members of the 1856–1857 convention were mainly responsible, the truth of this conclusion is by no means as

---

[11] Rabasa, *El juicio constitucional*, p. 255.

[12] It should be noted that Vallarta was not altogether without support in his interpretation of article 97. In this connection, see José María Lozano, *Tratado de los derechos del hombre, estudio del derecho constitucional patrio en lo relativo a los derechos del hombre, conforme a la Constitución de 1857 y a la ley orgánica de amparo de garantías de 20 de enero de 1869*, p. 438.

[13] Rabasa, *El juicio constitucional*, pp. 258–259. Although Rabasa's book deals exclusively with the Constitution of 1857, his conclusions about article 101 are also applicable to article 103 of the present constitution. The latter article was copied verbatim from the previous constitution, and was neither discussed in the convention debates in 1917, nor commented upon in the exposition of motives or the report of the study committee assigned to review the Carranza draft.

incontrovertible as he claimed.[14] It has been observed, however, that the frequent references to judicial practice in the United States, both in the exposition of motives and on the convention floor, are capable of being interpreted in this manner. Even conceding that the convention might have erred in the drafting of article 101, Rabasa held that, properly interpreted, the guarantee contained in article 14 provided the necessary authorization for expanding the constitutional application of *amparo*.

Although there are a number of differences between the present article 14 and that of the 1857 Constitution, the provisions upon which Rabasa's thesis was based are substantially equivalent. The earlier article provided that "no person may be judged or sentenced except by laws enacted prior to the act and applied exactly to it by tribunals previously established by law," while paragraph 2 of the present article states: "no person shall be deprived of life, liberty, property, possessions, or rights without a trial by a duly created court in which the essential formalities of procedure are observed and according to laws issued prior to the act."[15]

Both forms of the article establish due process of law as an essential element in the relation between government and governed, and it is on the significance that should be attached to the word "law" in this context that Rabasa's interpretation turns. To summarize, he held that two different constitutional uses of the term must be distinguished. As employed in article 101 (103), the reference is to a mere legislative act, whether valid or not. This is proven by the fact that the article explicitly authorizes the federal courts to determine the question of validity when this point is raised in the *amparo* suit. In article 14, however, the reference is to "law" in the strict sense, that is, to those enactments deriving customarily from the legislative branch, which are both formally and materially valid. In accordance with this interpretation, Rabasa concluded: "The Constitution, when it speaks

[14] It is particularly interesting to note that Ignacio Vallarta was a member of the convention and frequently referred to the fact in justifying his constitutional opinions.

[15] For the 1857 provisions, see Felipe Tena Ramírez, *Leyes fundamentales de México, 1808–1857*, p. 608.

of laws in the sense of norms (for instance, as in article 14) cannot be considered as referring to any legislative act whatsoever but only to those which in origin and content fall within its purview and which in conformity with it are valid. An unconstitutional law cannot be law in the language of the Constitution unless we admit that [that document] depreciates and nullifies itself by its own terms."

That conformity with the Constitution should be an indispensable characteristic of law in this sense seems to be a necessary consequence of the principle of constitutional supremacy, which is explicitly established in articles 126 and 133, respectively, of the two constitutions under consideration. Consequently, since article 14 requires that all governmental acts capable of affecting the juridical status of individuals must be based on previously existing law, and since it also requires that this law be in every material and formal aspect in conformity with the Constitution, it follows that any act that redounds to the injury of an individual and that is in any manner inconsistent with the Constitution directly violates article 14 and is properly subject to attack in *amparo*. Given the initial definition of the term "law" and the consequences of the principle of constitutional supremacy, this conclusion appears to be logically indisputable. If fully adopted by the courts, the Rabasa thesis would clearly suffice to establish a review jurisdiction equivalent in constitutional scope to that exercised in the United States. In this interpretation, the jurisdictional deficiencies of article 101 (103) are only apparent, and the courts can be considered to possess, at least in principle, an adequate instrument for extending judicial authority to such matters of primary constitutional concern as maintaining the separation of powers and supervising the exercise of those powers delegated to the respective branches of government.

The Rabasa thesis, in conjunction with similar interpretations of article 16, has been generally accepted by leading commentators, although in some cases this acceptance seems to be based more upon a desire to extend the scope of judicial review by any plausible means than upon the intrinsic merits of the argument.[16] As noted above, it

16 For examples of the treatment given this question in the commentaries, see Burgoa, *El juicio de amparo*, pp. 209–210; Ricardo Couto, *Tratado teórico-práctico*

is by no means certain that the framers of the 1857 Constitution intended to establish a general system of judicial review, and it is equally doubtful that the guarantee contained in article 14 was intended to assure anything more than a strict adherence to lawful procedure in adjudication. Despite these possible grounds for refutation, the Supreme Court has adopted the interpretation in principle and, largely, in practice. By way of illustration, it was held in the case of *Lee Santiago* that the enforcement of a state penal statute prohibiting the sale of narcotics violated article 14 because section XVI of article 73 of the Constitution grants exclusive powers to the federal government in the field of public health and sanitation and that, as a result, this offense could be penalized only in conformity with federal law.[17] In a more explicitly explanatory sense, the Court has stated: "Although, in principle, *amparo* is inadmissible against the violation of article 31 . . . because, in accordance with the terms of article 103, section I, of the Constitution and article 1, section I, of the Amparo Law, this article does not contain an individual guarantee claimable as such in *amparo*, its violation can nonetheless be alleged when the violative act also infringes the guarantees contained in articles 14 and 16 of the Constitution."[18] It is interesting to observe further that the substantive interpretation of article 14, and that of article 16 as well, not only extends the scope of judicial review of the federal Constitution but also permits the federal courts to exercise similar review powers in defense of the State constitutions. For example, the Court, in considering a case that involved a conviction for murder based partly upon procedural laws enacted by the permanent deputation of the Coahuila State congress, held that

the power to enact, reform, and repeal laws pertains exclusively to the legislative branch, which cannot, constitutionally, delegate these functions to the permanent deputation that operates during the recess of the con-

---

*de la suspensión en el amparo con un estudio sobre la suspensión con efectos de amparo provisional*, p. 39. Miguel Lanz Duret, *Derecho constitucional*, pp. 351–352; and Felipe Tena Ramírez, *Derecho constitucional mexicano*, p. 516.

[17] Suprema Corte, 32 *S. J.* 1877 (1931)

[18] Suprema Corte, *Carmona Leopoldo y coags.*, 118 *S. J.* 197 (1953).

gress . . . Articles 3, 67, and 70 of the Constitution of the state of Coahuila determine, respectively, the manner in which sovereignty is exercised in that federative entity, the powers of the legislative branch, and the powers of the permanent deputation, and nowhere among these is to be found an authorization whereby the aforesaid deputation may enact laws . . . Consequently, the permanent deputations of the thirtieth and thirty-first congresses of the state of Coahuila could not legally enact the Organic Law of the Public Ministry nor the Code of Criminal Procedures.[19]

Since the individual guarantees act as limitations upon any governmental authority, the logic of the substantive interpretation necessitates this further extension.

The general practice of alleging simultaneous violations of articles 14 and 16 and the failure of Supreme Court decisions, in the majority of cases, to distinguish clearly between the different contributions of these two articles to decisions reached, limits substantially the number of specific applications of article 14 that are available for citation. Even in the cases noted above, with one exception, violations of article 16 were also claimed. Because of this tendency to employ the articles in conjunction, an evaluation of the extent to which the substantive interpretations have actually extended judicial review to the general body of the Constitution will be deferred until article 16 has been considered.

*Article 16—Expansion of* Amparo *via the Concepts of "Competent Authority," and "Legal Basis and Justification"*

The expansion of the scope of *amparo* through the interpretation of article 16 has been based on three guarantees contained in the first sentence of that article: "no one shall be molested in his person, family, domicile, papers, or possessions except on the authority of a written order issued by the competent authority stating the legal basis and justification for the action taken." Since the jurisdictional claims based on article 16 differ both in scope and the reasoning employed in deriving them, depending on whether the reference is to the con-

---

[19] Suprema Corte, *Ayala Ascensión*, 64 S. J. 257 (1940). For similar rulings, see idem. *Solís Montes Estanislao*, 64 S. J. 2928 (1940); *González J. Carmen y coags.*, 69 S. J. 5162 (1941); and *Martínez Alberto y coags.*, 68 S. J. 184 (1941).

cept of "competent authority" or to that of "legal basis and justifica-tion," these two aspects of the article will be dealt with separately.

In determining the significance that should be attributed to the term "competent authority," the Supreme Court, following a thesis develop-ed originally by Vallarta, has distinguished between three types of competence: the constitutional, the jurisdictional, and *competencia de origen*, that is, that which derives from the legitimacy of the responsi-ble authority.[20] The last of these attempted to equate the competence of the authority with the legitimacy of the incumbent official's title to office. Although at one time accepted by the Court as included within the meaning of article 16, it was successfully and permanently deleted by Vallarta from the number of permissible definitions on grounds that can be more pertinently considered when examining the limita-tions imposed on the *amparo* suit by the doctrine of political questions. For the remaining types of competence, the Court, again in conformity with the opinion advanced by Vallarta, has held: "Constitutional com-petence, that is, that which refers to the scope of the powers [delegated to] the various governmental branches, is the only type protected by means of the individual guarantees."[21] In terms of article 16 then, a competent authority is one that acts within the sphere of its constitu-tionally delegated powers. To exceed these powers, to usurp those allocated to other governmental branches or subdivisions, or to contra-vene an express constitutional prohibition, when to do so results in one of the acts of molestation listed by article 16, divests the authority of competence and renders the act subject to attack in *amparo*.[22] Thus, by way of illustration, if the federal Congress should enact a tax not included among those expressly sanctioned by article 73, which sets forth the powers conferred upon the legislative branch, any attempt to

[20] For Vallarta's conclusions about the meaning and scope of article 16, in this point virtually identical in both the 1857 and 1917 constitutions, see particularly the *Amparo Guzmán* in Vallarta's *Cuestiones constitucionales*, I, 122–146.

[21] Suprema Corte, *Jurisprudencia definida de la Suprema Corte de Justicia en sus fallos pronunciados del 1 de junio de 1917 al 3 de septiembre de 1948, Apéndice al tomo XCVII del Semanario Judicial*, thesis 223, p. 431 (cited hereafter as *Apén-dice*). The thesis is repeated, although in shorter and less explanatory form in Suprema Corte, *Jurisprudencia de la Suprema Corte*, thesis 227, II, 436.

[22] Suprema Corte, *Díaz Solís Lucila*, 106 *S. J.* 2074 (1950).

collect it would inflict an injury of the sort envisaged by article 16, and the act could be voided in *amparo*. The legal situation would, of course, be similar in the event of any of the other transgressions noted above.[23] As in the case of the substantive interpretation of article 14, the protection afforded the organic and other nonguarantee sections of the Constitution by this provision of article 16 is indirect, *amparo* being granted only if it appears that the initial constitutional violation also constitutes a direct infraction of the competency requirement. Where the rule of *stricti juris* applies, the obligation to demonstrate this fact rests necessarily with the complainant.

In his discussion of this topic, Burgoa concludes that the "competent authority" guarantee extends the sphere of judicial authority to all those constitutional articles that either confer power or establish prohibitions. To judge by the list of articles cited as subject to this defense, however, it is evident that he does not believe it capable of being extended to the entire body of the Constitution.[24] To be sure, the articles listed—71, 73, 74, 76, 79, 89, 103, 104, 105, 106, and 117—include the majority of those whose violation would be likely to produce an actionable personal injury, but the logic of the interpretation is capable of sustaining even more inclusive conclusions. Since, in a constitutional state, all governmental authority, in conformity with the principle of constitutional supremacy, derives from the Constitution, it is reasonable to conclude that no official agency can be considered

---

[23] Suprema Corte, *Cooperativa Manufacturera de Cemento Portland, "La Cruz Azul," S. C. L., Informe, 1956* (Informe de la segunda sala), p. 48, in which the Supreme Court declared a federal tax on cement unconstitutional, provides a specific example. For additional illustrations, see Suprema Corte, *Ferrocarril Noroeste de México, Aserraderos González Ugarte S. A., y coags.*, 116 S. J. 287 (1953); idem, *Unión Nacional de Productores de Azúcar, S. A. de C. V.*, 115 S. J. 445 (1953); and idem, *Regional Platanera de Paso de Talaya, S. de R. L. de I. P. y G. V.*, 114 S. J. 182 (1952). The latter cases are concerned with unconstitutional State infringements upon powers granted exclusively to the federal government. It should be noted that in these cases, as in others of the type under consideration, an act violating the "competent authority" provisions is equally inconsistent, given the substantive interpretation, with the "legal basis and justification" guarantees as well as with the provisions of article 14. Since the printed case reports rarely distinguish between these guarantees, which are, in any event, generally equivalent, it is difficult to cite cases illustrating separate applications of these provisions.

[24] Burgoa, *El juicio de amparo*, pp. 207, 214.

competent to perform any act inconsistent in any way with the fundamental law. If this contention is valid, it follows that any unconstitutional act performed by an authority, regardless of the nature of the provision violated, constitutes, given the requisite personal injury, an actionable infraction of the "competent authority" guarantee. This provision would, consequently, possess the same inclusiveness claimed for article 14 and, as will be seen, for the "legal basis and justification" provisions of article 16. It must be confessed, however, that neither case material nor the commentaries provide support for an omnicompetent jurisdiction based on this interpretation of constitutional competence.

Turning to the remaining guarantees contained in article 16, it will be seen that the reasoning employed in their interpretation is essentially the same as that advanced by Rabasa about article 14. Probably the most convinced exponent of the virtues of these guarantees, not only as a basis for a general defense of the Constitution but also as a defense of the entire legal order, is Ignacio Burgoa, who asserts that "The juridical effectiveness of the guarantee of legality [the inclusive term used for these guarantees is *causa legal*, "legal cause"] resides in the fact that by means of it the entire Mexican system of positive law is protected, from the Constitution itself to the most trivial administrative regulation."[25] The presentation adopted here follows in general the course of Burgoa's argument.

An act, of the sort envisaged by article 16, must have a legal basis (in the original, a written order "*que funde . . . la causa legal*") in order to be valid. This requirement encompasses, according to Burgoa, three different elements of legality: the act must be derived from a law specifically authorizing its performance, the authority responsible for the act must be empowered explicitly to perform it, and the material conditions of execution must be in strict conformity with those prescribed in the authorizing law. In support of these contentions, the Supreme Court has held that "the authorities can do nothing that is not permitted by law,"[26] or, more explicitly, that: "The administrative

---

[25] Burgoa, *Las garantías individuales*, p. 471. For the author's overall treatment of this aspect of article 16, see pp. 471–475, and *El juicio de amparo*, p. 213.

[26] Suprema Corte, *Jurisprudencia de la Suprema Corte*, thesis 166, II, 347.

authorities have no other powers than those expressly conferrred upon them by the laws, and when they perform some act that is not properly based upon and justified by a law, this act should be deemed violative of the guarantees contained in article 16 of the Constitution."[27] Although the general rule formulated in these holdings is not as explicit in every respect as might be desired, the conclusions expressed above seem to be logically implicit in it. In any event, the vast number of cases citing article 16 and, in one way or another, touching upon these points provides ample corroboration.[28] It is evident from the opinions quoted that a merely formal compliance with the requirements of the article is not sufficient to sustain the validity of the act. With more explicit reference to this point, the Court has held that "the spirit of article 16 of the Constitution is not [merely] that court orders contain the legal precepts upon which they are based, but that there should really exist a justification for issuing them and a legal precept upon which to base them."[29] Nor is the mere existence of an adequate legal foundation for the act sufficient if the interested parties are not properly, and in adequate detail, informed of this in time to prepare their defense.[30] These rather stringent requirements are also applicable to acts of a discretionary nature, even when the exercise of discretion is expressly prescribed by law, as the Court has indicated in the case of *Establecimientos Emeur, S.A.*, holding that

the exercise of the discretionary power is subordinated to the rule of article 16 of the federal Constitution, insofar as this precept imposes on the

[27] Suprema Corte, *Olivares Amado*, 29 *S. J.* 669 (1930). Although the reference is to administrative authorities, the rule is equally applicable to the judiciary and, substituting the Constitution for statutory law, as the substantive interpretation requires, should be considered binding on the legislative branch as well.

[28] To cite only a few examples, see: Asociación Nacional de Funcionares Judiciales, *Pedro Yee Díaz*, 127 *BIJ* 141 (March 1958); idem, *Gilberto Corral*, 127 *BIJ* 143 (March 1958); idem, *María Cristina Cerezo Campa de Orozco*, 133 *BIJ* 554, (September 1958) (cited hereafter as Asociación); Suprema Corte, *Ingenio de San Cristóbal y Anexas, S. A., Informe, 1957.* (Informe de la segunda sala), pp. 17–18. Also see Suprema Corte, *Jurisprudencia de la Suprema Corte*, thesis 810, IV, 1477.

[29] Suprema Corte, *Baetzner Federico y coag.*, 26 *S. J.* 252 (1929).

[30] For examples see: Suprema Corte, *La Cía. del Ferrocarril Sud-Pacífico de México*, 71 *S. J.* 5812 (1942), and Asociación, *Antonio Sánchez Reyes*, 133 *BIJ* 537 (September 1958).

authorities the obligation of [legally] basing and justifying those acts that are capable of molesting individuals in their possessions and rights and, although the aforesaid exercise presupposes a subjective judgment of the act, which neither can nor should be replaced by the opinion of the judge, nonetheless it is subject to the control of the latter . . . when it is not reasonable but arbitrary and capricious, and when it is notoriously unjust or contrary to equity. It can be added that this [judicial] control is admissible when, in the aforementioned judgment, the factual circumstances have not been taken into account or have been unjustifiably altered, as well as in cases in which the reasoning is illogical or contrary to the general principles of law.[31]

The majority of the cases cited above indicate that the two requirements—legal basis and justification—are concurrent, and the presence of one will not, in the absence of the other, suffice to validate an act of the type contemplated by article 16. Briefly defined, the "legal justification" rule (in the original, a written order "*que . . . motive la causa legal*") requires that the specific, factual situations to which a given law is applied must be included within the bounds of the general and abstract situation delineated by that law. The tendency and intent here is to prevent the application of statutes, by analogy, to situations to which they do not explicitly pertain. Thus, hypothetically, the collection of a levy on inheritances, which is justified on the basis of a statute enacting an income tax, would constitute a violation of this guarantee.

Given the obligation of public authorities to act solely and strictly in conformity with law, Rabasa's thesis on the scope and significance of article 14 is evidently equally applicable to article 16. This permits the conclusion that the guarantees under consideration can be construed as authorizing the extension of the review power to all those constitutional articles whose infraction is capable of producing the requisite personal injury. If constitutionality, both formal and substantive, is an indispensable characteristic of law, it follows logically that no valid act can be based upon, and justified by, statutes or reglamentos that lack this quality. Consequently, the performance of an official act that

[31] Suprema Corte, *Informe, 1956* (Informe de la segunda sala), pp. 46–47. Also see Asociación, *José María Vázquez Alba*, 132 BIJ 461 (August 1958).

is inconsistent with any part of the Constitution and that leads to the injury of an individual constitutes a direct infraction of article 16 as well, and the alleged violation may properly be considered and adjudged in *amparo*. The Court's concurrence in this reasoning was clearly expressed in the case of *García Cepeda Ricardo*:

Although it is true that article 31 of the Constitution is not included in the section on individual guarantees, the violation of the right that it established [also] violates those contained in articles 14 and 16, because it not only fails to apply exactly a precept of some secondary law but also denigrates article 31 itself, and the violation of that text cannot produce a [legally] based and justified order prejudicing anyone. For this reason, if the Supreme Court were to say that the judicial power is not authorized to remedy such a violation and that the remedy is to be found [only] in the ballot box, it would render section I of article 103 of the Constitution nugatory.[32]

Given the principle of constitutional supremacy, the above interpretation of article 16 is indisputably logical, although it should be noted that much the same criticisms advanced about the substantive interpretation of article 14 could be leveled against it. In evaluating the various proposals for extending the constitutional scope of *amparo* that have been examined in this chapter, it should be remembered that the elements of admissibility prescribed in articles 103 and 107 continue to be indispensable prerequisites for jurisdiction. It follows that some constitutional violations, and not necessarily the least important, are not susceptible to any judicial remedy. This result is, of course, inevitable, if judicial review is to be judicial in fact. To dispense with the principle that jurisdiction derives only from the existence of a genuine conflict of interest between adverse parties would be to transcend the conventional limits of the judicial process and revert to the political mode of constitutional defense exemplified historically by the Supreme Conserving Power.

The general guarantee of legality and constitutionality deduced from articles 14 and 16 is of more than theoretical significance as is abundantly demonstrated in the decisions of the Supreme Court. It must be

[32] Suprema Corte, 61 S. J. 2922 (1939). Also see idem, *Jurisprudencia de la Suprema Corte*, thesis 543, III, 1004–1005.

noted, however, that this judicial acceptance, seemingly unconditional in principle, has not been carried as far in practice as the inherent logic of the interpretation permits. The development of a generally consistent position on the jurisdictional implications of this substantive guarantee is of comparatively recent occurrence, dating mainly from the middle and late 1940s.[33] The vacillating character of the Court's conclusions on the issue prior to that period can be illustrated by comparing the ruling in the above-cited *García Cepeda* case with that in *Ferrocarriles Nacionales de México*. Both cases were decided in the same year and involved the same constitutional issue. In contrast to the conclusion reached in the former, the latter held that "section IV of article 31 of the Constitution does not constitute an individual guarantee, and its violation cannot provide grounds for the concession of *amparo*."[34] Judging by the case reports for approximately the last thirty years, however, it is permissible to conclude that at present the Supreme Court can be expected to hear and, unless grounds for dismissal are found, to decide the substantive issues presented by cases in which the complainant can, with some degree of plausibility, show a violation of articles 14 and 16 that resulted from a prior infraction of constitutional provisions not found in the individual guarantees. To this degree *amparo* can be considered to have become technically adequate to the exigencies of a general constitutional defense. Nonetheless, one notable exception to this expansion of jurisdiction must be noted. The Court has not yet seen fit to bring within the protective sphere of *amparo* the electoral rights contained in articles 35 and 36 of the Constitution. In this matter it continues to maintain that "the violation of political rights does not give grounds for the admissibilitiy of *amparo* because these [rights] are not individual guarantees."[35] There is abundant practical justification for evading jurisdiction in clashes between the ideal situation envisaged by the Constitution and the practices followed by the government Party of the Institutional Revolution (PRI) in an area so fundamental to the interests of the latter, but the logic

[33] In illustration of one aspect of this development, see Servando J. Garza, *Las garantías constitucionales en el derecho tributario mexicano*, pp. 75–86.

[34] Suprema Corte, 62 *S. J.* 2724 (1939).

[35] Suprema Corte, *Jurisprudencia de la Suprema Corte*, thesis 345, III, 654.

of the exclusion from the *amparo* jurisdiction requires some critical scrutiny. This subject, however, can be considered more appropriately when dealing with the limitations to which the *amparo* jurisdiction is subject. Lastly, in evaluating the practical significance of the jurisdiction derived from articles 14 and 16, it seems that the most persuasive evidence for its effectiveness and for the increasing willingness of the Court to use it as a curb on arbitrary and irregular governmental procedures, aside from the testimony of the cases themselves, is provided by the restrictive amendments to the *amparo* and judiciary laws enacted in December 1957. Certainly, there would be little point in attacking a mere theory with such heavy legislative artillery.[36]

*The Constitutional Limits of the* Amparo *Jurisdiction*

Having examined the various interpretations by which the *amparo* suit has been transformed from an extraordinary defense of civil liberties into the foundation for a general system of judicial review, it is necessary to turn next to the limitations on the action. The most significant and far-reaching of these derives undoubtedly from those extra legal political practices and traditions whereby the spirit rather than the letter of the Constitution is violated. Certainly, in executive-legislative relations and the practice of federalism there is an irreconcilable variance between fact and constitutional intent. Constitutional infractions

[36] Thus far, the jurisdiction conferred by articles 14 and 16 has been used most frequently to combat violations of section IV, article 31, and various sections of article 73, the latter listing the powers delegated to the federal Congress. Virtually all of these cases have been concerned with the validity of tax measures. In addition, however, there have been numerous cases presenting issues based on articles 49, 60, 65, 70, 72, 74, 75, 76, 77, 89, 94, 117, 118, 123, 124, and 130. The following cases can be cited in illustration: Suprema Corte, *Artículos Mundet para Embotelladores, S. A.,* 85 *S. J.* 2973 (1945); *Aviles Bravo Manuel y coags.,* 89 *S.J.* 1546 (1946); *Cemento Portland Blanco de México,* 108 *S. J.* 1888 (1951); *Cia. Maderera de Miravalles, S. de R. L.,* 109 *S. J.* 2096 (1951); *López de Castillo Experanza,* 110 *S. J.* 362 (1951); *Cortés López José,* 114 *S. J.* 798 (1952); *Regional Plantanera de Paso de Telaya, S. de R. L. de I. P. y C. V.,* 114 *S. J.* 182 (1952); *Olliver Juan,* 116 *S. J.* 437 (1953); *Rodríguez Vda. de Villalabos María Luisa,* 116 *S. J.* 617 (1953); *Cine Roxy y coags.,* 119 *S. J.* 2660 (1954); *Martínez Esteban y coags.,* 121 *S. J.* 1890 (1954); *Rangel V. Fernando y coags.,* 121 *S. J.* 164 (1954); *Cervecería Central S. A., y coags.,* 121 *S. J.* 2680 (1954); and *Artículos Mundet para Embotelladores, S. A., Informe, 1957* (Informe de la segunda sala), p. 36.

of this kind, however, are usually compatible with formal compliance and readily elude judicial control even in the absence of political pressure on the courts. Aside from cases that involve inherently nonjusticiable constitutional questions, this class of limitations relates more directly to the content of judgments and the independence and originality of judges than to the technical and theoretical scope of jurisdiction and can be dealt with better in a later chapter. It is also preferable to postpone consideration of the purely technical limitations prescribed in the Amparo Law or derived from the formalities of judicial procedure, since these deal more with the disposition of individual cases than with the general jurisdictional competence of the courts. The following pages, therefore, are concerned exclusively with those jurisdictional limitations imposed by the Constitution, whether continuously or only intermittently in effect, and with the exclusion of "political questions" pursuant to a doctrine formulated, in large part, by the Supreme Court itself.

*Explicit Jurisdictional Exclusions—Article 27*

Although technically included among the individual guarantees, section XIV of article 27 stipulates an explicit exception to the usual rules of admissibility in *amparo*. The provisions in question state that "landowners affected by decisions granting or restoring communal lands and waters to villages, or who may be affected by future decisions, shall have no ordinary legal right or recourse and cannot institute *amparo* proceedings. Persons affected by such decisions shall have only the right to apply to the federal government for payment of the corresponding indemnity." The strict exclusion of the judiciary from this field is further evidenced by article 33 of the Agrarian Code, which, in conformity with section XIII of article 27, provides that the president is the supreme agrarian authority and states that when acting in this capacity "his final resolutions cannot in any case be modified." The final resolutions referred to are listed as those that grant or restore lands or waters, those that enlarge grants previously made, those that create new centers of agricultural population, those that recognize communal property rights, and those that recognize or establish nonaffectable properties in accordance with the terms of the code.[37] In effect, presidential orders of the types indicated establish res judicata in the specific cases to which they pertain. This is true even when the resolutions in question exert their effects on small agricultural properties in exploitation despite the special status and protection afforded these holdings in paragraph 3 and in section XV of article 27. The first of these states that in the process of breaking up and distributing large estates the rights of small landowners engaged in operating their properties should at all times be respected, while the second provides that "the mixed commissions, the local governments, and any other authorities charged with agrarian proceedings cannot in any case affect small agricultural or grazing properties in operation, and they shall incur liability for violations of the Constitution if they make grants that affect them."

Notwithstanding the apparent intent of these provisions to limit the meaning of the term "landowner" (*propietario*), as used in section XIV, to the owners of large estates (*latifundios*), the Supreme Court, in a series of cases exploring the scope of the limitation, has established *jurisprudencia* affirming its altogether unconditional character. The relevant thesis states:

Section XIV of article 27 of the Constitution excludes from the cognizance of the judicial power any controversy that may arise from a presidential decision granting or restoring lands or waters, even one whose unconstitutionality derives from the fact that small agricultural properties are affected thereby. In accordance with the absolute terms employed in the drafting of the aforesaid precept and following the principle of interpretation . . . that where the law itself does not distinguish, no distinction can be made, it is evident that small landowners cannot be excepted from that general statement, since the text alludes to 'landowners,' whether they be large or small, excluding them from the right of access to the *amparo* suit.[38]

---

[37] *Código agrario*, p. 15. The present statute was originally published in the *Diario oficial* of 27 April 1943.

[38] Suprema Corte, *Jurisprudencia de la Suprema Corte*, thesis 749, IV, 1366–1367. Also see thesis 103, II, 229, and idem, *Felipe I. Martínez y coag., Informe, 1942* (Informe de la segunda sala), p. 22. Burgoa, in *El juicio de amparo*, pp. 400–403, argues that *amparo* should be admissible against a distribution of

The absolute character of this exclusion has been somewhat modified, however, by constitutional amendment, and the area of its application explored and, to a degree, limited by judicial decision. With the intent of affording a judicial defense to small holders, a third paragraph was added to section XIV in 1947, providing that "owners or occupants of agricultural or stockraising properties in operation, who have been issued or to whom there may be issued in the future certificates of nonaffectability, may institute *amparo* proceedings against any illegal deprivation or agrarian claims on their lands or waters."[39] Since the concession of such certificates remains entirely in the hands of the agrarian authorities, whose discretion in the matter is subject to no form of judicial intervention, the practical value of the provision is somewhat doubtful. The long and complicated procedure specified by law would also be enough to discourage all but the most persistent applicants.[40] Nonetheless, an inadequate defense is doubtless better than none, and the certificate, once obtained, serves to confer on small agricultural holdings the same degree of legal stability and protection against arbitrary administrative impositions that may be enjoyed by other forms of individually owned property. This seems to be the case theoretically at least. In practice, there are indications that agricultural property, even when so protected, occupies a more precarious status than other types of property. One student of this question has stated that as of 1957, approximately 160,000 certificates of nonaffectability had been granted covering some 5 million hectares. Since the *Reglamento de inafectabilidad* provides for both types, this total includes presumably both temporary and permanent certificates. Given the usual

---

lands affecting the small properties defined in section XV. Gabino Frago, in the *Informe, 1942* (Informe de la segunda sala), pp. 7–10, presents a detailed defense of the Court's position.

[39] See the summary of agricultural decisions in the *Informe, 1943* (Informe de la segunda sala), p. 9.

[40] The provisions on certificates of nonaffectability are contained in Title II, articles 21–41, and Title III, articles 58–75, pp. 160–168 and 174–181, of the *Reglamento de inafectabilidad agrícola y ganadera*, in the above cited edition of the *Código agrario*. The law was originally published in the *Diario oficial* of 9 October 1948. For a general commentary on the provisions of article 27, section XIV, see Angel Caso, *Derecho agrario*, pp. 217–219.

figure of some 7 million hectares sown to crops, it also seems probable that the larger part of the properties protected by these certificates must consist of semiarid grazing land.[41]

The Supreme Court has not ventured to contest the plenary power of the president to grant or restore communal lands or waters to villages, regardless of the size of the private properties affected. It has held, further, that the same immunity from judicial restraint applies to resolutions enlarging existing *ejidos*, but it has ruled, in strict conformity with the terms of section XIV, that resolutions not directed to achieving one or another of the above purposes are subject to attack in *amparo*.[42] The suit is also admissible when the complaint alleges injuries resulting from the improper execution rather than the substance of a presidential order granting or restoring lands or waters.[43] This latter ruling, however, is not applicable to irregularities that occur in executing the provisional resolutions issued by subordinate agricultural officials. Orders of this type, although producing material effects, are not final until ratified by the president and, pending this approval, are subject to modification or recision in an administrative appeal prescribed by the Agrarian Code. A suit initiated against the improper execution of such resolutions would fail, consequently, to satisfy the rule established in section III, subsection (a), of article 107, that *amparo* is admissible, in general, only against final judgments or awards against which no ordinary recourse is available.[44] For the same reasons, the *amparo* suit has also been held to be inadmissible against the substance of such provisional resolutions.[45]

Although the Court has been unable or unwilling to extend the protection of *amparo* to the agricultural proprietor, except in the limited instances noted, the position of the *ejido* is altogether different.

---

[41] Julian Rodríguez Adamo, "El problema agrario, bases constitucionales, realizaciones, estado actual," in Antonio Martínez Báez, *La constitución de 1917 y la economía mexicana: Cursos de invierno 1957*, p. 92.

[42] Suprema Corte, *Jurisprudencia de la Suprema Corte*, thesis 413, III, 784, and thesis 416, 786–787.

[43] Ibid., thesis 104, II, 229–230, and thesis 415, III, 785. Also see idem, *Bananera Tuxpan, S. de R. L.*, 62 S. J. 578 (1939).

[44] Suprema Corte, *Jurisprudencia de la Suprema Corte*, thesis 393, III, 736.

[45] Suprema Corte, *Informe, 1943* (Informe de la segunda sala), p. 10.

Briefly, the Court has concluded that the term "landowner," as employed in section XIV, does not include the *ejido*, and that the exclusion of *amparo*, consequently, does not apply when an *ejido* is the complainant. In accordance with this ruling, it has been held that *amparo* is admissible when the residents of an agricultural village claim preferential rights to lands that have been granted by presidential resolution to another village, or when a presidential order modifying a previous grant or restitution of lands is protected.[46] As previously noted, the privileged status of the *ejido* as complainant in *amparo* was greatly extended in the Amparo Law and constitutional amendments adopted in 1963.

Given the absolute exclusion in section XIV, there appear to be no constitutional grounds, with the possible exception of paragraph 3 and section XV of article 27, upon which the Court could validly base a more effective and extensive defense of agricultural property rights, even if it were inclined to do so.

In view of the fundamental position occupied by the issue of land reform in the program of the Mexican Revolution, the pressure on governments to translate this aspiration into reality, and the revolutionary implications of a shift from a private to a communal form of land tenure, it is easily understandable that there has been impatience with the customarily dilatory processes of litigation and fear of a conservative reaction from the courts, at least during the earlier stages of the reform. Despite these considerations, however, the original version of article 27 presupposed no incompatibility between accomplishing land reform and the continued availability of *amparo* to persons adversely affected by expropriation. The provisions contained in the present section XIV appeared originally in the form of an amendment to article 10 of the Agrarian Law of 1915, enacted in 1931, and promulgated in January 1932.[47] Since it may be objected that a statutory provision cannot validly limit the admissibility of *amparo*, it should be explained that the original text of article 27 incorporated the Agrarian Law of

---

[46] Ibid., pp. 4–6.

[47] For the text of the amendment see the *Diario oficial* for 15 January 1932, or Manuel Fabila Montes de Oca, *Cinco siglos de legislación agraria, 1493–1940*, pp. 541–543.

1915 as a "constitutional law," that is, as a part of the Constitution itself. The alteration was effected, consequently, in conformity with the procedure prescribed for constitutional amendment in article 135. Section XIV itself was added in the course of the general revision to which article 27 was subjected in 1933–1934.

Although the complicated history of Mexican agrarian policy lies outside the proper scope of this study, it should be observed that the position taken by the Supreme Court prior to 1929 in this class of *amparos* tended generally to favor the cause of the *hacendados*, or large landowners. With the exception of the period occupied by the presidency of Alvaro Obregón, the Court's preference for conservative solutions was generally in accord with the cautious and somewhat unenthusiastic attitude of the various administrations in office during the 1920s. During the brief presidency of Emilio Portes Gil, however, the creation of *ejidos* was pursued with vigor, and the Court responded by establishing *jurisprudencia* that apparently ruled out the grant of *amparo* except in questions of evaluation and compensation and in cases involving violations of the Agrarian Law itself. With the elevation of Pascual Ortiz Rubio to the presidency in 1930, land reform seemed destined to come to an early end. His administration is, in this respect, chiefly notable for issuing a series of decrees that set termination dates for further applications for distribution of communal lands. The agrarian forces in the National Revolutionary Party, threatened by the unsympathetic attitude of the administration and anticipating a reversion to conservatism on the part of the Court, responded by pushing through the amendment to the Agrarian Law. Presumably this victory was made possible by the equivocal attitude of Plutarco Elías Calles, the real head of the government at that time. Considering the policies subsequently followed by Lázaro Cárdenas, however, it is doubtful that the Court could have been a serious obstacle for very long to the continuation of land reform.[48]

Aside from the fact that no established Mexican government need fear any serious judicial opposition to its agrarian policies, the contin-

---

[48] For a more extensive account of this period see Eyler N. Simpson, *The Ejido: Mexico's Way Out*, pp. 109–120, and Frank Tannenbaum, *Mexico: The Struggle for Peace and Bread*, pp. 136–153, 182–192.

ued presence of section XIV in the Constitution could be criticized on the practical ground that it tends to discourage the development of small and medium scale private ownership farming, a type of agriculture more productive generally—in Mexico as well it appears—than collectivism. Since Cárdenas, however, the mystique of collective farming has been merged so indisolubly with the idea of agrarian reform, that public discussion of the issues on their merits and within a political context has been virtually impossible. It is probably fortunate that actual government policy has in this respect frequently departed in a drastic manner from the theoretical commitment to communalism. The possibility of reintroducing a judicial defense for small holders through *amparo* is reduced further by the rapid population growth that has resulted in increased pressure on the available supply of arable land, despite the countervailing effects of industrial growth and extensive irrigation and reclamation projects. This, taken in conjunction with the fact that the peasant sector continues to comprise a major source of organizational and electoral support for the presidentially dominated, one-party political system first perfected by Cárdenas, indicates that the subject of rural land tenure remains so politically explosive that it precludes any significant limitation of absolute executive discretion in the foreseeable future.

## Other Explicit Jurisdictional Exclusions

Although certainly the most far reaching in its effects, the explicit exclusion of *amparo* prescribed in section XIV of article 27 is not the only provision of its type to be found in the Constitution. Technically similar prohibitions are imposed in articles 3, 33, 60, and 111. To review these briefly, section II of article 3, dealing with education, provides that "private persons may engage in education of all types and grade levels, but in elementary, secondary, and normal education, and in any kind or grade designed for laborers and farm workers, they must previously obtain, in every case, the express authorization of the public power. Such authorization may be refused or revoked by decisions against which there can be no judicial proceedings or recourse." This exclusion was originally introduced in the amended version of article

3 ratified in December 1934, while the present provisions were included in the amendment of December 1946.

Article 33 confers special powers upon the president in the control of aliens, stating that "the federal executive shall have the exclusive power to compel any alien whose remaining he may deem inexpedient to abandon the national territory immediately and without the necessity of previous legal action." The full extent of the limitation imposed on the judiciary by this article is somewhat obscured by the ambiguity of its phrasing, but within its proper area of application the discretion entrusted to the president is apparently unhampered by any procedural restraints.[49] In effect, the most summary of expulsions, if undertaken on the direct authority of the president, would not constitute an injury in the legal sense of the term or a violation of guarantees. Nonetheless, since the preliminary portions of article 33 equate aliens with citizens for the purposes of the individual guarantees that do not relate to political activity, there seems to be no impediment to initiating an *amparo* suit directed against ancillary injuries that are not rendered irreparable by the execution of the presidential order. It also seems reasonable to conclude that the suit should be admitted when citizenship is itself a question at issue, since, whatever the extent of the president's discretion in dealing with aliens, article 33 confers no powers applicable to citizens. Proper procedure in a situation of this kind appears to necessitate the admission and examination of the complaint subject to subsequent dismissal upon proof of the plaintiff's status as an alien. These considerations derive some support from the ruling in *Wong Ying Antonio*, in which the Court held that when the validity of naturalization papers is contested the burden of proof rests with the authorities and, by necessary implication, confirmed the right of judicial intervention when such questions are at issue.[50]

[49] See Suprema Corte, *Jurisprudencia de la Suprema Corte*, thesis 473, III, 908, which holds that suspension (in effect, an injunction) is inadmissible against the execution of such a deportation order. It can perhaps be inferred that deportations ordered by subordinate authorities would be subject to consideration in *amparo* unless subsequently ratified by the president. Should the latter occur while a case is in progress, dismissal would presumably be proper.

[50] Suprema Corte, 36 S. J. 1321 (1932).

Unlike the instances considered previously, the prohibitions contained in articles 60 and 111 relate primarily to questions of governmental organization rather than to the legal rights and obligations of individuals. Article 60, dealing with the organization of the federal Congress, provides that "each chamber shall be the judge of the elections of its members and shall decide any questions about them. Its decisions shall be final and unimpeachable."

Article 111, governing the impeachment process, establishes the final and unassailable character of the findings of the Chamber of Deputies and the decisions of the Senate in such cases. The exclusion of the judiciary in both of these instances follows naturally from the principle of separation of powers incorporated in the Mexican Constitution and has its equivalent in other similarly organized constitutional systems.

*Intermittently Operative Limitations—The Suspension of Guarantees*

Potentially, the most sweeping limitation upon the *amparo* jurisdiction is to be found in the emergency provisions of article 29, which states:

In the event of invasion, serious disturbance of the public peace, or any other event that may place society in great danger or conflict, only the president of the Mexican Republic, with the consent of the Council of Ministers and with the approval of the federal congress, and during adjournments of the latter, of the Permanent Commission, may suspend throughout the country or in a determined place the guarantees that present an obstacle to quickly combatting the situation; but he must do so for a limited time, by means of general preventive measures[, and] without these suspensions being limited to a specified individual. If the suspension should occur while the Congress is in session, the latter shall grant such authorizations as it deems necessary to enable the executive to meet the situation. If the suspension occurs during a period of adjournment, the Congress shall be convoked without delay in order to grant them.

In the most general sense, the suspension of an individual guarantee deprives it of its status as law and, consequently, of its enforceability in the courts for the period during which the suspension is effective. The governed may no longer, except at their own risk, exercise the rights defined by the guarantee in question, nor is the government obliged to respect them.[51] Nonetheless, despite the clarity with which the legal effect of this action can be stated, its use in specific instances raises a number of rather difficult questions about the permissible scope of the suspension, the authorities empowered to act under its authorization, and the procedures of initiation, implementation, and termination. The answers to these questions, insofar as they can be ascertained, must be deduced largely from the measures adopted in initiating and implementing the suspension of guarantees decreed in June 1942, in response to the emergency arising from the declaration of war on German, Italy, and Japan. Before examining the events of the war period, however, it should be noted that article 29 establishes two limitations on the extent to which the individual guarantees may be suspended. The requirement that suspension should be general rather than individual in its application preserves that provision of article 13 that states that "no one may be tried by private laws," while logic demands the inference that article 29 itself may not be suspended.

On 30 May 1942, President Manuel Avila Camacho, having secured the necessary prior consent of the Council of Ministers, presented to a special session of Congress a three-point proposal: he requested authority to declare war on the Axis powers, asked for approval to suspend certain specified individual guarantees, and requested delegation of extraordinary legislative powers to himself. With the celerity customarily displayed in dealing with urgent executive measures, the Congress considered and passed the proposed legislation during the course of a single sitting.[52] Both the declaration of war and the suspension decree became effective upon publication in the *Diario oficial* on 2 June. The latter measure authorized an unqualified suspension, throughout the national territory and applicable to all persons residing there, of the guarantees contained in article 4, paragraph 1 of article 5, articles 6, 7, 10, 11, 14, 16, 19, 20, 21, paragraph 3 of article 22, and article 25. These guarantees were to remain suspended for the duration of the state of war or, at the election of the president, for a

---

[51] For a commentary on this point see Burgoa, *Las garantías individuales*, p. 123.
[52] Ibid., pp. 127–128.

period not to exceed thirty days from the date of cessation of hostilities. Because of the ambiguity of these terms in both municipal and international law, the precise intent of the Congress on this point is rather uncertain, but presumably the actual termination of combat by surrender or armistice was meant rather than the conclusion of peace treaties. Such, at least, was the interpretation adopted in ending the suspension in 1945. Authority to establish limits on the extent of the suspension and to provide for the conditions of its employment was committed entirely to the discretion of the president, who was further empowered to enact any legislation required for defending the territorial integrity, sovereignty, dignity, and fundamental institutions of the country.[53] In practice, this meant not only legislation barred customarily by the terms of the individual guarantees but also measures falling within the normal competence of the Congress.

In appraising the legal effects of the suspension of guarantees during the war, two different periods must be distinguished. The first of these occupied the brief interval between the publication of the suspension decree on 2 June, and the promulgation of the corresponding regulatory legislation, the *Ley de Prevenciones Generales* (Law of General Precautionary Measures), on the thirteenth. The second period extended from the latter date until 1 October 1945, when Congress officially terminated the state of suspension. During the interval between the publication of the suspension decree and the appearance of the regulatory law, the guarantees listed in the former were presumably in abeyance completely, and *amparo* actions based on the violation of the guarantees totally inadmissible. It follows from this assumption that even arbitrary and unauthorized violations of rights were temporarily excluded from judicial examination and control.

The *Ley de Prevenciones*, promulgated by President Avila Camacho, under authority of the extraordinary legislative powers conferred by the Congress, specified in detail the areas within which the individual guarantees cited in the suspension decree were to remain inoperative and the manner in which the powers derived from the state of sus-

---

[53] The above summary of the suspension decree is based on the text printed in Manuel Andrade, ed., *Constitución política mexicana*, pp. 156-1–156-2, a standard (loose-leaf) compilation of constitutional and statutory materials.

pension were to be exercised. It was clearly stated that only the president could initiate actions that were based on and derived their validity from the suspension of guarantees. All subordinate officials, federal, state, and local, were restricted to a purely administrative role and permitted to act solely as executors of the emergency legislation emanating from the presidential office.[54] In declaring a price control statute enacted by the Coahuila State legislature unconstitutional, the Supreme Court stated: "It is the will of the fundamental law that the suspension of guarantees should be strictly reserved to the federal authorities . . . local authorities are not permitted to legislate in this field even under the pretext of instituting within their own territories legal dispositions decreed by the president of the Republic for the federal district." Although not stated explicitly in the statute, article 29 suggests that the president's discretion should be considered limited to issuing legislative measures of general applicability. If this interpretation is sound, it follows that in the strictly administrative area the president was obliged to act in conformity with the terms of the measures he himself had formulated in his legislative capacity.[55] Certainly, an executive order of individual application would violate the requirement that suspension be effected only by means of "general preventive measures." Thus, aside from the specific exceptions contained in the various emergency enactments, the individual guarantees were restored to their normal status, and *amparo* again became admissible if they were violated. The guarantees of procedural and substantive due process (*garantías de legalidad*) in articles 14 and 16, which were among those restored in this manner, were undoubtedly of the greatest significance in determining the extent of jurisdiction regained by the courts. For cases arising under the emergency legislation itself, however, the President intended evidently to exclude *amparo* altogether. To this end, article 18 of the *Ley de Prevenciones* directed the courts to reject any complaint challenging either the emergency laws themselves or acts based upon them. Certainly not all of the legislation emanating from the executive

---

[54] Suprema Corte, *Francisco O'Reilly y coags., Informe, 1943* (Informe de la segunda sala), p. 72.

[55] This also follows from the restoration of the "legal basis and justification" guarantees of article 16.

was classified as emergency in character. On the contrary, in conformity with article 29, the *Ley de Prevenciones*, and its regulatory law, the Supreme Court held that only those measures issued by the president pursuant to the powers granted in article 3 of the suspension decree, that is, those serving to regulate the scope, the manner of application, and the specific employment of suspension, could be classed as emergency laws. The suspension decree also authorized the president to legislate in areas falling within the normal competence of Congress, but measures of this type, it was held, did not possess emergency status and were subject to the usual constitutional limitations applicable to acts of Congress.[56] The second paragraph of article 18 further instructed the courts to dismiss any cases already in process of adjudication upon notification by a federal authority that the act complained of was based on provisions of the *Ley de Prevenciones*. The federal authority referred to was presumably that responsible for the alleged injury and would include state and local authorities as well when they were acting as federal auxiliaries in the enforcement of emergency legislation.[57] Aside from the obvious incongruity in empowering a party to a case to determine the manner of its disposition, the constitutionality of this article is highly questionable. It established, in effect, a blanket presumption of validity for all emergency legislation and for all administrative acts based ostensibly on such legislation. By creating a new rule of inadmissibility, article 18 deviated from the proper regulatory purpose of the *Ley de Prevenciones* and directly limited the jurisdictional provisions of articles 103 and 107 of the Constitution, which was an exercise of power manifestly in excess of that granted by article 29. To demonstrate this conclusion, it is only necessary to recall that while the latter article permits the temporary suspension of individual guarantees and the transfer of legislative powers to the executive, with the concomitant effects of these actions on the number

---

[56] Suprema Corte, *Fernando Coronado y coags.*, *Informe, 1945* (Informe de la segunda sala), pp. 118–119. Also see idem, *Compañia del Ferrocarril de Nacozari, Informe, 1945* (Informe de la segunda sala), pp. 119–120; idem, *Pedro Cañas Bustamante, Informe, 1943* (Informe de la segunda sala), p. 11; and idem, *Elsie Schroeder, Informe, 1943* (Informe de la segunda sala), pp. 72–73.

[57] Andrade, *Constitución política*, pp. 156-3–156-13.

and variety of situations capable of giving rise to *amparo* suits, it does not authorize either the president or the Congress to alter or dispense with any other provisions of the Constitution. It has previously been indicated that rules of inadmissibility must be derived from the Constitution itself. It follows that new grounds of inadmissibility can be established only by the process of constitutional amendment and not, as in the present case, by statute.[58] From this, it can be deduced that, while the temporary inoperativeness of individual guarantees limits necessarily the area within which the judicial branch may function, the courts cannot validly be denied the right to determine in individual cases whether one of the guarantees that continues in force has been violated by acts or laws represented as emergency measures. This is not to deny that the proper application of an emergency law produces a situation in which *amparo* is inapplicable, but in such a case the inadmissibility of the suit arises not from statutory provisions but because the guarantee affected has ceased to have legal existence, and its violation can produce no actionable injury. Interpreted in this fashion, article 18 expressed a truism, namely, that where no injury has been inflicted there can be no suit. In practice the Supreme Court upheld consistently its right to determine this. The position taken by the Court is clearly summarized in the case of *Epitacio Leonardo Blanco y Susano Paredes*, in which it was held:

> it does not suffice that the responsible authority state that it has acted in conformity with and under the authorization of the *Ley de Prevenciones*. [On the contrary] it is necessary that it justify its acts, since the aforecited law has not repealed article 149 of the *amparo* law, which imposes this obligation on responsible authorities, nor the right of the complainant to present proofs. The district judge should not decree the dismissal called for by article 18 of the *Ley de Prevenciones* but should assure himself that the provisions of that statute have been correctly applied by the authorities competent to do so.[59]

[58] The above argument is substantially similar to that presented by Burgoa, *Las garantías individuales*, pp. 154–157.

[59] Suprema Corte, *Informe, 1945* (Informe de la primera sala), p. 66. Also see *Martín Pérez Alemán, Informe, 1945* (Informe de la primera sala), p. 66; *Guillermo Luque Salanueva, Informe, 1944* (Informe de la segunda sala), p. 102, and *Ruíz y García Sucesor, Informe, 1944* (Informe de la segunda sala), pp. 102–103.

Had article 18 exercised the effects it was apparently intended to have, the mere designation of a law or act as an emergency measure would have prevented any consideration by the Court.

A more detailed treatment of the jurisdiction actually exercised by the courts under the regulations established by the *Ley de Prevenciones* and subsequent emergency legislation would be of little value in assessing the extent to which the *amparo* jurisdiction may be limited by the suspension of guarantees. On the whole, the situation prevailing during the interim period of unlimited suspension is most indicative of the possibilities here. Despite the arguments which would preserve an active and inviolable role for the courts during such periods, it is obvious that they may be almost completely deprived of jurisdiction. It is easily possible to imagine a situation, such as an invasion or a major rebellion, in which the physical security of the government would be directly threatened, when all or the greater part of the individual guarantees, other than that prohibiting private laws, could be entirely and indefinitely suspended. Under such circumstances, the *amparo* suit would, for all practical purposes disappear until more normal conditions were reestablished. Given the existing Mexican political structure and tradition, the area within which *amparo* will be permitted to function in time of emergency will be determined exclusively by the executive branch which means, in effect, by the president.

Of greater practical importance is the question of whether emergency legislation can be used to modify permanently the scope and applicability of individual guarantees. Uncertainty on this point stems from policies pursued in alleged conformity with the terms of the congressional decree of 28 September 1945, which terminated the state of emergency and restored the full enjoyment of constitutional rights. According to article 6 of this decree, however, executive orders that had been issued during the emergency for regulating governmental intervention in the economy were given blanket congressional ratification and emerged in the guise of ordinary statutory law. Among the effects has been the perpetuation by the Ministry of Foreign Affairs of a policy originally established in the Emergency Decree of 1944. By this policy the ministry exercises a fully discretionary authority over the conditions under which permission for the organization or reorganization of corporations engaged in virtually all types of economic activities is granted or withheld whenever there is foreign capital participation or the possibility of such participation. Whatever justification might be suggested for such a procedure, there is little or no reasonable doubt that it limits the scope of the guarantees contained in article 4 of the Constitution as it was previously interpreted. Despite this, the validity of the policy was not questioned in *amparo* until 1962, in the case of *Química Industrial de Monterrey S.A.*[60] Unfortunately, perhaps, the Supreme Court did not address itself to the constitutional question proper, that is, the ability of the Congress to extend indefinitely the application of laws that, though valid under the conditions of a declared emergency, under ordinary circumstances violate individual guarantees. Instead, the Court, pursuing the principle of judicial parsimony, confined itself to questions of legality arising from the interpretation of the relevant statutes. In finding for the plaintiff corporation, the Court pointed out that article 1 of the Emergency Decree of 1944 stated specifically that the effects of the decree were to be limited to the period of the suspension of guarantees. Article 5 of the decree of 1945, which terminated the suspension of guarantees, provided in turn that emergency measures so limited were not to be considered as receiving congressional ratification. The Court concluded, therefore, that article 6 of the latter decree could refer only to the ratification of emergency measures not limited to the period of suspension, and, as a result, that the provisions of the Emergency Decree of 1944 lapsed with the legal termination of suspension.

Although the Court did not deal directly with the principal constitutional issue involved here, it is safe to predict its position if such a question should be submitted in inescapable form. It was previously noted that the Constitution cannot be amended by simple statute, but the modification of individual guarantees would certainly constitute such an amendment. The ratification by Congress of emergency decrees previously issued by the executive does not differ substantially from the ordinary legislative process and, consequently, is bound by

[60] Suprema Corte, 66 *S. J.* 25 (1963). Also see the equivalent decision in *Playtex, S. A.*, Amparo en revisión 3596 (1964).

constitutional limitations that the courts, in *amparo*, have a right to enforce. To legitimize the violation of individual guarantees, therefore, the provisions of article 29 of the Constitution must be properly invoked. The legitimacy of such violations continues only during the period of the emergency and lapses entirely with its termination. The individual guarantees constitute, except in legally established emergency periods, the minimum of rights that the government must recognize. It may legitimately expand but not reduce them.

*Intermittently Operative Limitations—the Amending Clause*

In a formal sense, the Mexican Constitution must be included among those classified as rigid. Article 135 provides that "The present constitution may be added to or amended. In order that the additions or amendments shall become a part thereof, it shall be required that the Congress of the union, by a vote of two-thirds of the individuals present, agree to the amendments or additions and that they be approved by a majority of the legislatures of the States. The Congress of the union shall count the votes of the legislatures and shall announce those additions or amendments that have been approved."

Notwithstanding these provisions, the Constitution has proven in practice to be not merely flexible but fluid, having been amended over a hundred times since its promulgation in 1917. This ease in amending the Constitution derives mainly from the domination the president exercises over the structure and processes of Mexican government. If no serious opposition to a given proposal arises within one or more of the "sectors" into which the governing Party of the Institutional Revolution (PRI) is divided, or among major interest groups such as the industrial and commercial chambers, none can be expected in the Congress and the state legislatures. Should the latter display unexpected symptoms of independence, however, the president, acting through the federal Senate, may always avail himself of the power granted in section V, article 76 of the Constitution, and dismiss the existing state government, appoint a provisional governor more to his taste, and call new elections. Needless to say, the outcome of such elections is never in doubt. The majority of these alterations and additions have been of relatively minor importance, but their number is indicative of the extraordinary ease with which such changes can be made and suggests that constitutional amendment, potentially at least, can be a serious limitation on both the scope and the long-run significance of judicial review. Such results may be achieved in two ways, by depriving the courts of jurisdiction in certain fields, or by reversing established judicial interpretations of the Constitution. Thus far, the amendment of article 3 and the addition of section XIV to article 27 offer the only instances of the first of these procedures. Since these exclusions have already been discussed at some length, only the second procedure will be considered at this point. One of the most conspicuous instances of the sort is provided by the amendment of article 49 in 1938. It was observed in dealing with the suspension of guarantees that article 49, in its original form, stated that "the supreme power of the Federation is divided for its exercise, into legislative, executive, and judicial. Two or more of these powers shall never be united in one single person or corporation, nor shall the legislative power be vested in one individual except in the case of extraordinary powers granted to the executive, in accordance with the provisions of article 29."

Despite the clear intent of this provision, the Congress persisted in granting such powers in the absence of the specified conditions, while the Supreme Court condoned the practice in *jurisprudencia*, holding that it represented merely a form of legislative-executive cooperation and did not violate the prescribed separation of powers.[61] Possibly recognizing that presidential control of legislation was sufficiently complete without the assistance of this device, President Lázaro Cárdenas proposed and secured the acceptance of an amendment that added to article 49 the following statement: "In no other case will extraordinary powers to legislate be granted to the executive." By 1950, it had become evident to the Aleman administration that the Cárdenas amendment, at least as interpreted by the Supreme Court, was forcing an in-

---

[61] Suprema Corte, *Jurisprudencia de la Suprema Corte*, thesis 466, III, 913–914. The continued presence of this thesis in the current compilation of *jurisprudencia* indicates that the Court is prepared to resurrect it in the event of a reversion to this practice. In the light of recent cases, it would be difficult to explain its presence on any other grounds. See Suprema Corte, *Artículos Mundet para Embotelladores, S. A., Informe, 1957* (Informe de la segunda sala), p. 36.

conveniently rigid adherence to the formalities of separation of powers. Dissatisfaction with this state of affairs derived primarily from its effect on administering the international trade and currency controls associated with the postwar industrialization program. In order to more effectively bring the direction and volume of Mexican trade into conformity with the fluctuations of the international market, legislation was enacted granting the president extensive discretionary powers over tariff rates and other economic controls. Confronted with this legislation, the Court found that it violated articles 73 and 49, and, consequently, articles 14 and 16. In the case of *Cía. Maderera de Miravalles, S. de R. L.*, for example, the Court held that

> sections VII and XXIX of article 73 of the Constitution forbid the Congress to authorize the president to modify export tax rates. The power to tax foreign commerce and to levy the taxes necessary to cover the appropriations budget belongs exclusively to the Congress. The president of the Republic can in no case impose taxes, and it is unconstitutional to delegate such powers to him. If he modifies an export tariff rate, that modification implies the creation of a new tax that, for the aforesaid reasons, is in violation of the Constitution.[62]

In 1951, the Court's position was reversed by the amendment of articles 49 and 131. The final sentence of the first of these was altered to read: "In no other case, except as provided in the second paragraph of article 131, will extraordinary powers to legislate be granted," while the latter provided that

> the executive may be empowered by the Congress of the union to increase, decrease, or abolish tariff rates on imports and exports, which were imposed by the Congress itself, and to establish others; likewise to restrict and to prohibit the importation, exportation, or transit of articles, products, and goods, when he deems this expedient for the purpose of regulating foreign commerce, the economy of the country, the stability of domestic production, or for accomplishing any other purpose to the benefit of the country. The executive himself, in submitting the fiscal budget to Congress

---

[62] Suprema Corte, 109 *S. J.* 2096 (1951). Also idem, *Ramón Hernández Reyes*, 81 *S. J.* 5753 (1944), and *Cía. de Industrial de Matamoros, S. A. de C. V.*, 103 *S. J.* 995 (1950).

each year, shall submit for its approval the use that he has made of this power.

Should the remaining limitations on the delegation of legislative powers prove equally burdensome, it may be presumed that similar correctives will be applied. The only other example of this use of the amending power, in 1934 and 1946, has been previously considered in examining article 104 and the *recurso de súplica*.

It should also be pointed out again that the amending power can be employed as an indirect check on the judiciary as well as in the direct fashion treated here, which was clearly illustrated in the 1928 and 1934 alterations in the provisions on appointments, terms, and removals of federal judges.

When one considers the ease with which the Mexican Constitution can be amended, it is, at first glance, surprising that the courts have suffered so little restraint from this source. In the instances cited, the intent has been either largely precautionary, as in the case of section XIV of article 27, or it has been to correct an inconveniently protracted judicial adherence to the discarded policies or practices of the executive branch. Because none of these amendments has been designed to resolve conflicting executive-judicial views on matters of major policy significance, it is possible to infer that such differences have not arisen in practice. Even in the case of the situation that led to amending articles 49 and 131, in 1951, the position held by the Supreme Court was in conflict with the procedure adopted by the executive rather than with the substance of the policy involved. As long as the Court refrains from passing judgment on questions of policy, it is not probable that the president will often have occasion to seek amendments that impose jurisdictional limitations. Amendments reversing specific constitutional interpretations may, perhaps, be more likely, but the record does not indicate that such heroic measures will be frequently employed.

## Political Questions

The literature of jurisprudence provides an extensive array of ambiguous attempts to distinguish systematically between political and justiciable questions. For present purposes, however, the former may be defined, in the most inclusive sense, as those either expressly or by necessary implication reserved by the constitution for the final and discretionary decision of the executive or legislative branches of government. This definition has the advantage of indicating the practical consequences of the distinction as well as evading the difficult, if not impossible, task of demonstrating substantive differences between the questions actually incorporated in each category. The preceding pages have examined under other headings those situations in which the Constitution has left little doubt of the intent to confer unrestricted discretion upon the political agencies of government. In the following pages, consideration is given to those cases in which the Supreme Court itself has found it advisable to exclude *amparo* on the ground that the question posed is essentially political.

Both the Supreme Court and the federal Congress have so construed the scope of the *amparo* action that it excludes jurisdiction in the field of political rights, that is, those rights that relate to the exercise of the suffrage and to the holding of elective or appointive public office. Sections VII and VIII of article 73 of the *amparo* law provide specifically that the suit shall be inadmissible:

VII. Against the resolutions or declarations of the presiding officers of polling places, counting boards, or electoral colleges in the matter of elections;
and

VIII. Against the resolutions or declarations of the federal Congress or of either of its chambers, of the legislatures of the states or of their permanent committees or deputations, in the election, suspension, or removal of officials, in those cases in which the corresponding constitutions confer upon them the power to decide such questions in a sovereign or discretionary manner.

As has been previously indicated, the inadmissibility of the *amparo* suit must be founded on express or implied constitutional exclusions, not merely on statutory prescriptions. For the provisions of sections VII and VIII, this constitutional support is not always clearly apparent. Since the political rights affected are contained in articles 35 and 36 of the Constitution, it is, of course, obvious that they are not physically included among the individual guarantees and consequently do not fall directly within the scope of *amparo* as defined by section I of article 103. Because of the substantive interpretations of articles 14 and 16, however, this fact is not, in itself, sufficient to justify the exclusion. The only explicit constitutional support for the inadmissibility of *amparo* in these cases is provided by article 60, which makes each chamber of the federal Congress the sole and final judge of the elections and qualifications of its own members, and by article III, which governs the impeachment process. Insofar as section VIII refers to the powers of the federal Congress, additional constitutional support may be implied from the following provisions of articles 74, 76, and 109.

Article 74. The exclusive powers of the Chamber of Deputies are: I. to constitute itself as an electoral college in order to exercise the powers assigned to it by law in the election of the president of the Republic . . . V. To take cognizance of accusations against public officials mentioned in this Constitution, for official crimes, and in proper cases to present impeachment before the chamber of senators; and to constitute itself as a grand jury in order to decide whether to proceed against any of the public officials who enjoy constitutional prerogative, when they are accused of common crimes . . . VII. To declare whether the petitions for removal of judicial authorities made by the president of the Republic are justified, under the terms of the final part of article III.

Article 76. The exclusive powers of the Senate are: . . . V. To declare, whenever the constitutional powers of a state have disappeared, that the condition has arisen for appointing a provisional governor, who shall call elections in accordance with the constitutional laws of the said State. The governor shall be appointed by the Senate from a list of three proposed by the president of the Republic, with the approval of two-thirds of the members present, and during adjournments, by the Permanent Commission, according to the same rules. The official thus appointed cannot be elected constitutional governor in the elections held pursuant to the call that he issues. This provision shall govern whenever the constitution of a state does not make provision for such cases . . . VII. To constitute itself as a grand jury to take cognizance of official crimes of the officials which this Constitution expressly designates . . . XI. To declare whether the petitions made by the president of the Republic for removing judicial authorities are justified, under the provisions of the final part of article III . . .

Article 109.   If the offense [i.e., common crimes committed by senators, deputies, ministers of the Supreme Court, secretaries of the Cabinet, the attorney general, or the president] is of a common order, the Chamber of Deputies acting as a grand jury shall determine by an absolute majority of votes of its total membership whether there are grounds for proceedings against the accused. If the finding is negative, there shall be no grounds for any further proceedings; but such decision shall not be an obstacle to continuing the prosecution of the charge, whenever the accused has relinquished his immunity, since the decision of the chamber in no way prejudges the merits of the charge. If the finding is affirmative, the accused shall thereby be suspended from office and is immediately subject to action by the ordinary courts, except in the case of the president of the Republic, who may be impeached only before the Chamber of Senators, as in the case of an official offense.

The decisions reached in the cases defined in article 109 are stated by article 111 to be final. In all other respects, the constitutionality of sections VII and VIII is decidedly questionable. Certainly, there is nothing in the Constitution that directly suggests that the decisions of the electoral officials named in section VII are intended to be judicially unimpeachable. Those provisions of section VIII that deal with the powers of state legislatures present an even more complex question of interpretation. The proviso that *amparo* is inadmissible only in the event that the appropriate constitution confers sovereign or discretionary powers suggests clearly that in the absence of such constitutional authorizations actionable private rights exist. From this it could be inferred that the Congress, in enacting this section of the Amparo Law, did not intend to affirm the existence of any inherent and fundamental distinction between the juridical characteristics of political rights and individual guarantees. Rather, it intended to confirm the exceptional and exclusively constitutional nature of such departures from the customary rule of legality guaranteed by articles 14 and 16. The federal constituent authority is indisputably competent to create exceptions in favor of both the federal and state legislative or executive branches as it has done for the federal Congress in the instances noted. In the case of the state legislatures, however, no similarly explicit constitutional authorizations are to be found. In their absence and consistent with the wording of section VIII, it is apparently assumed that the constituent authorities of the states are competent to create universal restrictions on the admissibility of the *amparo* suit. Article 103 of the federal Constitution, in conformity with article 1, establishes the admissibility of the suit whenever an individual guarantee is violated by an authority at any level of government. The imposition of such restrictions by a state constitution would necessarily modify the constitutional scope of *amparo* and, in consequence, violate not only article 103 but also the supremacy and amending clauses in articles 133 and 135. If the premises of this argument are sound, it follows that the statutory provisions in question should be considered unconstitutional. This is not to say that a state constitution may not validly confer discretionary authority on the legislative branch in the area under consideration. When this is done, however, it is proper to apply the ruling of the previously cited *Establecimientos Emeur* case, that the exercise of such powers is subordinated to the rule of legality and may be counteracted by the federal courts when "it is not reasonable but arbitrary and capricious and when it is notoriously unjust or contrary to equity."[63]

Although the conclusion expressed above conforms with the general rule on inadmissibility and with the apparent sense of the terminology in section VIII, it is possible to derive from article 40 of the Constitution a result more consonant with the purpose of the statute. Article 40 states that "it is the will of the Mexican people to organize themselves into a federal, democratic, representative Republic composed of free and sovereign states in all that concerns their internal government, but united in a federation established according to the principles of this fundamental law." Nothing, assuredly, is more intimately associated with the internal government of a state than the selection and tenure of its officials. The intervention of the federal judiciary in these matters would necessarily limit the freedom of action promised by

---

[63] Suprema Corte, *Informe, 1956* (Informe de la segunda sala), pp. 46–47.

article 40 and could be construed as violating its intent. So interpreted, article 40 provides a definite constitutional foundation for the inadmissibility of *amparo* in such cases. Even so, it is unlikely that the Congress entertained these views in enacting section VIII, since this interpretation presupposes the general and automatic inadmissibility of the suit and would require neither federal legislative sanction nor inclusion in the state constitutions for it to be effective.

The Supreme Court itself has not questioned the constitutionality of these statutory provisions or, insofar as it has been possible to determine, subjected them to any detailed interpretation.[64] Relevant are the comments of Lic. Francisco Díaz Lombardo, former president of the Supreme Court, on the Court's refusal to accept jurisdiction in a suit initiated by the federal government against the government of the state of Guanajuato. He asserted that the free and unrestricted right to choose their own officials is a necessary consequence of the sovereignty possessed by the governments of the states and of the federation within their own proper spheres of authority. In conclusion, he said that neither government, nor any agency of either government, could be considered empowered to intervene in any electoral process or question falling within the jurisdiction of the other.[65]

The *jurisprudencia* established by the Supreme Court in the field of political rights presents similar problems of ambiguity. As a general rule, it has been stated that "the violation of political rights does not give grounds for the admissibility of *amparo* because these [rights] are not individual guarantees."[66] On the precise significance to be at-

---

[64] For an example of their application in litigation see Suprema Corte, *Arrieta Federico,* 52 *S. J.* 103 (1937).

[65] Suprema Corte, *Informe, 1928* (Informe de la presidencia), pp. 23–24.

[66] Suprema Corte, *Jurisprudencia de la Suprema Corte,* thesis 345, III, p. 654. The effect of this rule is somewhat modified by thesis 346, III, p. 656: "Even when political rights are in question, if the act complained of may also involve the violation of individual guarantees, a fact that cannot be judged *a priori,* the complaint . . . should be admitted . . ." See also Suprema Corte, *Mendoza Eustaquio y coags.,* 10 *S. J.* 475 (1922) that: "although the Court has established that *amparo* is inadmissible against the violation of political rights, this *jurisprudencia* refers to cases in which federal protection is sought against authorities exercising political functions and whose acts are directly and exclusively related to the exercise of rights of that nature. It cannot be applied to cases in which *amparo* is sought against judicial

tributed to this rule, the Court has advanced conflicting opinions. In *Ríos Martínez Cuauhtémoc,* it was held that this thesis "refers only to those acts performed in the exercise of a sovereign and unlimited authority," in other words, acts either expressly or by necessary implication reserved by the Constitution for the final and discretionary decision of the executive or legislative branches, or of the states.[67] As was indicated in considering sections VII and VIII of article 73 of the Amparo Law, not all rights of a political character can be considered reserved in this manner. The implication, therefore, is that in some cases in which political rights are violated *amparo* might be admissible. In a number of more recent cases, however, the Court has declared that its general thesis on political rights "is applicable not only to cases in which the authorities concerned enjoy sovereign and discretionary powers . . . but in any case involving such rights."[68] From these decisions it necessarily follows that the exclusion of *amparo* is absolute and unqualified irrespective of the specific character of the political rights involved. Given the apparent rationale of the *jurisprudencia*—that the political rights in question are not physically included among the articles that contain the individual guarantees—the latter ruling seems both more logical and more consonant with actual practice than the former. Because of the substantive interpretations of articles 14 and 16, however, such a purely literal application of the provisions of section I of article 103 is intellectually and juridically unsatisfactory. There are, of course, limited cases in which there is an express or clearly implied constitutional intention to confer final and discretionary authority upon the political agencies of government. Excluding these, however, the rights

---

decisions that, although affecting political rights, may also violate individual guarantees." Nonetheless, the exclusion of political rights as such from the *amparo* jurisdiction remains unaffected by these decisions.

[67] Suprema Corte, 55 *S. J.* 1476 (1938).

[68] Supreme Corte, *Chávez Anselmo, Jr.,* 87 *S. J.* 3283 (1946). Also, idem, *Castro J. Medardo y coags.,* 87 *S. J.* 3283 (1946), *Carrola Antuna Enrique,* 85 *S. J.* 2687 (1945), and Suprema Corte, *Federico Fernández, Informe rendido, 1942* (Informe de la segunda sala), pp. 35–36. The latter states that *amparo* is also inadmissible when the right claimed is exclusively and necessarily derived from a political right, although not itself political.

defined in articles 35 and 36 are not obviously distinguishable in kind
from those other constitutional provisions, also lacking in the character
of individual guarantees, which nonetheless find a judicial defense in
the general guarantees of legality. The following ruling indicates that
the court has not been unaware of this incongruity:

> The *jurisprudencia* sustained by this Supreme Court has held that the
> violation of political rights does not give grounds for the admissibility of
> *amparo* because these [rights] are not individual guarantees. It is not pos-
> sible to confound the two because the latter are set forth in the first 29
> articles of the Constitution, and in none of these is the right to exercise a
> public, electoral office guaranteed. Furthermore, the individual guarantees
> are limitations imposed on the public power toward all the inhabitants of
> the Republic, regardless of nationality, sex, judicial capacity, etc., whereas
> the constituent authority conceded political rights exclusively to Mexican
> citizens.[69]

Even if this were relevant to the general question of exclusion, the
assertion that the exercise of political rights is dependent upon citizenship, whereas no such stipulations attach to the enjoyment of the individual guarantees, is not altogether true. Those provisions of articles
8 and 9 that deal with the rights of political petition and association
are explicitly contingent upon citizenship, as are sections of articles 11
and 27. Nor are the individual guarantees entirely devoid of other
conditions, direct and indirect, which are of a similarly limiting character.[70] The mere existence of a condition prerequisite to the enjoyment
of a right is not, therefore, enough to rule out the application of
*amparo*. It is equally inappropriate to stress the intrinsically political
or nonpolitical character of a right as a basis for determining the admissibility of the suit. At least, this is a reasonable conclusion if the

[69] Suprema Corte, *Antuna Benito, Jr., y coags.*, 69 *S. J.* 4731 (1941). Also, idem,
*Huerta José G.*, 47 *S. J.* 33 (1936), where political rights are defined as prerogatives and obligations of citizenship. No more explicit statement of the Court's reasoning, concluding that a right contingent on citizenship falls outside the scope of
the guarantees of legality, appears to be available.

[70] See, for example, article 3, which prohibits clerics from intervening in primary,
secondary, and normal education; article 4, which authorizes the imposition of
standards of professional competence for the exercise of certain vocations; and various provisions of articles 27 and 28.

customary definition of political rights be accepted, that is, rights involved in forming or administering government. Certainly, such rights as freedom of speech, press, assembly, and petition must be subsumed under this definition. Rights so exclusively political in function as suffrage and the occupation of public office have at most times and in most places been confined to citizens. This does not, in any self-evident way, imply an intrinsic juridical distinction between these and any other legally recognized rights.

In defense of the Court's position, Ignacio Burgoa asserts that the two types of rights are totally different in juridical nature. Political rights, as he defines them, are powers conferred by the state upon citizens enabling them to intervene actively in the political process, either through the vote or by standing for public office. The exercise of such rights is periodic rather than continuous, dependent upon the occurrence of a condition, namely an election. In the intervals between elections these political rights lie dormant; they are, in effect, nonexistent until the recurrence of the condition. The individual guarantees, on the other hand, are limitations imposed by the state on its own sovereignty, establishing areas within which the governed, regardless of nationality or other condition, may at any time act freely.[71] Although Burgoa insists that the force of this argument must convince any logical person of the validity of the Court's ruling on political rights, several objections are in order. In the first place, even if these distinctions are accurate, it does not follow automatically that the violation of a political right fails to occasion a consequent, and actionable, infraction of the general guarantees of legality in articles 14 and 16. The only point actually demonstrated is that the functions and purposes, the manner of exercise, and the scope of application of these rights can be differentiated in various ways. The logical progression from premise to conclusion is unstated and obscure. Nor can considerations of logic be dispensed with in this case, since the decisions of the Court, as well

---

[71] *El juicio de amparo*, p. 377. It should be noted that Burgoa conceives of individual rights as proceeding from the state and deriving their force and significance from it rather than, in the natural law and social contract sense, preceding the state and conditioning its creation. From a practical juridical point of view, this position would be difficult to contest.

as the implications of Burgoa's argument, reject unequivocally the possibility that the Constitution confers sovereign and discretionary authority on the political branches of government in all of the situations envisaged in articles 35 and 36. It remains, then, to examine the distinctions cited in order to determine whether a conclusion justifying the inadmissibility of *amparo* can reasonably be inferred from them.

The exercise of political rights, Burgoa says, is contingent upon two conditions, citizenship and an election. As stated in dealing with the case material, however, the association of a right with a condition precedent implies in no way the nonjusticiability of violations of that right or, more properly, of the resultant violations of the guarantees of legality, when the condition has been fulfilled. To establish the validity of the contrary conclusion in the particular case at hand, it is necessary to demonstrate the existence within the Mexican legal system of a general principle to that effect. That no such principle exists has already been sufficiently shown. Indeed, it would be difficult to imagine such an unworkable rule being incorporated in any legal system.

The second ground of distinction, which seems to be based on the function of the rights in question and the intention of the state in granting them, is more suggestive than the first but equally questionable as to the conclusions drawn. As defined, there is an implication that political rights are no more than revocable privileges granted by the State as a matter of grace, whereas, individual guarantees, although equally derivative from the will and authority of the state, are, by virtue of an act of sovereign self-limitation, irrevocably vested in the individuals to whose benefit they redound. From this, one is intended to infer, presumably, that although individual guarantees constitute limitations on the power of the State, political rights, in a judicially enforceable sense, do not. Although there is nothing intrinsically impossible in such an arrangement, the Constitution affords no reliable evidence of such intent unless the provisions of article 103 are subjected to very literal interpretations. This, in turn, would be incompatible with the actual evolution of the *amparo* jurisdiction.

Attempts to find logical consistency in the Court's position on political rights are probably fruitless and are certainly irrelevant. As in previously noted instances, the explanation is political rather than juridical. It resides in the domination of the political system by a co-optively recruited elite, which acts through the instrumentality, among others, of the Partido Revolucionario Institucional and demands an effectively uncontested control of the electoral process. The defense of political rights under the aegis of *amparo* must await the appearance of genuinely competitive politics.

Although political rights are entirely excluded from the *amparo* jurisdiction, two classes of quasi-exceptions to this general rule remain to be examined. In the case of *Nájera Rojas Mariano,* the Court has stated:

> It is true that there is *jurisprudencia* to the effect that the violation of political rights does not give grounds for an *amparo* action, since individual guarantees are not involved; but it should be noted that the second chamber of the Supreme Court, restricting the scope of that thesis, has modified it so that when political rights are claimed, if the complainant can only be deprived of them by means of a proceeding previously established by the law governing such rights, the *amparo* suit may not be dismissed on grounds of inadmissibility. Instead, the merits of the question should be studied for the purpose of determining whether the act complained of is constitutional. [To do otherwise] would amount to leaving the enforcement of the law regulating these rights to the exclusive discretion of the authority [concerned]. If the case in question involves the dismissal of a judicial employee in a state in which the relevant law requires that the dismissal be justified in a proceeding, it is clear that the guarantees granted the complainant in article 14 of the Constitution have been violated if these requirements are not fulfilled.[72]

There is, evidently, no real inconsistency between this decision and the *jurisprudencia* that it refers to. In a strictly legal sense, the violation of political rights in such circumstances is irrelevant. The infraction complained of consists solely of failure to apply a governing statute, a procedure clearly in contravention of the guarantees of legality and within the scope of *amparo*. The admissibility of *amparo* in such a case assumes nothing more than the indisputable right of legislative bodies

---

[72] Suprema Corte, 45 *S. J.* 893 (1935). Also see *Balderas Manuel y coag.,* 46 *S. J.* 6027 (1935), and *Arrieta Federico,* 52 *S. J.* 103 (1937).

to impose enforceable statutory limitations in situations in which un-restricted discretion would otherwise be the rule.

Finally, *amparo* has been held admissible, despite the apparently political nature of the rights involved, in cases arising from the re-moval of the elected municipal officials referred to in article 115 of the Constitution.[73] In these cases, the Court has based its decision on the contention that the offices in question, although occasionally en-tailing functions of a political character, are essentially administrative. From this, one infers presumably that the holder of such an office possesses proprietary and personal rights in it and, as a result, may legitimately claim the protection of articles 14 and 16.[74] Since articles 35 and 36 refer to all elective and appointive offices, with specific reference to those at the municipal level, it is impossible to clearly reconcile this position with the general jurisprudential rule on political rights. The Court has been of two minds on the subject, holding in earlier cases that no distinction can be drawn between those rights derived from municipal office and those derived from any other public employment.[75] Because of the uncompromising rejection of all juris-diction in the field of political rights, proclaimed in the above-cited case of *Chávez Anselmo, Jr.*, it is doubtful that the Court would pres-ently entertain this exception.

Before terminating this examination of the limits of the *amparo* jurisdiction, very brief consideration must be given to the applicability of the action in cases arising from the conduct of foreign relations. Unfortunately, the pertinent case material is exceedingly sparse and only partially relevant, but other statements emanating from the Court indicate that the executive and legislative branches, when acting in this field, are held to possess a sovereign and unlimited discretion.[76]

---

[73] Municipal presidents, aldermen, and syndics (*síndicos*).

[74] Suprema Corte, *Méndez Jesús*, 85 S. J. 2894 (1945), *Cerón Guadalupe y coags.*, 55 S. J. 1039 (1938), and *Sarmiento José A. y coags.*, 47 S. J. 5351 (1936).

[75] *Tintos Florencio*, 46 S. J. 4618 (1935). Also see *Alcaraz Gustavo S.*, 46 S. J. 4618 (1935), 4050. It should be noted, of course, that personal rights in an office can be conferred by legislation. Where this has been done *amparo* would be admis-sible in conformity with the first of the exceptions noted above.

[76] See particularly the remarks of Lic. Salvador Urbina, formerly president of the Court, in *Informe, 1945* (Informe de la presidencia), p. 13.

It is to be expected, therefore, that *amparo* suits alleging injuries that result from implementing foreign policy would be rejected because they pose political questions. The Court has, however, reserved authority to determine the constitutionality of particular domestic applications of treaty provisions, stating as the general rule in such cases that "treaties, which have the character of constitutional law, cannot be considered as having greater authority than the Constitution itself."[77] On the evidence available, it is not possible to delimit the position of the Court in this field in greater detail.

[77] Suprema Corte, *Ramírez Ramón*, 117 S. J. 896 (1953). Also see *Valenzuela Pedro Mario*, 103 S. J. 613 (1953), and *Pelayo María del Rosario*, 118 S. J. 73 (1953). The reference to treaties as constitutional law means only that, by the terms of article 133, treaties form a part, with the Constitution and federal statutes, of the supreme law of the land.

## Chapter 6

# *Amparo* Against Laws

IT HAS BEEN SEEN that an act of authority detrimental to the constitutionally guaranteed rights of a private person, or the patrimonial rights of a public person, may be attacked in *amparo* on one or both of two grounds: the unconstitutionality of the act itself or the unconstitutionality of the law upon which it is based. From the provisions of section I, article 103 of the Constitution, which states that the federal courts shall decide all controversies arising "from laws or acts of the authorities that violate individual guarantees," the Supreme Court has evolved a further jurisdictional rule. The Court has held that in certain cases the unconstitutionality of a law may be attacked in the absence of any administrative act of enforcement or judicial act of application. It is this form of the suit that is technically referred to as "amparo against laws" (*amparo contra leyes*).[1] Although

[1] These statements suggest that there are certain similarities between *amparo* against laws and the jurisdictional possibilities afforded in the United States by actions that enjoin the enforcement of allegedly unconstitutional laws and, in an even more limited sense, actions that seek declaratory judgments on constitutional questions.

the doctrinal basis for this jurisdiction was established by the Court, formal statutory authority for its exercise was not granted until the passage of the new Amparo Law of 1935, and indisputably explicit constitutional authorization appeared only with the amendments of 1950.[2] Since neither the statutory nor constitutional authorizations indicate clearly the precise circumstances under which this jurisdiction is to operate, the following discussion is based primarily on *jurisprudencia* and the commentaries of publicists.

Neither article 103 nor article 107 establishes any procedural distinctions between the admissibility or trial of *amparo* suits contesting the enforcement or application of allegedly unconstitutional laws and that of suits questioning their constitutionality in the absence of such enforcement or application. It is presumed, therefore, that the general rules on admissibility set forth in these articles are equally applicable in either case. It is necessary, therefore, to demonstrate in *amparo* against laws that the law in question constitutes an authoritative act in the constitutional sense of that term, a fact usually self-evident, and that its mere existence violates an individual guarantee, or guarantees, and is materially prejudicial to the interests of an identifiable private person or to the patrimonial interests of a similarly identifiable public person.

The views presently prevailing in the Supreme Court about *amparo* against laws are summarized in the following citation from the case of *Villera de Orellana María de los Angeles y coags*:

Section I of article 103 of the Constitution and section I, article 1 of the Amparo Law established the admissibility of *amparo* against laws or against the acts of authorities that violate individual guarantees; [also] section I of article 22, section VI of article 73, and section I of article 114 of the Amparo Law confirm admissibility of the suit against laws that, by their mere issuance, violate guarantees. Furthermore, the jurisprudencia of the Supreme Court, interpreting section I, article 103, and section I, article 107 of the Constitution . . . has established . . . [:] despite the general rule requiring an act of execution as a preliminary to impugning

2 Section VII, article 107: "When *amparo* is sought . . . against laws. . . ." Because of the accepted technical meaning of the term "*amparo* against laws," this seems sufficiently explicit.

a law, the *amparo* suit is admissible when the precepts of the law acquire by their mere promulgation an immediately obligatory character; that is, when [the precepts of a law] contain a principle of execution that is carried into effect by the very existence of the law without the necessity of subsequent concrete applications, inasmuch as the persons or entities obligated, in obedience to the law, to act in a designated manner are perfectly identified by virtue of the pure legislative act and of those [acts] relating to its promulgation and publication. The law may be impugned when its precepts, independent of other acts of authority, impose an obligation to act or to refrain from acting on a well-defined portion of the members of the community. It is to be noted further that because of the recent amendments to the Amparo Law, the present section VI of article 73, establishes that the suit is inadmissible against laws that, by issuance alone, inflict no injury on the complainant but that require a subsequent act of authority in order to produce such injury. Consequently, in conformity with the principles established by jurisprudencia as well as the terms of the present text of the aforecited section VI, the admissibility of the suit against laws necessitates that these carry within themselves a principle of immediate execution, that is, that no intermediate or subsequent act of authority be necessary in order to inflict an injury on the complainant.[3]

The provisions of the Amparo Law cited by the Court state: section I, article 22—that *amparo* against laws may be initiated at any time within a period of thirty days following the promulgation of the law; section VI, article 73—that the suit is inadmissible when the law, by merely being issued, does not inflict an injury on the complainant; and section I, article 114—that original jurisdiction in *amparo* against laws shall be exercised by the federal district courts.

Since a personal injury must exist before there can be any jurisdiction, the Court has held further that the law must actually be in force on the date of the alleged injury. Thus, if any of the procedures required for this purpose, that is, proper passage, signature of the chief executive, counter-signature of the appropriate departmental secretary, promulgation, or publication have been omitted, the statute is not

---

[3] Suprema Corte de Justicia, 123 *S. J.* 783 (1955). Also see *Aldrete José y coags.*, 61 *S. J.* 466 (1939); *Menchaca Melchor y coags.*, 70 *S. J.* 4740 (1940); *Rojas Alberto P. Jr.*, 109 *S. J.* 1115 (1951), and idem, *Jurisprudencia de la Suprema Corte*, thesis 97, II, 215.

legally in force, and the suit is inadmissible. In these circumstances, any attempt at enforcement may be contested in a suit against the act of application, based on violation of articles 14 and 16 of the constitution.[4]

It is also essential that the contested regulation be a law in the constitutional sense of the term. Reasoning from the separation of powers principle incorporated in both the Mexican federal and state constitutions, the Court has held that the status of law attaches only to the statutory enactments of constituted legislative bodies and, presumably, to legitimate exercises by the executive of extraordinary legislative faculties. Administrative regulations, therefore, although they may be indistinguishable from formal legislation in substance and effect, are not laws in the technical sense and may only be attacked by the injured party following specific enforcement of the regulation on him.[5]

The admissibility of *amparo* against laws has therefore been established as a general jurisdictional principle both in *jurisprudencia* and by statute in those provisions of the Amparo Law cited by the Court. Both the Court and the Amparo Law are quite explicit, however, in stating that *amparo* cannot be considered admissible in every case in which the charge of unconstitutionality might be leveled against a statute but only in those instances in which the law inflicts an injury on the complainant without the necessity of any intermediate or subsequent acts of authority, that is, when the law in question is self-executing (*auto-aplicativo*).[6] In the general, theoretical sense implied by the concept of popular sovereignty that underlies the Mexican Constitution, it could be argued that unconstitutional acts injure every citizen, and that every constitutionally dubious statute should, as a result, be subject

---

[4] Asociación Nacional de Funcionarios Judiciales, *Ricardo López y coags.*, 110 *BIJ* 718 (October 1956).

[5] For rulings, see: Suprema Corte, *Fraccionadora Nacional, S. A., Informe, 1957* (Informe de la segunda sala), pp. 13–14, idem, *Vázquez Negri Rafael*, 119 *S. J.* 3278 (1953), Asociación, *Luz López de Arrendondo*, 130 *BIJ* 325 (June 1958), idem, *Compañía Gustavo Levy Sucs., S. A.*, and *Editorial Sol, S. A.*, 131 *BIJ* 404 (July 1958).

[6] In this connection, see Suprema Corte, *Garza Flores Hnos., Sucs.*, 28 *S. J.* 1208 (1930).

to attack in *amparo*. The mere existence of an unconstitutional statute does not in itself, however, establish, *erga omnes,* that personal link upon which the concept of legal injury depends. In the absence of such injury, a suit against the law, no matter how flagrantly unconstitutional it may be, cannot prosper. The practical application of this rule has been clarified in decisions holding that the district courts, in considering petitions for suits of this character, should not presume to decide a priori whether a contested law is self-executing but should admit the suit. In considering the allegations made by the parties and the evidence presented by them, the courts can decide this point during the course of trial. If any of the constitutional, statutory, or jurisprudential grounds of inadmissibility appear in the course of this examination, the case is to be summarily dismissed (*sobreseido*).[7] Given the fundamental character of the factor of personal injury in the admissibility of any *amparo* suit, further consideration must be given to the equivalence between personal obligation and personal injury that the Court has postulated, as well as to the precise nature of those obligations about which this equivalence can be said to exist.

As the *Orellana* and allied decisions demonstrate, the Court has attempted to discriminate between self-executing and non–self-executing laws. It has specified a number of conditions that must exist in the former while being entirely or partially absent in the latter. In summary, these are (1) the provisions of the statute must identify clearly and unmistakably, by establishing explicit classes, those persons to whom it is applicable; (2) the persons so identified must be subjected, *ipso jure*, to an obligation. The compulsory character of this obligation is completely independent of any prior, intermediate, or subsequent acts of authority except those involved in passing and promulgating the law itself; (3) compliance with this obligation would necessitate performing an act not previously required or abstaining from an act formerly permissible; and (4) such compliance would result in a prejudicial modification of rights vested in the person of the obligor. As this restatement implies, the Court's use of the term "immediately obligatory" in the *Orellana* and allied cases should not be

---

[7] Suprema Corte, *Robles Javier y coag.*, 70 S. J. 836 (1941).

interpreted to mean an absence of any temporal interval between the promulgation of the law and the moment in which the obligation becomes effective. The intention is rather to indicate that the creation by the law of a definite and binding obligation may not be in any way conditional on any attendant authoritative act external to the statute itself; in other words, the obligation must arise directly and exclusively from a correspondence between the situation defined in the statute and that actually occupied by a particular individual. By way of illustration, a statute automatically extending the contractual term for the payment of outstanding mortgage debts would clearly meet all four requirements. All holders of mortgages are individually and immediately affected and are subjected, *ipso jure*, to obligations undeniably prejudicial to their vested contractual rights. A law of this sort would oblige mortgagees to refrain from demanding payment on the due dates fixed by contract and would deny them access to normal legal remedies if they should still endeavor to secure it. In the absence of a right to attack the law directly via *amparo*, the mortgagee's only recourse would be an ordinary foreclosure action against the mortgagor, followed by a suit for *amparo* against the adverse judgment he would undoubtedly receive in such a case. This result follows, since the courts, in suits other than *amparo* and in those rare and essentially theoretical situations previously discussed in chapter three, possess no powers of judicial review and have no choice but to apply the statutes as written. Given a statute of this general type, therefore, the obligor is totally precluded from exercising his right except as the possible end product of a lengthy and expensive judicial process involving two separate suits. When, as in these situations, the enjoyment of a right is contingent on the cooperation of administrative and judicial authorities, the immediacy and material reality of the injury springing from the statutory prohibition of such cooperation is sufficiently clear.[8] In the absence of *amparo* against laws, the injury would be partly irreparable. However, to be considered self-executing, in conformity with the four criteria summarized above, it is not essential that a law materially deprive the persons obligated by it of the power to exercise previously

---

[8] Suprema Corte, *Sánchez Vda. de Terán Ricarda*, 29 S. J. 1536 (1930).

established rights. Thus, assuming the concurrence of the other criteria cited, a statute that directed corporations to distribute a percentage of profits to their employees would clearly be considered self-executing, although the object of the affected right, that is, the profits, would remain within the physical control of the obligor and subject to the same discretionary dispositions that would exist if the law had never been enacted. With a law of this character, therefore, the occurrence of an injury, in the material sense, is contingent on compliance with the obligation, whether this be voluntary or exacted by judicial or administrative action.[9] This being the case, it might be argued that suits against the law shall fall under the jurisprudential prohibition of suits directed against future acts. As noted in chapter IV, this ground of inadmissibility does not apply when the injurious act is both imminent and certain, as would be the case here, whether as the result of suits brought by employees benefited under the statute or as the result of administrative enforcement.[10]

It is clearly impossible, empirically, to establish a general rule, comparable to the laws of physics, whereby one could determine infallibly the exact moment in time at which a legal injury might be said to have occurred. Determining this necessarily depends on the precepts of a particular system of positive law, as fixed by those agencies competent to establish the content of that law. In *amparo* against laws, this has

---

[9] Voluntary compliance with an obligation of this general character would deprive the obligor of the right to initiate an *amparo* suit. Such, at least, is the necessary consequence of sections XI and XII, article 73, of the Amparo Law, which establishes that *amparo* is inadmissible when there has been express or tacit consent to the act complained of. Furthermore, if the suit were not available against the law, the obligor would risk not only the injury entailed in the terms of the obligation itself but also the application of whatever penalties might be prescribed for noncompliance.

[10] That the Supreme Court does consider laws of this type to be self-executing is evidenced by such decisions as *Cía. Industrial de Atlixco, S.A.*, 69 S. J. 1416 (1941), wherein a statute that would impose a special tax on bachelors is cited as a hypothetical example; and *Jurisprudencia de la Suprema Corte*, thesis 247, II, 482, which states: "Solely because a law abrogates concessions granted by the Congress or the executive of a State, the holders of such concessions are . . . injured. Consequently, it can be said that the law begins to exert its effects from the date of its promulgation."

been determined in general terms in the Amparo Law itself and elaborated in detail by the Supreme Court. As the situations examined indicate, the Court has concluded that an injury (*perjuicio*) occurs in any case in which the law imposes an immediate, direct, and personal obligation that abrogates or modifies rights legally vested in the person of the complainant. Within these limitations, therefore, the creation of the obligation and the occurrence of the injury must be considered simultaneous and equivalent acts. Nonetheless, in determining whether a given statute is self-executing, it is necessary not only to know if a personal obligation exists but also to look at the character of the objects to which that obligation refers. A law prohibiting burglary, for example, imposes an immediate obligation on everyone within the jurisdiction but can hardly be considered self-executing for that reason unless there has been a previous recognition in positive law of an individual right to commit that act. There can be no equivalence between obligation and injury if there is no legally recognized right vested in the person of the obligor.

Although the admissibility of *amparo* against laws has been conclusively established both by statute and in *jurisprudencia*, a question remains about whether this recourse is available only to those persons who are in the situation governed by a self-executing law at the time it is promulgated or whether it is equally available to all who come to occupy such a situation during the life of the law. Although logic and equity might require the latter of these alternatives, practice and the terms of article 22, section I, of the Amparo Law have opted for the former. The statutory provisions in question provide that the term within which the *amparo* complaint must be filed shall be fifteen days from the day following that in which the complainant shall have been properly notified of the injurious act, except in "those cases in which, by its mere issuance, a law may be subject to protest in *amparo*, since then the term for filing the complaint shall be thirty days counted from the time the law itself shall have entered into force."

It should be noted that, in conformity with the amendments to the Amparo Law enacted in 1950, it is no longer absolutely vital that a complainant determine for himself whether a law is self-executing. Article 73, section XII, of the Amparo Law now provides that persons who fail to initiate suit against a law, and who have the right to do so, should not be considered as having given tacit consent to the validity and applicability of the law but may subsequently sue against the first act of application. Prior to the amendments, a failure to institute suit against a self-executing law within the statutory period constituted tacit consent and, consequently, a bar to any future suit against either the law or its application.

Further problems are posed by the possibility that a law may contain some provisions that are self-executing and others that are not. May *amparo* be sought against such a law and, if so, is the complainant relieved of all liability under it, or only of liability under those provisions that are self-executing? Pertinent decisions are scarce and only partly helpful in resolving these questions. Concerning the first, the Court has stated that "although the Supeme Court has resolved that the *amparo* suit is inadmissible when the mere issuance and promulgation of a law is protested, except in those cases in which the precepts of the law acquire an immediately obligatory character by promulgation alone, it is also true that in establishing that theory no distinction was made between those cases in which only some rather than all of the precepts of the law contain a principle of execution, nor has the Court considered it reasonable to make a distinction of that nature."[11]

The conclusion that *amparo* is admissible against a law that is only partially self-executing emerges clearly from this ruling. Neither *jurisprudencia* nor the *Semanario Judicial* provides any direct and conclusive guide in answering the second of these questions. General principles of judicial interpretation are, however, sufficient to settle the point. If the self-executing and non–self-executing provisions of a law are so intimately related that neither is capable of standing alone as an independently enforceable rule of behavior, a judgment declaring the unconstitutionality of the former results necessarily in annuling the effects of the latter as well. On the other hand, if the two are capable of an autonomous existence, the judgment in *amparo* against laws should be limited to the self-executing provisions, leaving consideration of the remainder of the statute for a later suit against the first act

[11] Suprema Corte, *Sierra Torres José*, 29 S. J. 737 (1930).

of application. In the first instance, the courts are confronted with a logically indivisible whole, in the second, with the equivalent of two distinct statutes. In the latter case, the provisions of article 73, section VI, of the Amparo Law prohibiting suits against laws that do not automatically injure the complainant should apply to exclude consideration of the non–self-executing sections of the law.

Precisely the same reasoning is applicable to the situation that would arise if a complainant were to comply voluntarily with certain provisions of a law while protesting the constitutionality of others. Should the provisions complied with be separable from those protested against, there should be no objection to a suit directed against the latter, assuming that they are self-executing. However, since compliance constitutes consent, if the law in question were indivisible, the grounds of inadmissibility set forth in sections XI and XII of article 73 of the Amparo Law would apply.[12]

As noted in chapter three, one of the most fundamental procedural rules governing the use of *amparo* and testifying to its charter as an extraordinary remedy is the inadmissibility of the suit as long as the complainant has access to other administrative or judicial remedies, whereby the act allegedly violative of guarantees may be modified, revoked, or annulled. Clearly, this rule cannot be applied to *amparo* against laws. To do so, the complainant would be compelled to avail himself of the procedural remedies afforded by the very statute whose constitutionality he proposes to attack, an act constituting consent and resulting in the inadmissibility of the *amparo* suit. Since it is hardly possible that the procedural provisions of a law, assuming that these are not themselves the object of protest, could exist independently of its substantive content, this conclusion is not incompatible with that reached in the case considered above. For these reasons, the Court has ruled that "there is no obligation to exhaust the ordinary remedies established in a law before having recourse to *amparo* when the unconstitutionality of the law is the principal ground of the suit."[13]

As discussed in chapter two, the Supreme Court has been severely

---

[12] This conclusion is at least partially supported by *Jurisprudencia de la Suprema Corte*, thesis 95, II, 213.

[13] *Jurisprudencia de la Suprema Corte*, thesis 96, II, 214. This rule also applies

handicapped in its handling of all *amparo* suits contesting the constitutionality of laws since the adoption of the 1958 amendments to the Amparo and Judiciary laws. In *amparo* against laws, the district courts retain original jurisdiction, but the requirement that all appeals from their decisions in such cases be heard by the Supreme Court sitting *en banc* has resulted in interminable delay in securing final judgments. It does not seem likely that the 1968 amendments, which return such appeals to the appropriate chamber whenever the full Court has already established the constitutionality of the law in *jurisprudencia*, will do much to remedy this situation. Such delay necessarily encourages malicious litigation, results in effective denials of justice, and must frequently prove similarly damaging to the interests of law enforcement.

---

to *amparo* against an act of application when the principal ground of protest is the unconstitutionality of the law on which the act is based.

*Chapter 7*

# *Amparo* as Cassation

$A$LTHOUGH RELEVANT only in a formal sense to the practice of judicial review, a brief examination of the cassation function of *amparo* is indispensable for an understanding of the practical significance and use of the suit. Because of the individual guarantees contained in article 14 of the Constitution, the Mexican federal courts, primarily the Supreme Court and the collegial circuit tribunals, have been compelled to accept a universal appeals jurisdiction operating through the medium of *amparo* and technically applicable to every judicial and quasi-judicial decision handed down by any court or administrative tribunal in the land. Cases of this sort comprise more than half of the *amparo* suits annually filed with the Supreme Court and provide virtually all the business transacted by the collegial circuit tribunals.[1] By cassation is meant the power to review and annul judicial or quasi-judicial decisions on the basis of error in selecting, applying,

[1] This estimate is only approximate because the statistics published by the federal judiciary do not differentiate sufficiently to allow complete accuracy. The above is, if anything, an understatement of the burden imposed by cases of this type.

or interpreting secondary legislation, that is, all laws except articles of the Constitution itself. Since the issues under review in these cases are strictly legal ones, considerations of fact, merit, and equity are rigorously excluded, as is any question about the substantive constitutionality of the laws applied.

## Constitutional Basis—Article 14

The constitutional foundation for the cassation function of *amparo* is to be found in the following provisions of article 14:

No law shall be given retroactive effect to the detriment of any person.

No person shall be deprived of life, liberty, property, possessions, or rights without a trial by a duly created court in which the essential formalities of procedure are observed and in accordance with laws issued prior to the act.

In criminal cases no penalty shall be imposed by mere analogy or constructively. The penalty must be decreed in a law in every respect applicable to the crime in question.

In civil suits the final judgment shall be according to the letter of the juridical interpretation of the law; in the absence of the latter, it shall be based on the general principles of law.

For present purposes, only those individual rights, established in article 14, that are relevant to the definition of the cassation jurisdiction need be further examined. These can be listed as follows: (1) the prohibition of ex post facto laws and of the retroactive application of laws otherwise valid; (2) the guarantee of procedural due process; (3) the prohibition, in criminal trials, of offenses and penalties created by analogy; (4) the prohibition, in criminal trials, of offenses and penalties created by judicial construction; and (5) the prohibition, in civil suits, of judgments not founded on the letter of the law, on its juridical interpretation, or in the absence of a relevant statute, on general principles of jurisprudence.

Concerning the first of these, little need be said. The prohibition extends clearly both to the retroactive application by the courts of law that are themselves valid for regulating actions that occur after the laws become effective and to the judicial application of laws that are intended by the enacting authorities to produce retroactive effects. Contrary to the situation prevailing in the United States, these prohibitions apply to both criminal and civil law.[2]

It is also unnecessary to examine in detail the guarantee of procedural due process. In the most general sense, this provision guarantees to defendants in criminal trials and to all parties in civil actions a course of legal proceedings in conformity with those rules and principles established in the Mexican legal system for enforcing and protecting private rights. As a consequence, it follows that if such proceedings are to be valid, a suit must be tried and the judgment or sentence rendered by a court possessing proper jurisdiction of the subject matter at issue. The parties must be properly notified, served, represented, and heard in their own interest; the proceedings and decisions of the court must be fair, unbiased, and unaffected by coercion, intimidation, or fraud. It should also be noted that this right demonstrates conclusively that the cassation jurisdiction of the federal courts extends not only to correcting substantive error in the final judgment or sentence but also to reviewing and correcting material flaws in procedure.[3]

In criminal actions, the third paragraph of article 14 establishes, in the strictest possible terms, the traditional rule of *nullum crimen, nulla poena sine lege* ("there is no crime, there may be no punishment in the absence of a law"). That the terms of this paragraph, despite the absence of explicit reference to that effect, do in fact extend to defining crimes as well as to applying penalties seems to be a necessary inference from the logical relation of cause and effect existing between the concepts of delict and sanction. Consequently, for the courts to consider a given act a crime and, therefore, a sufficient reason for imposing a punitive sanction, a law must exist that characterizes the act and that establishes the penalty to be inflicted when it is performed. Correlatively, a court cannot legitimately impose a punishment in the absence of a law that prescribes explicitly the sanction corresponding to the delict defined therein.

---

[2] Suprema Corte de Justicia, *Jurisprudencia de la Suprema Corte*, thesis 925, V, 1724. Also see idem, *La Cía. del Puente de Nuevo Laredo, S. A.*, 72 S. J. 3496 (1942).

[3] For an illustrative list of procedural errors that may give rise to an *amparo* suit, see articles 159 and 160 of the Amparo Law.

In order to better define and defend these rights, paragraph 3 of article 14 strictly prohibits penalties to be imposed that are based on analogy or judicial construction. By analogy is meant the application of a law to a state of affairs not explicitly governed by it, but which nonetheless presents some essential similarity or affinity with the situation to which the law does pertain. In the various fields of civil law, for example, it is customary judicial procedure, when a situation regulated by no existing law arises, to have recourse to laws dealing with different subject matter but governed by the same general principle. Thus, in the absence of a law specifically defining the nature and extent of private rights in such intangibles as stocks and bonds, the law of real property might be applied. Similarly, in the field of criminal law, a court confronted with an act considered *malum in se*, but not identified as a crime by any existing statute, might feel impelled to apply another law or laws governing acts of the same general nature and type. Although it may be well founded morally, such a procedure would be a flagrant violation of article 14 and, if proven, a writ of *amparo* would properly issue against the sentence imposed.

More difficulty is attached to clarifying the prohibition of "constructive" crimes and penalties. Unfortunately, the term "construction," with the connotations it bears in Anglo-American law, does not convey adequately the meaning of the original Spanish expression *mayoría de razón*, literally, superiority, or weight, of reason. Every law, of course, has its *ratio legis*, that is, some reason or occasion for its enactment. This reason or occasion, in Aristotelian terms, constitutes its "final cause" or purpose. To illustrate, a law authorizing the organization of labor unions and collective bargaining could have the promotion of peaceful and equitable relations between capital and labor as its ultimate purpose. Should an actual situation arise that threatens such peaceful relations, although in a way entirely unrelated to the rights of organization and collective bargaining, a court, in the absence of more pertinent legislation, might nonetheless endeavor to apply this law on the ground that it is the legislative intent rather than the letter of its decree which should be served. Such elastic application of existing laws to meet situations differing fundamentally in character from those for which the law was envisaged, but similar in ultimate effect, is what is meant by *mayoría de razón*. In this hypothetical instance, the only similarity between the case at hand and the state of affairs abstractly described and regulated by law is to be found in the general character of the problem,—here, industrial strife—that the legislative authority wished to solve, rather than in specific elements of the two situations themselves. In applying laws by analogy, on the other hand, some substantial similarity must exist between the elements of the situation abstractly contemplated by the law and the facts of the concrete case; for example, there is a similarity of circumstances entailed in the theft of an intrinsically valuable article and the theft of money. Whenever a court proceeds on the basis of analogy or construction, its decisions necessarily contain an element of legislative discretion. Fundamentally, it is this quasi-legislative function, no matter how attenuated, that paragraph 3 of article 14 seeks to proscribe in criminal litigation.[4]

Paragraph 4, which prescribes the conditions of legal procedure in civil suits, extends actually to a much broader area of adjudicative activity than its terms would suggest. In practice, the regulations set forth in this paragraph govern not only suits arising under the terms of the federal and state civil codes but also all other fields of law, except criminal, wherein private rights may be created, modified, or extinguished. Furthermore, not only regularly established courts of law are bound by these rules, but also any administrative tribunal or agency that either regularly or occasionally performs a judicial function must comply with them.[5] Thus, the general guarantee of legality established in paragraph 2, conditioned by paragraph 4, applies to every proceeding, except the criminal, which is essentially judicial in character; that is, it applies to all those proceedings wherein private rights are authori-

[4] These distinctions are based primarily on the discussion in Ignacio Burgoa, *Las garantías individuales*, pp. 450–453.

[5] The provisions of paragraph 4 of article 14 extend to fields of law outside those covered in the civil codes and to tribunals other than those incorporated within the regular judiciaries of the federation and of the states. This is attested by such a vast multitude of cases that extensive individual citation would be tedious. For pertinent examples, however, see Suprema Corte, *Judisprudencia de la Suprema Corte*, thesis 623, IV, 113; Ibid., V, thesis 986, p. 1799; thesis 991, p. 1803; and thesis 1112, p. 1992. Also see Suprema Corte, *Gutiérrez López Gabino*, 81 S. J. 2867 (1944), and *Secretaría de Educación Pública*, 88 S. J. 2543 (1946).

tatively adjudicated and from which, as a result, the deprivations contemplated by the article emerge.

Whenever possible, paragraph 4 directs that the law should be applied literally, that is, in strict conformity with the legally established definitions of its terms and the customary rules of grammatical construction. Obviously, given the limitations of language, situations will arise frequently in which this procedure would produce absurd, contradictory, or ambiguous consequences. In such cases, adjudicative bodies may have recourse to the juridical interpretation of the law. This requires that the legally established hierarchy of interpretive techniques be followed and correctly applied. Thus, if the conclusion reached is logically incompatible with the technique employed, or if the latter is not selected from the established order of precedence, the final judgment will not have been reached in conformity with the judicial interpretation of the law, and the issuance of a writ of *amparo* will be in order. By necessary inference, these rules serve also to protect the parties to litigation from judgments not founded on laws properly applicable to the case at hand, or motivated by other considerations than legal ones.[6] Finally, situations arise occasionally which the positive law makes no sufficient provision for resolving. To avoid decreeing dismissals, whenever such lacunae appear, paragraph 4 authorizes decisions based on the general principles of law, but does not indicate, however, how these decisions are to be reached. Although the source and content of such general principles of law has long been the subject of controversy among philosophers of the law, it is sufficient for present purposes to indicate that the procedure favored in practice derives these rules by inductive reasoning from the institutions and postulates of the positive law. The positive law in question need not be exclusively Mexican. Practice indicates, at least, that it is permissible to derive such principles from foreign legal systems when these are substantially similar to the Mexican system in origin and general character.[7]

[6] Suprema Corte, *Aguilar Félix*, 22 *S. J.* 42 (1928).

[7] For an example of borrowing of foreign precedents, see some of the arguments employed by the Supreme Court in *Cía. Mexicana de Petróleo "El Aguila," S. A., y coags.*, 62 *S. J.* 3021 ff (1939).

## Jurisdiction

Under the Constitution of 1857, all *amparo* suits were initiated in the district courts. The 1917 Constitution, however, introduced the present jurisdictional distinction between "direct" and "indirect" *amparo*. The former consisted of suits tried in original jurisdiction and single instance before the Supreme Court itself, the latter were suits initiated in the district courts and subject to appeal. Under the terms of the original section VIII of article 107 of the Constitution, the Supreme Court was required to exercise this original jurisdiction when the act complained of consisted of a final judgment in either a civil or criminal case. In order to reduce somewhat the burden imposed on the Supreme Court, the constitutional and statutory amendments of 1950 divided the direct *amparo* jurisdiction between the Supreme Court and the concurrently created collegial circuit tribunals. At the same time, final awards granted by the Conciliation and Arbitration commissions in labor cases were added to final civil and criminal judgments as acts subject to attack via direct *amparo*. Since these judgments are normally contested on the ground that they violate article 14, the cassation function is performed primarily, although not exclusively, in direct *amparo*.

Under the amendments of 1950 and in conformity with article 107, section V, of the Constitution and article 158 of the Amparo Law, the Supreme Court was to exercise original jurisdiction in all suits directed against final civil and criminal judgments and awards of the Conciliation and Arbitration commissions when error in the judgment itself was claimed. Article 158 bis, section II, provided a single exception to this rule for those civil and criminal cases in which the final judgment was based on the application of a law that made no provision for appeal. In accordance with section VI, article 107 of the Constitution, article 158 bis of the Amparo Law conferred original jurisdiction on the collegial circuit tribunals in the exceptional cases noted, whether the complaint was directed at errors of procedure or at substantive flaws in the judgment, and in all others in which the final judgment or award was contested on grounds of procedural error occurring during the course of trial. Against procedural error, however, *amparo* was, and remains, admissible only if the complainant has been wholly or partially deprived of those defenses that should legally be available to him, and provided that this deprivation has affected the conclusions set forth in the judgment.[8] The direct *amparo* jurisdiction of both the Supreme Court and the collegial circuit tribunals was further defined by paragraph 2, section II, of article 158 bis. This article reiterated the provisions of paragraph 4, article 14, of the Constitution, while adding that *amparo* is also admissible against civil judgments and arbitral awards incorporating persons, pleas, objections, or things not properly a part of the original proceedings or, when expressly omitted or denied, excluding those that should have been included.

Should the complainant have wished to claim both procedural violations and error in the judgment itself, both of these allegations had to be included in the same complaint and filed with the appropriate collegial circuit tribunal, which then proceeded to consider the former only. If the tribunal found against the complainant, the suit was transferred to the Supreme Court for consideration of the alleged errors in the judgment.[9]

The complications and potentialities for delay inherent in this bifurcated jurisdiction have been previously noted. Painful experience dictated that a substantial proportion of the modifications introduced in the constitutional and statutory amendments of 1968 should be directed to clarifying and simplifying the jurisdictions of the Supreme Court and the collegial circuit tribunals. As provided in the present section V, article 107, of the Constitution, *amparo* against definitive judgments or awards, whether the alleged violation of rights occurs during the course of the trial or is contained in the judgment or award itself, shall be tried directly and in single instance before the Supreme Court in the following cases: (1) in criminal jurisdiction, when the suit is directed against definitive resolutions handed down by federal tribunals, including military courts, and against comparable decisions of state courts

---

[8] Although the Amparo Law does not attempt to give an exhaustive enumeration of those procedural errors, articles 159 and 160 provide lengthy lists of illustrative examples.

[9] Amparo Law, article 44, paragraph 2 (prior to the 1968 amendments).

when the sentence complained of imposes the death penalty or imprisonment in excess of five years. (2) in administrative jurisdiction, suits directed against definitive judgments of federal tribunals, whether judicial or administrative, when the violations complained of are not susceptible to reparation by any ordinary legal procedure.[10] (3) in civil jurisdiction, when the suit is directed against definitive judgments decreed by federal tribunals, or, in the case of mercantile suits, definitive judgments handed down by both federal and state courts; and in other cases arising from civil litigation in state courts as may be provided for by law. The Supreme Court is, furthermore, the only court authorized to hear *amparo* suits directed against definitive judgments, whatever their origin, that concern marital status or that affect the stability of the family. It has also been explicitly provided that, in civil judgments arising from litigation in which the Federation is involved, *amparo* may be sought by any of the parties including the Federation when acting in defense of its patrimonial interests. (4) in labor jurisdiction, when the suit is directed against awards decreed in collective conflicts by the Central Committees of Conciliation and Arbitration of the various states; against any award handed down by federal conciliation and arbitration authorities; and against awards granted by the Federal Conciliation and Arbitration Tribunal for Workers in the Service of the State.

Section VI, article 107, provides in turn that in all *amparo* suits directed against definitive judgments or awards and not included among the cases listed in section V jurisdiction is to be vested in the collegial circuit tribunal within whose area the responsible authority resides. This is the case whether the alleged violation of guarantees has occurred during the course of the trial or is contained in the judgment itself.

Whatever the nature of the violations protested, direct *amparo* may not be initiated until a final judgment, or award, has been rendered or a sentence imposed.[11] Article 46 of the Amparo Law defines final

10 The 1968 amendments provide for the first time explicit constitutional authorization for creating administrative courts.

11 Amparo Law, article 161. Also see Suprema Corte, *Jurisprudencia de la Suprema Corte*, thesis 456, III, 880.

judgments as those which resolve the principal point or points at issue in a suit and against which the law affords no ordinary recourse by which they may be modified or reversed. This would apply to suits for which the law provided trial in single instance only, and to those in which recourses such as appeal have been exhausted.[12] The second paragraph of article 46 supplements this definition by considering as final those civil judgments handed down in first instance in which the parties themselves have expressly surrendered their right of appeal or other recourse, providing that this renunciation is legally permissible. From this definition, it follows that judicial decisions that do not settle the principal points at issue, even though the suit is terminated, cannot be considered final. In these cases, the complainant's proper recourse is to the district courts.[13]

Although the statutory and jurisprudential definitions of the term "final judgment" imply jurisdiction of the Supreme Court, or the collegial circuit tribunals in cases contesting the legality of definitive decisions rendered by administrative agencies acting in a quasi-judicial capacity, the Amparo Law, even as recently amended, has determined otherwise. Original jurisdiction in *amparo* actions directed against administrative decisions continues to rest in the district courts with the exception of arbitral awards in labor cases and the decisions of administrative courts.[14] Sections III, IV, and V, of article 114 of the Amparo Law also assign original jurisdiction to the district courts in *amparo* actions contesting the following: (1) acts of judicial, administrative, or labor tribunals executed out of court or after the termination of a suit; (2) acts taking place during the course of trial, which, if executed, would be irreparable; and (3) acts effected during the course of trial or out of court, which adversely affect persons not parties to the suit, if the law does not establish an appeal or other means of defense available to such third parties, whereby the judgment or other detrimental action affecting them may be modified or reversed.[15] Con-

---

[12] For the definition of final judgments, see also *Jurisprudencia de la Suprema Corte*, thesis 995, V, 1807.

[13] *Jurisprudencia de la Suprema Corte*, thesis 1003, V, 1824.

[14] Amparo Law, article 114, section II.

[15] Not included in this grant of jurisdiction is the so-called *"juicio de tercería,"*

sistent with these considerations, the Supreme Court has affirmed that the direct *amparo* suit against a final judgment is inadmissible when the judgment is contested on the ground that the complainant was deprived of the right to a hearing through absence of proper legal notification or summons and, consequently, did not act as a party to the original action although he had a right to do so. Again, the complainant's proper recourse is to the district courts.[16] Where violations of article 14 are alleged, whether jurisdiction falls to the Supreme Court, the collegial circuit tribunals, or the district courts, the questions presented for consideration relate usually to the selection, interpretation, and application of secondary legislation and, as a result, their resolution would constitute an exercise of the cassation function as previously defined.

## The Stricti Juris Rule

The trial of all types of *amparo* suits, with the exception of the criminal, is governed in some degree by the rule of *stricti juris*. Since the application of this principle is particularly rigid in civil *amparo*, the example *par excellence* of the cassation function, its nature and consequences deserve examination in some detail. As used in *amparo*, the rule of *stricti juris* (*estricto derecho*) requires the courts to confine their attention to and base their decisions exclusively on those conclusions of law (*conceptos de violación*) wherein the plaintiff, in his formal written complaint, endeavors to demonstrate that his constitutional rights have been violated by the contested act. Where the rule applies, the courts are strictly forbidden to add anything to or correct any defect in the complaint.

The general authorization for applying this rule in *amparo* is derived by implication from paragraphs 2, 3, and 4, section II, of article 107 of the Constitution. More explicitly, article 79, paragraph 2, of the Amparo Law provides for *stricti juris* in civil *amparo* in the fol-

---

that is, a suit in which the law relevant to the subject matter in litigation makes provision for the entry of affected third parties as actual participants, in their own right and interest. Also see Suprema Corte, *Fuentes Leopoldo de Suc. de y coag.*, 13 *S. J.* 999 (1923).

16 Suprema Corte, *Jurisprudencia de la Suprema Corte*, thesis 427, III, 815.

lowing terms: "The *amparo* suit for inexact application of the law against acts of judicial authorities of the civil order is of strict law and, consequently, the judgment decreed in it . . . must be directed to the terms of the complaint without correcting it or adding anything to it." This applies not only to correcting substantive defects, but even to correcting errors in citing the constitutional guarantees violated. Hypothetically, even though a complainant should demonstrate beyond doubt that his rights under article 14 have been violated, his suit would be dismissed if he claimed mistakenly a violation of article 16 instead. Paragraph 1 of article 79, however, permits this sort of error to be corrected in all other types of *amparo* suits. The courts are permitted by article 178 of the Amparo Law to instruct the complainant to supply any omitted formal elements whose inclusion in the complaint is required by article 166. If he does not do so within a period not to exceed five days, the suit must be dismissed. In performing this function, however, the courts do not advise the complainant about the nature of the arguments he should employ, but indicate merely the missing item.

Thus, if the *amparo* suit is to prosper, the complaint, in addition to meeting all technical requirements, must argue conclusions of law that are not only accurate and valid in themselves but also sufficient to refute the legal grounds on which the contested judgment or procedural ruling is based. In illustration of these points, the Supreme Court has held that "if the complainant does not properly specify conclusions of law, or if he fails to identify those legal dispositions that were not applied or were improperly applied by the responsible authorities . . . the suit must be considered inadmissible because it lacks sufficient grounds to permit a decision about whether the contested judgment actually violates individual guarantees."[17] The Court has ruled further, that in *amparo* against a judgment of this sort "it is not sufficient to

---

[17] *Rodríguez de Castellanos Josefina*, 73 S. J. 3771 (1942). Also see *Orozco Juan José* 44 S. J. 3408 (1935). The Court has decided, however, that the rule of *stricti juris* is not to be carried so far as to require the dismissal of suits in which the complainant has merely neglected to specify by number the statutory provisions violated. It is enough if they are unmistakably identified in some other manner. *Jurisprudencia de la Suprema Corte*, thesis 94, II, 210.

prove that one or various conclusions of law on which the judgment is based are illegal. It is necessary to demonstrate that all the foundations on which it rests violate the law. If one of them is legitimate, it will be sufficient to confirm the judgment."[18] It is not even necessary that the conclusions of law remaining in support of the judgment be legally valid. If the plaintiff fails to attack and refute them in his written complaint, the courts cannot enter ex officio into an examination of their possible unconstitutionality.[19] Considering the extraordinary complexity of the procedural rules governing civil *amparo*, if a complainant is to emerge victorious from such a suit he must be either rarely fortunate or blessed with the services of one of the few attorneys skilled in this specialized field.

The limitations examined above in civil *amparo* apply equally to all varieties of administrative *amparos* except for those concerned with protecting communal agrarian rights. More explicitly, the only exceptions to the rule of *stricti juris* are the following provisions of paragraphs 2, 3, and 4, section II, of article 107 of the Constitution:

A defect in the complaint may be corrected when the act complained of is based on laws declared unconstitutional by the *jurisprudencia* of the Supreme Court.[20]

A defect in the complaint may also be corrected in criminal matters and in behalf of workers in labor disputes, when it is found that there has been a manifest violation of the law against the injured party, who is left without defense, and in criminal matters, likewise, when the conviction has been based on a law not precisely applicable to the case.

In *amparo* suits in which the acts protested deprive or may deprive *ejidos* or *ejidatarios*, or other centers of rural population that de facto or de jure live communally, or members of such communities, of the property, or possession and enjoyment of their lands, waters, pastures, and woodlands, defective complaints shall be corrected in conformity with the dispositions of the law regulating articles 103 and 107 of this Constitution.

As indicated in paragraph 2, if the complainant in a labor *amparo*

---

[18] *Jurisprudencia de la Suprema Corte*, thesis 100, II, 226.

[19] *Orozco Juan José*, 44 S. J. 3408 (1935).

[20] Added by amendment in 1950–1951. For an illustration of this exception in the highly formalistic field of civil *amparo*, see Suprema Corte, *Angeles Isidro*, 116 S. J. 447 (1953).

is the employer, the rule of *stricti juris* is fully applicable.[21] In labor and criminal cases, the worker or the accused, as the case may be, is usually considered to be the weaker party in financial standing, educational attainment, familiarity with legal process, and access to competent legal advice. This discrepancy between reality and the standard assumption of procedural equality between the parties to litigation serves to justify these special exceptions to the complicated formalities entailed in trial *stricti juris*.[22] An additional justification for correcting defective complaints in criminal *amparos* derives from the principle of *nullum crimen, nulla poena sine lege*, established in article 14 of the Constitution. This, of course, has no relevance to the field of labor law. Presumably similar considerations of practical equity motivated the addition, in 1963, of paragraph 4, section II, of article 107.

It should be noted, finally, that where the rule of *stricti juris* governs the trial in first instance, it is also applicable on appeal. That is, the Supreme Court or appropriate collegial circuit tribunal is required to confine its attention, in conformity with the principles examined above, to the injuries the complainant alleges to have been inflicted in the judgment handed down by the district court.[23] Conversely, where correction of defective complaints is permitted on first instance, it is likewise permitted on appeal.

Unquestionably, applying *stricti juris* can result in serious injustices, since technical oversights on the part of the complainant, or his attorney, may require the courts to ignore probable, or even flagrant, illegalities when these are improperly contested or omitted from the complaint. The maxim *jura novit curia* is thus rescinded in these cases, leaving the judge in the position of a referee empowered to do nothing more than evaluate the skill of the contending attorneys. Without engaging in the perennial controversy about whether the defense of

---

[21] For a detailed summation of the rules applicable to correcting defective complaints in labor *amparos*, see Suprema Corte, *Zúñiga Justino*, 116 S. J. 139 (1953).

[22] Cámara de Diputados, *Diario de los debates de la Cámara de Diputados*, XLI Legislatura, I, no. 18, p. 11. These arguments are taken from the *exposición de motivos* presented by President Alemán in support of the constitutional amendments of 1950–1951.

[23] Suprema Corte, *Jurisprudencia de la Suprema Corte*, theses 62, 63, 64, 65, and 66, II, 133–136, 138–139, and theses 927 and 1025, V, 1728, 1851.

legality is a proper function of *amparo*, applying *stricti juris* in such a manner is incompatible not only with the stress on the individual litigant and the tutelary purpose for which the *amparo* action was devised but also with the ends customarily pursued in cassation. Unlike *amparo*, cassation is not basically concerned with the interests of individual litigants, but is intended to serve the law itself by providing the means whereby uniformity of interpretation and application can be maintained. Consistent with this, proceedings in cassation are marked by a rigorous formalism. To apply equitable principles that might come to light by concentrating on the extralegal merits of the case, to introduce new factual allegations, or to weigh any matter not present on the face of the record or in the relevant law, are necessarily and properly excluded. As construed in *amparo*, the *stricti juris* rule results in excluding the relevant and the irrelevant alike. By restricting the courts to evaluating the sufficiency and validity of the conclusions of law advanced in the pleadings and to those conclusions alone, they are compelled to countenance multiple and inconsistent interpretations. Where the courts are not permitted to base their conclusions on any legal precept, which they, in their own discretion, consider relevant to resolving the situation established in the record, they cannot possibly achieve the legal uniformity and consistency to which cassation is dedicated. In logic, therefore, *stricti juris* in *amparo* can neither be explained nor justified as an adaptation of the principles of cassation.[24]

Because of the discrepancy between the effects of *stricti juris* and the traditional purposes of *amparo*, it is hardly surprising that the rule has been the target of continuous and bitter criticism.[25] Nonetheless,

[24] Nonetheless, this conclusion is expressed or at least implied in a number of the general commentaries on *amparo*. For the statutory origin and development of the *stricti juris* rule in *amparo*, see articles 780 and 824 of the *Código de procedimientos federales de 1897*, and article 767 of the *Código de procedimientos civiles de 1909*. Also see Felipe Tena Ramírez, "El amparo de estricto derecho y la suplencia de la queja," in *Problemas jurídicos y sociales de México*, pp. 34 ff.

[25] See particularly the preface by Felipe Tena Ramírez to Juventino V. Castro, *La suplencia de la queja deficiente en el juicio de amparo*, pp. 7–38. See also Mariano Azuela, "Trayectoria y destino del juicio de amparo," *El Foro*, April–December 1954, pp. 137–139; J. Ramón Palacios, "El mito del amparo," *Foro de Mexico*, no. 48 (March 1957), pp. 92–101, and no. 49 (April 1957), pp. 46–62; and Ignacio

attempts have been made to justify it on both legal and practical grounds.

The principal legal argument for *stricti juris* holds that if the courts are permitted to base their conclusions on reasoning not adduced by the parties themselves in the complaint or response or during the course of trial, the adversaries of the complainant, that is, the responsible authority and injured third parties, are deprived of the opportunity of rebuttal and are placed, consequently, in an indefensible position. In support of this argument, it is frequently stated that the relation between the parties in civil *amparo* differs noticeably and, perhaps, significantly, from that in most other forms of *amparo*. In civil *amparo*, the responsible authority is the court responsible for the contested judgment. The participation of this court in the *amparo* suit is normally limited to providing a copy of the judgment and a statement of the reasoning on which it is based. In practice, the latter may be omitted. Contrary to the situation of the responsible authorities in most other types of *amparo* suits, the court has no personal interest to defend. The party most intimately concerned, other than the complainant himself, is the complainant's adversary in the original suit. As an "injured third party," this person is permitted by the Amparo Law to intervene in the suit by presenting a brief, but his status is more that of *amicus curiae* than party. Although this might appear, on the surface, to justify the stringent limitations placed by *stricti juris* on both court and complainant, it must be observed that the injured third party will have opportunity, if *amparo* is granted, to recontest the issues of the original suit, as well as the reasoning on which the *amparo* is based, on retrial. It is not true, therefore, that he is deprived of effective means of defense.

It is sometimes argued further that if the decision were based on the discretion of the court, the judge would, of necessity, assume the status of party to the action, alter the character of the controversy, and, in

---

Medina, "La sentencia civil impugnada en amparo en el derecho mexicano," *Foro de México*, no. 54, (September 1957), pp. 25–26. Criticisms of the *stricti juris* rule are frequently coupled with a more general attack on the whole concept of *amparo* as a defense of legality. The classic work in this latter area is Emilio Rabasa's previously cited *El artículo 14*.

effect, rule on his own cause.[26] On strictly practical grounds, there is
something to be said for the first of these contentions. In those legally
ambiguous areas from which litigation is most likely to arise, it is not
altogether true, empirically, that the "judge knows the law" despite
the usual formal presumption to that effect. Indeed, since the judicial
process itself serves as the instrumentality through which the law is
discovered or formulated and the legal truth established, it would be
inaccurate to say, in any absolute sense, that anyone "knows it." In
many situations, it is not impossible that the knowledge and dis-
cernment of counsel may exceed that of the court, and the lack of
opportunity to refute the reasoning of the judges, even if they were to
be so instructed, might result in a decision of doubtful validity. Nonetheless, in the vast majority of cases in which the legality of a judicial
decision is contested in *amparo*, the parties will have had opportunity
already to confront and refute not only the arguments of opposing
counsel but also any interpretations advanced ex officio by the courts
at both the trial and appeal stage. It is not very likely, therefore, that
striking and unanticipated interpretations would subsequently be encountered in *amparo*. Also, since it is the Supreme Court which rules
on the majority of these cases, flagrant judicial error would not be
expected. The probability of oversight or incompetence on the part of
counsel is likely to be considerably greater than a similar failing on the
part of the courts. In any event, it would be impractical, if not fatal, to
base the content of procedural law on the assumption that the courts are
manned by incompetents.

Also, from a more purely legalistic point of view, the arguments
supporting *stricti juris* are less than conclusive. In carrying out the
cassation function, as in all other forms of *amparo*, the courts are required to examine an act performed by a public authority in order to
determine whether its legal consequence violates a constitutional guarantee or guarantees. In cassation, as has been seen, guarantees will be
considered to have been violated whenever a judicial or quasi-judicial

[26] For a more extended statement of these arguments, see Burgoa, *El juicio de
amparo*, pp. 236–237.

authority decides a case on grounds inconsistent with the standards of legal selection and interpretation decreed in article 14 of the Constitution. The fundamental question at issue here is not to give an equal handicap to the participants in a legal horse race but to determine the proper location of the power for an authoritative interpretation of the law in its specific application to concrete situations. In all developed legal systems, the problem has normally been resolved by vesting this power in the judiciary, that is, in an instrumentality of the State, rather than by vesting it in the parties. To deny the courts the faculty of independent judgment is not so much a protection of the procedural equality of the parties, which is otherwise adequately secured in any event, as a partial reversion to the primitive principle of self-help. For purposes of clarification, it should be added that articles 149 and 169 of the Amparo Law lay the burden of proof on both plaintiff and defendant. The former is obliged to prove the existence of the act complained of and demonstrate its unconstitutionality; the latter must disprove the existence of the act or demonstrate its constitutionality. When permitted, the correction of defective complaints extends only to the second obligation imposed on the plaintiff—demonstration of unconstitutionality—and then only when, in the opinion of the court, the facts as proven necessarily entail a violation of guarantees. The rights of the defendant would clearly be infringed if the courts were permitted to introduce, ex officio, new questions of fact, but this is never allowed. Under the *stricti juris* rule, the courts are permitted to interpret the law only to the degree necessary to determine the validity and adequacy of the allegations contained in the briefs. In effect, this amounts to vesting the real power of decision in these cases in the parties rather than in the judiciary. Logically, the validity of both the arguments cited above in support of *stricti juris* depend on accepting one of three manifestly inadmissible premises: (1) that the judicial process, properly understood, is a sublimated form of trial by combat, wherein the courts serve as nothing more than impartial referees and witnesses to the success of superior force; (2) that the courts are incompetent; and (3) that judgments, when based on judicial discretion in the interpretation of the law, are likely to be vitiated by bias or venal self-interest. If the first premise were accepted, the *stricti juris* rule should clearly be applied to all litigation and not merely to some. If either of the other two were true, *stricti juris* would prove a most inadequate remedy.

It is very doubtful that the origin of *stricti juris* in *amparo* can be attributed to such legalistic considerations as those examined above. In the light of the evidence that is available, it appears that the rule was adopted in a vain attempt to stem the flood of suits resulting from the admission of the civil *amparo* jurisdiction. If this is to be a justification, it is vitiated both by its futility, evidenced by the Supreme Court's annual statistical record of cases, and by the injustices that result from applying it.

It should be noted finally, that, in the majority of the cases in which the practice is permissible, the decision to correct a defective complaint lies entirely within the discretion of the courts. Paragraphs 2 and 3, section II, article 107 of the Constitution, and paragraphs 2 and 3, article 76 of the Amparo Law, state that the courts "may" (*podrá*), not that they must, correct such complaints, and judicial interpretation has supported the literal implications of this grammatical form. The courts are only authorized to correct defective complaints in the situations covered by these constitutional and statutory provisions, in cases in which the act complained of rests on a law whose unconstitutionality has been established in *jurisprudencia* or in which the complainant has been rendered defenseless by a manifest violation of the law. Equity, the principle of equality before the law, and the interests of uniformity in interpretation would therefore recommend a mandatory rather than discretionary provision for exercising this function. Thus far, however, the only move in this direction is contained in the above-cited paragraph 4, section II, article 107 of the Constitution and the corresponding fourth paragraph of article 76 of the Amparo Law. Both were added by amendment in 1963 and relate exclusively to agrarian cases. In these instances, the courts are explicitly directed to correct defective complaints. The Spanish term employed here is *deberá*, that is, "must" or "shall."

An additional restrictive formality, potentially destructive of the rights of litigants, was applied to civil and administrative *amparo* in the constitutional and statutory amendments of 1950–1951, with further amendment in 1963 and 1968. Section V, article 74 of the Amparo Law, in conformity with paragraph 4, section II, and section XIV, article 107 of the Constitution, provides at present for dismissing suits or discontinuing appeals or other motions in the following instances:

In direct *amparo*, and in indirect *amparo* in the course of trial before district judges, when the contested act originates with civil or administrative authorities, and when the constitutionality of a law is not involved, if, whatever the stage at which the suit has arrived, no procedural act has been performed, nor any motion presented by the complainant, during a period of three hundred days including Sundays and holidays.

In *amparos* on appeal (*revisión*), the procedural inactivity of the appellant or his failure to introduce appropriate motions during this period will result in discontinuing the appeal. In such cases, the appellate court will confirm the judgment of the court below.

Procedural inactivity on the part of the *ejidos* or other communal centers of agrarian population, or on the part of members of such *ejidos* or population centers, will not be a cause of dismissal of the suit or discontinuance of any motion.

The dismissal of such suits necessarily means that the legal questions they present and the personal interests they represent can receive no final judicial resolution, but this result has been justified by supposing that the complainant's failure to act could reasonably be assumed to indicate his tacit abandonment of the case. Although this assumption may be true in some instances, when one considers the interminable delay resulting from the Supreme Court's inordinate work load—and it is to the Supreme Court that the rule of *stricti juris* has applied primarily in practice—it is more likely that such procedural inactivity on the part of the complainant derives from the exhaustion of his funds or of his hopes of ever securing a judgment rather than from the issue becoming moot. In any event, neither justice for the individual nor uniformity of legal interpretation is served by this procedure. At best, nothing is accomplished except some temporary or relative reduction in the backlog of undecided cases burdening the courts, and the annual statistical reports submitted by the Supreme Court indicate the ultimate futility of such a remedy for this problem. It is doubtful that the dilemma can be solved except by vesting the cassation jurisdiction outside the Supreme Court. Technically, at least, there is no insuperable objection to transferring the cassation function to an expanded system of circuit courts, subject to supervision by the Supreme Court in order to assure jurisprudential uniformity. It must be confessed, however, that until now this proposal has met with little enthusiasm in either the Mexican Congress or legal profession, although the opposition has been less adamant than the opposition to reestablishing the writ of cassation and creating a separate court to handle such cases. Certainly the reallocation of jurisdictions between the Supreme Court and the collegial circuit tribunals, introduced in the 1968 amendments, promises no solution. The aforecited provisions of sections V and VI, article 107 of the Constitution, indicate that the redistribution of jurisdictions has simply substituted for the old distinction—between injuries inflicted in definitive judgments and those produced by procedural error —a distinction based on the importance of the parties or of the legal subject matter of the case. It is doubtful that this will have any perceptible effect on the volume of the Supreme Court's business, although the backlog should be temporarily ameliorated by resurrecting the auxiliary chamber. Despite any short-run effects of the amendments, the continued growth of the Mexican economy and the increase in population, with the consequent increase in social complexity and conflict, can hardly fail to produce increases in litigation, which will wipe out any gains achieved by mere mechanical tinkering.[27]

## The Effect of Amparo against Final Judgments

In conformity with article 80 of the Amparo Law, the issuance of a writ of *amparo* restores to the injured party the full enjoyment of the individual guarantee or guarantees violated by an act of public authori-

[27] For a more extensive commentary on these questions, see Cámara de Diputados, Comisión de Estudios Legislativos de la XLIV Legislatura, "Dictámen de las comisiones unidas primera de puntos constitucionales y primera de justicia, del Senado de la República, relativo a la reforma de la Constitución Política de los Estados Unidos Mexicanos, en sus artículos 94, 98, 102, 105 y 107 fracción VIII, inciso IV," *Iniciativas, dictámenes de comisiones del Senado de la República, discusiones y opiniones relativos a reformas a la constitución política de los Estados Unidos Mexicanos en la organización del poder judicial federal y en materia de amparo.* See particularly p. 9.

ty. Article 190 provides also that in direct *amparo* the judgments of the Supreme Court and collegial circuit tribunals must deal exclusively with legal questions posed in the complaint, must be founded on the constitutional precept whose application is at issue, and must specifiy the act or acts against which the writ is issued. As has been seen, in *amparo* suits that are of the nature of cassation, the question posed is the legality of the selection, interpretation, and application of law by judicial or quasi-judicial agencies. Consequently, granting *amparo* in these cases does not constitute a definitive settlement of the merits of the original suit. On the contrary, the *amparo* writ, directed to the court responsible for the contested judgment, identifies the legal errors committed, indicates the interpretations that should rule, and directs the continuation or resumption of the original suit. The judgment that follows must, of course, be compatible with the legal conclusions established in the writ of *amparo*.

*Chapter 8*

# Procedure in *Amparo*

⌒⌒⌒⌒

THUS FAR, the procedural law governing the trial of *amparo* suits has been described and analysed only in enough detail to obtain an accurate understanding of the juridical principles and constitutional functions of the action with which we have been primarily concerned. For this limited area of interest, a detailed examination of the entire complex and frequently ambiguous field of *amparo* procedure would be both tedious and inappropriate.[1] Nonetheless, if a clear and comprehensive view of the practical operation of *amparo* is to be attained, a systematic summary of the major procedural steps involved in the suit is indispensable. It should be noted, however, that the apparent brevity and simplicity of the rules summarized is misleading. A substantial number of inconsistencies, real or apparent

[1] In my opinion, the best single treatment of the entire field of *amparo* procedure is to be found in Ignacio Burgoa's *El juicio de amparo*. For those interested in specialized points of procedure, a number of other leading works have been listed in the bibliography. In approaching such works, however, a word of warning is in order: namely, that in Mexican and other Latin American legal commentaries the distinction between *lex lata* and *lege ferenda* is frequently anything but clear.

contradictions, obscurities, and active controversies have been intentionally excluded.

*Jurisdiction*

At the risk of repetition, it is desirable to begin with a review of the jurisdictional powers allocated to the federal courts. As discussed in the preceding chapter, the direct *amparo* jurisdiction assigned to the Supreme Court and the collegial circuit tribunals includes all suits directed against: (1) final civil judgments; (2) final criminal sentences, including those of military courts; (3) final judgments of both judicial and administrative tribunals in administrative matters; and (4) awards granted by conciliation and arbitration commissions and tribunals in labor cases.[2] Appeals from decisions rendered by district courts in indirect *amparo* are also divided between the Supreme Court and the collegial circuit tribunals. The former exercises jurisdiction in the following cases: (1) when the constitutionality of a law, federal, state or local, is contested. This applies both in *amparo* against self-executing laws and to suits directed against the first act of application.[3] Prior to the 1968 amendments, articles 84 and 92 provided that when the complainant, both in the initial trial and on appeal, contested the constitutionality of a law and alleged the violation of secondary legislation as well, the Supreme Court would hear *en banc* that part of the appeal that dealt with the first of these questions, while the appropriate chambers or collegial circuit tribunals retained jurisdiction over the latter.

[2] Article 107, sections V and VI, of the Constitution; article 158 of the Amparo Law; chapter II, articles 24, 25, 26, and 27, and chapter III bis., article 7 bis., of the Judiciary Law. Since the distribution of direct *amparo* jurisdiction between the Supreme Court and the collegial circuit tribunals has been examined in detail in chapter seven, the subject will not be treated further here. It should be noted, however, that subsections (b) and (c), of section V, provide for direct *amparo* jurisdiction in administrative, civil, and mercantile matters to be elaborated or modified by ordinary congressional legislation. The rules governing the assignment of cases to the Supreme Court's four chambers and to the full Court have also been discussed enough, in chapter two, and require no further analysis. Also see, Suprema Corte de Justicia, *Jurisprudencia de la Suprema Corte*, thesis 228, II, 439–440.

[3] Article 107, section VIII, subsection (a), of the Constitution; and article 84, section I, subsection (a), of the Amparo Law. Also relevant is article 92 of the Amparo Law.

As the law is presently written, this remains true except in those cases in which the Supreme Court, *en banc,* has already established the constitutionality or unconstitutionality in *jurisprudencia.* If this is the case, jurisdiction falls to the appropriate chamber of the Court, although each chamber, if it concludes that there is adequate reason to change the *jurisprudencia* in question, may resubmit the point to the full Court.

Basing itself primarily on article 92, the Supreme Court has held further that its own jurisdiction extends to appeals that contest the dismissal (*sobreseimiento*) by district courts of suits challenging the constitutionality of self-executing laws. This ruling seems to negate the apparent intent of article 84, section I, subsection (a), and article 85, section I, of the Amparo Law. These provide, respectively, that the Supreme Court shall exercise jurisdiction over appeals from *amparo* judgments in which the act complained of is an allegedly unconstitutional law, while the collegial circuit tribunals shall decide appeals contesting, among other things, the dismissal of an *amparo* suit.[4] The Court has held also that when the complainant has not cited a given law as one of the acts complained of, although he has alleged the unconstitutionality of that law in order to contest the validity of some other act, jurisdiction falls to the collegial circuit tribunals. This conclusion follows from the contention that jurisdiction is determined by the nature of the acts complained of rather than the arguments employed to demonstrate their unconstitutionality.[5]

Subsection (c), section VIII, article 107, as amended in 1968, provides further that the Supreme Court shall take jurisdiction when the complaint is directed against the president of the Republic on the ground of the alleged unconstitutionality of administrative regulations (*reglamentos*) promulgated by him under the authority granted in section I, article 89 of the Constitution. Since the constitutional provisions in question cover all federal administrative regulations, this

---

[4] See Suprema Corte, *Cía., Manufacturera de Driles y Lonas, S. A.,* 120 S. J. 1313 (1954); *Jiménez María Guadalupe,* Revisión 6029/1947 (decided September 1954); *Hernández Vda. de Vega María,* Revisión 3546/1953 (decided September 1954), and *Guerrero de Caballero Isabel,* Revisión 4766/1949 (decided February 1953).

[5] *Comercial del Yaqui, S. A.,* 120 S. J. 1795 (1954).

amendment abrogates, in the main, previous Supreme Court decisions that held that appeals from suits contesting the constitutionality of *reglamentos* should be heard by the collegial circuit tribunals.[6] This conclusion was based on a definition of the constitutional sense of the term "law," which restricted it to enactments of legally constituted legislative bodies. Since subsection (c) refers only to *reglamentos* originating from the presidency of the Republic, it is to be assumed that the Court's *jurisprudencia* will remain effective when the case concerns the constitutionality of *reglamentos* issued by state governors or local officials; (2) when the act complained of involves a situation described by sections II and III, article 103 of the Constitution, that is, when it is claimed that a state has usurped powers constitutionally assigned to the federation or vice versa;[7] (3) when, in agrarian matters, the acts complained of, regardless of the authority from which they emanate, affect communal or small property rights of *ejidos* or other communal centers.[8] (4) When, in administrative *amparos*, the responsible authority is federal, subject, however, to such explicit allocations of jurisdiction between the Supreme Court and collegial circuit tribunals in this area as may be provided by congressional enactment.[9] The last paragraph of Section VIII, article 107, as amended in 1968, provides further that the collegial circuit tribunals shall have jurisdiction in appeals from *amparo* cases contesting the acts of administrative authorities of the federal district and territories. This revokes previous Supreme Court rulings stating that all officials and governmental institutions in the federal district as well as the governors

[6] See Suprema Corte, *Cortés Leopoldo y coags.*, 117 S. J. 185 (1953), for a succinct statement of his position.

[7] Article 107, section VIII, subsection (b), of the Constitution, and article 84, section I, subsection (b), of the Amparo Law. The latter provides further that the appeal in this case shall be heard by the Supreme Court *en banc*.

[8] Article 107, section VIII, subsection (d), of the Constitution, and article 84, section I, subsection (d), of the Amparo Law.

[9] The amended text of article 84 of the Amparo Law now provides that the Supreme Court hear *amparo* appeals arising from federal administrative actions when the amount in question exceeds 500,000 pesos, or when, in the judgment of the Supreme Court, the question at issue is of extraordinary importance to the national interest. This latter provision is the only example to date of a purely discretionary jurisdiction for the Supreme Court.

and their immediate subordinates in the territories were, in the constitutional sense, federal, and consequently, that jurisdiction over *amparo* appeals (*revisiones*) arising from their acts were to be vested in the Court rather than in the circuit tribunals.[10] In the event that both federal and state or local officials are charged in the same suit, the Supreme Court has concluded that its own jurisdiction extends to reviewing the acts of the latter as well as those of the former.[11] Finally, in appeals from indirect *amparo* judgments dealing with civil, criminal, and labor questions and in those concerned with the administrative acts of state and local authorities, with the exception just noted, jurisdiction falls to the collegial circuit tribunals.[12] A specific exception to this rule is given in article 107, section VIII, subsection (f), of the Constitution, and article 84, section I, subsection (f), of the Amparo Law, which provide that the Supreme Court shall hear appeals from judgments in criminal *amparos* in which the act or acts complained of consist solely of violations of article 22 of the Constitution.[13] Except for the cases noted, jurisdiction over appeals from *amparo* judgments rendered by district courts falls to the collegial circuit tribunals, whose decisions are final and without recourse.[14]

In all *amparo* suits, excepting those described above, jurisdiction normally lies with the federal district courts. Article 114, sections I–VI, of the Amparo Law—as interpreted in *jurisprudencia*—allocates this jurisdiction as follows: (1) suits against self-executing laws; (2) suits against acts not originating in judicial, administrative, or labor tribunals; (3) suits against the acts of judicial, administrative, or labor tribunals when executed outside of or after the termination of judicial proceedings; (4) suits against acts perpetrated during the course of a judicial proceeding or during hearings of administrative or labor

[10] See Suprema Corte, *Martínez Miguel,* 110 S. J. 924 (1951), and Burgoa, *El juicio de amparo,* fn. 281, p. 332.

[11] See *Castro de Garcia Natalie y coags.,* 119 S. J. 3578 (1954).

[12] Article 107, section VIII, paragraph 2, of the Constitution, and article 85 of the Amparo Law.

[13] Article 22 lists a number of prohibited punishments, all irreparable once inflicted.

[14] Article 107, section VIII, paragraph 2, of the Constitution, and article 85 of the Amparo Law.

tribunals when these would, if executed, cause irreparable injury to persons or things; (5) suits against acts executed within or outside a judicial proceeding that affect persons not parties thereto when the law does not establish in the interest of the latter any ordinary means of defense that can modify or revoke such acts; (6) suits against laws or acts of federal or state authorities as contemplated by sections II and III of article 103 of the Constitution; and (7) suits against final civil judgments or arbitral awards when the injured party, because of failure or illegality of notification, has taken no part in the proceedings. The judgments must then be attacked as having infringed the right to a hearing, and the proceedings as a whole, or all acts relating to the execution of the judgment, as may be appropriate, must be contested. As noted in chapter III, article 37 of the Amparo Law also makes provision for the participation of other courts, both federal and state, in a few special situations. Thus, a person claiming violation of the provisions of article 16 of the Constitution that relate to procedure in criminal investigations and prosecutions, or of articles 19 and 20, sections I, VIII, and X, paragraphs 1 and 2, also relating to criminal procedure, may seek *amparo* from either a federal district court or from the superior of the tribunal responsible for the alleged infractions.[15]

It will also be recalled that articles 38 and 40 of the Amparo Law confer a partial and strictly temporary jurisdiction upon state courts and upon federal courts below the district level when the infraction of constitutional guarantees occurs in a place where recourse to a district court is not immediately possible. In such cases, the selection of a court is determined by the domicile of the authority who executes or threatens to execute the act complained of. The court so selected is authorized to receive the complaint and, when the contested act threatens life, deprivation of personal liberty without judicial process, deportation, exile, any of the penalties prohibited by article 22 of the Constitution, or deprivation of agrarian rights, it may enjoin the execution of such acts for a period of seventy-two hours or for any additional

---

[15] Article 107, section XII, of the Constitution, and articles 83, sections II and IV, and 156 of the Amparo Law.

period that distance and communication facilities may impose in order to lay the case before the nearest district court.[16] The actual trial and final disposition of the suit must, of course, take place in the district court.[17]

Further jurisdictional questions arise in distributing cases between the various collegial circuit tribunals, the district courts, and within the Supreme Court itself. In conformity with articles 72 bis and 73 of the present Judiciary Law (1936, as amended) thirteen collegial circuit tribunals have been established, six in the federal district and one each in seven other territorially delimited areas. In *amparo*, each of these tribunals stands in a relation of hierarchical superiority to the district courts within its circuit. In both direct and indirect *amparo*, jurisdiction lies with that collegial tribunal within whose circuit the responsible authority is legally domiciled. In the federal district, however, this latter rule is supplemented by a further division of jurisdictions based on the juridical character of the case. Thus, one collegial circuit tribunal hears criminal *amparos*, two deal with administrative *amparos*, two with civil *amparos*, and one with labor *amparos*.[18]

The rules governing the jurisdiction of the various district courts are somewhat more complicated, although, as in the case of the collegial circuit tribunals, the territorial principle is basic. Thus, paragraph 1, article 36 of the Amparo Law states that "When, in conformity with the specifications of this law, the district judges are competent to hear an *amparo* suit, jurisdiction lies with that court within whose district the act complained of is executed or is to be executed." It may happen, however, that an *amparo* complaint will contest not only an act of material execution but also some or all of the acts precedent thereto; for example, general administrative orders and declarations, which do not directly affect the position of the complainant but provide the legal basis for those acts of execution that do prejudice his interests. Obviously, in such a case, the authorities cited as responsible may be legally domiciled in more than one judicial

[16] Amparo Law, article 39.

[17] For rules regulating the obligations of the common courts in exercising the powers granted in articles 38, 39, and 40, see article 144 of the Amparo Law.

[18] Also see article 107, section VI, of the Constitution.

district. On this problem, the Supreme Court has ruled that "when, among the acts complained of, only some may be materially executed and the others not, that district judge is competent to hear the suit within whose district the act of execution is to take place."[19] In the event that the act complained of is executed in two or more different judicial districts, jurisdiction lies with the potentially competent district court that first receives and takes cognizance of the *amparo* complaint.[20]

Finally, if the act complained of has not been executed or, even though some such act would eventually be forthcoming, the mere issuance of an order pertaining to the complainant suffices to prejudice his constitutional rights, the *amparo* suit should be filed with the district court exercising jurisdiction over the area within which the responsible authority is domiciled.[21]

The rules set forth above are intended not only as a guide for litigants but also for district judges. When an *amparo* complaint is received, the first obligation of the court is to determine its own competence in the light of the allegations made and the identity of the authorities cited as responsible. Should this examination indicate that jurisdiction properly lies with another court, the case must be immediately transferred. At this stage of the proceedings, consequently, the complaint is controlling. A mere denial by one or more of the responsible authorities that the act complained of exists does not suffice to justify a change of jurisdiction.[22]

When the complaint has been admitted and the formal hearing (*audiencia constitucional*) initiated, consideration must be given to the jurisdictional implications of the pleadings advanced by the responsible authority or authorities. Thus, if the latter allege that the act complained of is nonexistent or it is to be or has been executed outside of the territorial jurisdiction of the court, and the complainant submits no evidence to the contrary, the assumption of jurisdiction should be

[19] *Jurisprudencia de la Suprema Corte*, thesis 229, II, 441. Also see, Ibid., thesis 237, II, 451.

[20] Amparo Law, article 36, paragraph 2.

[21] Ibid., paragraphs 3 and 4.

[22] Suprema Corte, *Jurisprudencia de la Suprema Corte*, theses 233 and 234, II, 448–449.

revoked and the case dismissed or transferred to another district court as appropriate.[23]

Lastly, in cases that involve authorities located in two or more judicial districts or that contest acts which may be executed in two or more such districts, the Supreme Court has ruled that: "if any of the responsible authorities deny the acts attributed to them, and the complainant has in no manner controverted this denial, in the absence of pleadings from the other authorities, the responsibility [of the latter] for the acts complained of is to be presumed. In such a case, the judge of the district wherein the latter reside should declare himself competent to try the suit."[24]

In contrast to the rules thus far examined, the jurisdictions of the eight district courts operating in the federal district are determined not only by geography but also by the juridical character of the act complained of. Of these eight, three specialize in criminal law, three in administrative and labor law, and two in civil law. In addition to administrative and labor *amparos*, the three courts responsible for these fields also exercise jurisdiction over *amparo* suits contesting the constitutionality of laws and *reglamentos*.[25]

To conclude, jurisdiction at the district level may also be determined, in three different situations, by the special character of the responsible authority. To illustrate, when an indirect *amparo* suit is initiated against acts performed by a district court, jurisdiction lies, in the first instance, with any other district judge located in the same district. If there is no other judge in this category, however, the suit must be tried in the nearest adjacent district court within the jurisdiction of the collegial circuit tribunal to which the responsible authority is subordinate.[26] When the responsible authority is a unitary circuit tribunal, jurisdiction in indirect *amparo* is exercised by the district court that is nearest without being located in the same circuit.[27] Only the fact that *amparo*

---

23 Ibid., thesis 235, p. 450.
24 Ibid., thesis 236.
25 Judiciary Law (*Ley orgánica del poder judicial de la federación*), articles 40 and 42, section III.
26 Amparo Law, article 42, paragraph 1.
27 Ibid., paragraph 2.

is legally a separate and distinct suit would seem to justify so novel an arrangement as to submit the constitutionality of the acts of a superior court to the decision of its hierarchical inferior. It would clearly be improper, however, to vest such jurisdiction in a direct subordinate of the defendant circuit tribunal. Lastly, the same rules for determining jurisdiction apply if the act complained of arises from the execution of a district court order or from the judgments of officials acting as auxiliaries of the court.[28] The reasons for this arrangement seem sufficiently obvious, since to proceed otherwise would require the district court in question to determine the constitutionality of its own acts as well as those of its agents, a process hardly compatible with judicial impartiality.

In view of the discussions in chapters II and VII, little more need be said about the jurisdiction of the Supreme Court. As noted, the Amparo Law and Judiciary Law amendments of 1957 vested jurisdiction over the questions of the constitutionality of laws and invasion of sovereignties in plenary sessions of the Court. The 1968 amendments have altered this arrangement only by returning jurisdiction to the chambers when the constitutionality of the law has already been determined in the *jurisprudencia* of the full Court. Where these points are not at issue, jurisdiction lies with the four chambers into which the Court is normally divided with their areas of specialization, that is, criminal, administrative, civil, and labor law, prescribed in articles 24, 25, 26, and 27 of the Judiciary Law. In order to determine the juridical character of the issues posed in any given case and, consequently, the chamber that should exercise jurisdiction, the Court has established the following rule: "The jurisdiction of the chambers of the Supreme Court is determined by the nature of the act complained of, regardless of the nature of the proceeding from which it has emanated and the authority that may have been involved."[29]

The question of jurisdictional competence may be raised either by the courts themselves, ex officio, or, if they fail to do so, by the parties. Depending on the circumstances, the question may be pursued either

---

[28] Ibid., article 43.
[29] *Jurisprudencia de la Suprema Corte*, thesis 228, II, 439–440.

by or before the court with which the complaint has been lodged (*declinatoria*), or by or before the court of presumptive jurisdiction (*inhibitoria*). The usual rules of rank and status, as prescribed by the Amparo Law, suggest that the decisions of the Supreme Court are final in any contest between itself and a collegial circuit tribunal or district court, or between collegial circuit tribunals. In the same fashion, the decision of a collegial circuit tribunal is binding in any question of jurisdiction between itself and a district court, or between district courts within its circuit. However, if district courts, subordinate to different circuits, are involved, the decision rests with the Supreme Court. In the event of a jurisdictional dispute between Supreme Court chambers, the question is resolved by the Court in plenary session.[30]

### Parties

The parties to an *amparo* suit are identified in article 5 of the Amparo Law as : (1) the injured party or parties, that is, the complainant (*agraviado*); (2) the responsible authority or authorities; (3) injured third parties (*terceros perjudicados*); and (4) the Federal Public Ministry (*Ministerio Público Federal*). Of these, the first and second correspond most closely to the concept of necessary or indispensable parties as these terms are normally understood in the United States, that is, those "who not only have an interest in the subject matter of the controversy, but an interest of such a nature that a final decree cannot be made without either affecting their interests or leaving the controversy in such a condition that its final determination may be wholly inconsistent with equity and good conscience."[31] The position of the injured third party is essentially similar to that of the intervenor in United States procedure, while that of the Federal Public Ministry, the Mexican equivalent of the United States Department of Justice, most closely resembles that of the *amicus curiae*, although the intervention of this agency is by statutory right rather than by invitation of the court.

---

[30] For the regulations governing this aspect of jurisdiction, see the Amparo Law, articles 47–52, and article 56. For the consequences of a denial of jurisdiction at various stages of the proceedings, consult articles 50, 53, and 54.

[31] Henry Campbell Black, *Black's Law Dictionary*, 1276.

Because of the detailed examination of the status of complainant and responsible authority in chapter IV, little need be said here concerning them. For the former, it is enough to repeat that he may be either a real or a corporate entity, that he must have been the subject of some act of authority or of a law allegedly violating a constitutional guarantee, and that this violation must have resulted in a direct and prejudicial infringement of personal interests legally recognized as such.[32]

The Supreme Court, as has also been noted, has defined the term "authority" in the following manner: "The term 'authority,' for the purposes of *amparo*, comprises all those persons who, de jure or de facto, dispose of public power and who are materially enabled thereby to exercise public acts."[33] In turn, article 11 of the Amparo Law provides the general rule for determining which of the authorities so defined are to be considered "responsible": "The responsible authority is that one which decrees or orders, executes or endeavors to execute, the law or act complained of." This statutory prescription indicates that the complainant, if his suit is to succeed, must cite as defendants all those authorities materially involved in the act complained of. If he neglects to do so, the suit will be inadmissible according to the rule of tacit consent.[34] Even if some ground for litigation should remain, the courts would be unable to consider the constitutionality of the acts of authorities not cited and consequently not represented in their own defense.[35] It should also be clearly understood that the responsible authority is conceived in institutional rather than personal terms. As a result, the discharge, transfer, promotion, demotion, death, or other removal of the individual who has actually ordered or executed the act complained of, or any transfer of jurisdiction over the matter in con-

---

[32] See particularly the remarks in chapter IV about the status of public corporate persons as complainants. The discussion of sections II and III of article 103 of the Constitution is also relevant.

[33] *Jurisprudencia de la Suprema Corte*, thesis 179, II, 360.

[34] Amparo Law, article 73, section XII. Also see Suprema Corte, *Jurisprudencia de la Suprema Corte*, thesis 180, II, 361, and note the statutory exception in favor of communal agrarian *amparos* introduced in 1963.

[35] Suprema Corte, *Jurisprudencia de la Suprema Corte*, thesis 181, II, 363.

test, is no bar to the suit.[36] The public institution involved remains responsible regardless of changes in personnel.

A new and increasingly difficult problem has arisen with the proliferation of more or less autonomous government corporations created as an incentive to economic development and usually operating in areas traditionally considered private. In the main, the courts have held that these corporations do enjoy the legal status of private persons, and, as a result, their acts have not normally been subject to attack in *amparo*. Nonetheless, in those cases in which the law permits such a corporation to use coercive public authority in order to carry out its policies, injuries resulting from the use of this authority may be contested and the corporations cited as responsible authorities.[37]

In the most simple and general sense, the injured third party (*tercero perjudicado*) is a person who possesses some personal, legal interest in the preservation and perpetuation of the act contested by the complainant in *amparo*. More explicitly, the identity of those who may claim this status is determined by the nature of the proceedings from which the act complained of arises. The first of the classifications established by the Amparo Law identifies the injured third party as "the adversary of the plaintiff when the act complained of emanates from a noncriminal case or controversy, or any of the parties in the aforesaid suit when *amparo* is sought by a person not a party thereto."[38] Consistent with the rules developed for defining the characteristics of a definitive judgment, the cases and controversies referred to here include not only civil and mercantile suits but the judgments and awards handed down by administrative and labor tribunals.[39] The Supreme Court has subjected this statutory provision to a broad interpretation, holding that "this provision of the Amparo Law should be understood to designate as injured third parties all those who have rights opposed to those of the complainant and, consequently, an interest in preserving the act complained of. Otherwise, such persons would

---

[36] Ibid., thesis 183, II, p. 365. Also see Suprema Corte, *Montúfar Miguel*, 17 S. J. 798 (1925).

[37] Suprema Corte, *Jurisprudencia de la Suprema Corte*, thesis 992, V, 1804.

[38] Article 5, section III, subsection (a).

[39] See Suprema Corte, *Bustamante Luis Felipe*, 21 S. J. 1066 (1927).

be deprived of the opportunity to defend the prerogatives gained from the contested act."[40] In conformity with this ruling, injured third parties in *amparo* actions arising from judicial proceedings of the type described may have been either necessary or merely formal parties in the original suit.

The Amparo Law provides further that injured third parties include "the victim or those persons who, in conformity with the law, are entitled to an indemnity or to exact the civil liability arising from the commission of a crime, as the case may be, in *amparo* suits initiated against judicial acts in criminal trials, provided that such acts affect the aforesaid indemnity or responsibility."[41] Literally interpreted, this would exclude injured third parties from all criminal *amparos* except those that contest rulings on the motions of indemnity or civil liability. It is obvious, however, that the interests of such persons may be adversely affected by a grant of *amparo* against other rulings within a criminal trial or against the sentence itself. Conscious of the inequity inherent in this situation, the first, or criminal, chamber of the Supreme Court has held that the persons listed in the above-cited provisions of the Amparo Law should also be accorded the status of injured third parties in *amparo* suits that contest either the final sentence imposed in a criminal action or the formal order of imprisonment (*auto de formal prisión*). The existence and relevance of the specified legal interest must, of course, be proven. The constitutional basis for this expanded interpretation is found in the due process clause in article 14.[42]

In administrative *amparos*, presumably not those originating from the decisions of formally constituted administrative tribunals as authorized by the 1968 amendments, the law identifies injured third parties as "the person or persons who have solicited in their own behalf

---

[40] Suprema Corte, *Jurisprudencia de la Suprema Corte*, thesis 1074, V, 1939.
[41] Article 5, section III, subsection (b).
[42] The following cases establishing this interpretation are cited in Burgoa, *El juicio de amparo*, p. 285; Suprema Corte, 95 *S. J.* 987 (1948); 103 *S. J.* 352 (1950); 105 *S. J.* 975 (1950); and *Informe*, (1948), (Informe de la primera sala), pp. 73–74.

the act against which *amparo* is sought."[43] The *jurisprudencia* on this point adheres literally to the requirement that the injured third party, to be recognized as such, must have solicited the execution of the act complained of.[44] By logical extension, however, the Court has also recognized that those persons possess this character who have solicited the execution of an administrative act, the necessary consequence of which is the act complained of in *amparo*.[45] More recently, the administrative chamber has broadened its interpretation of this statutory provision even further: "Even though a person may not have originally solicited the execution of the acts complained of, if he maintains an interest opposed to that of the complainants, if the continuance of those acts benefits him, and if this was his position prior to the initiation of the *amparo* suit, he possesses the character of an injured third party within the meaning of article 5, section III, subsection (c), of the Amparo Law."[46]

Asserting that no one can contend that a law has been passed for his own special benefit, the Supreme Court has held that there can be no injured third parties in *amparo* against laws.[47]

Section IV of article 5 of the Amparo Law states that the Federal Public Ministry shall be a party in *amparo* suits that, in the judgment of that agency, involve the public interest. Although the term "public interest," as employed here, hardly lends itself to exact definition, President Alemán's remarks in the exposition of motives submitted in support of the amendments of 1950–1951 that the ministry "should dedicate its fundamental attention to essentially constitutional problems," indicates an important and far from merely formal role for that

[43] Amparo Law, article 5, section III, subsection (c).

[44] *Jurisprudencia de la Suprema Corte*, thesis 1073, V, 1935.

[45] *Unión de Empleados de Restaurantes y Similares*, 20 S. J. 215 (1927).

[46] Asociación Nacional de Funcionarios Judiciales, *Félix Pineda Sánchez*, 129 BIJ 272 (May 1958). The administrative chamber, in making this ruling, relied on two previous, similar decisions, both antedating the ruling collection of *jurisprudencia*. It is, therefore, necessary to assume that the latter is not considered incompatible with this conclusion, although, superficially, it seems to be.

[47] Suprema Corte, *Cía. Singer de Máquinas de Coser*, 106 S. J. 1085 (1950).

agency.[48] Furthermore, in the absence of any explicit exceptions in the Amparo Law itself, the procedural recourses available to the Federal Public Ministry should be at least equal to those afforded the other parties. This, however, has not been the case. In rejecting the right of the ministry to appeal an *amparo* decision, the Supreme Court has denied that that agency can have any direct interest in the subject matter of the suit and has characterized its role as that of a mere monitor of procedural correctness on the part of the parties.[49] Presumably the Court has adopted this conclusion not so much by anything in the law as by the actual practice of the Federal Public Ministry in its participation in *amparo*. The ministry's participation has normally been limited to a brief statement in support of the views of the complainant or those of the responsible authority. To judge by the commentaries, little legal ingenuity or originality is expended in the preparation of these briefs, which are frequently, if not customarily, ignored by the courts.[50] Nonetheless, it is necessary to submit copies of all *amparo* complaints to this governmental agency in order that it may determine, in each case, whether the public interest requires its intervention.

The impression conveyed by the foregoing remarks is more descriptive of the situation in indirect than in direct *amparo*. Technically, a court—judicial, administrative, or labor—is the responsible authority and, consequently, the adversary party in the latter type of suit. From a more realistic point of view, however, the interests actually in opposition are those of the complainant on the one hand and those of the injured third party and the Federal Public Ministry on the other. In practice, the participation of the responsible authority is limited to transmitting the record of the case to the Supreme Court or the appro-

[48] Cited in Burgoa, *El juicio de amparo*, p. 289.

[49] Suprema Corte, *Jurisprudencia definida de la Suprema Corte, Apéndice al tomo LXXVI* (1944), thesis 626, pp. 986–987. Although this thesis did not appear in the subsequent compilation of *jurisprudencia*, it continues to be cited in secondary works dealing with this question and is consistent with actual practice. Apparently, it is still considered good law.

[50] See Burgoa, *El juicio de amparo*, fn. 252, p. 288, and Felipe Tena Ramírez, *Derecho constitucional mexicano*, p. 487.

priate collegial circuit tribunal, or that part of it that relates to the act complained of.[51]

## Legal Capacity and Personality

Although not explicitly distinguished in the Amparo Law, these two terms differ sufficiently in their application and procedural significance to justify separate consideration. Since the analysis offered by Burgoa in his *El juicio de amparo* is especially clear and descriptive, its general outlines will be followed here.[52] As understood in Mexico, both in general and in the context of *amparo*, the concept of capacity incorporates two different elements: (1) status as a legal person, that is, a natural or artificial entity entitled to enjoy rights and contract obligations; and (2) procedural capacity, that is, the ability, as determined by law, to appear in court and employ, in one's own behalf, such procedures as the law affords and as are appropriate to the interest pursued. In Burgoa's interpretation, capacity is a general and abstract rather than a concrete and specific power. He defines personality, on the other hand, as the status or quality of party in a particular judicial proceeding. Personality, in turn, may be either original or derivative, that is, an individual may appear and act in his own behalf, or he may act in the interest and as the legal representative of another.

As a general rule, any natural person physically present or legally resident in Mexico and subject to its jurisdiction is presumed to possess legal capacity in the first of these senses, and any person in the full possession and enjoyment of his civil rights, within the meaning of the second.[53] In the case of artificial persons, however, such capacity must be explicitly accorded by law.

[51] This is the impression gained from discussion with members of the Supreme Court staff during the latter part of 1958. Also see Hector Fix Zamudio, *Estudio sobre la jurisdicción constitucional mexicana*, pp. 209–210, note 239, where this same point is made.

[52] Chapter X, pp. 291–311. See particularly, pp. 291–292.

[53] The first of these conclusions is implicit in articles 1 and 103 of the Constitution, and both are tacitly suggested by article 4 of the Amparo Law. The second is derived most explicitly from article 44 of the Code of Civil Procedures for the Federal District and Territories. See *Código de procedimientos civiles para el Distrito*

Among those who are normally denied the full, personal exercise of civil rights are minors.[54] Nonetheless, article 6 of the Amparo Law, presumably to lessen the chances of irreparable injury resulting from delay, provides a limited exception to this rule, stating that "a minor may request *amparo* without the intervention of his legal representative, when the latter is absent or disqualified; but, in this case, the judge, without prejudice to the issuance of orders that may be urgent, shall name a special representative to join in the suit." Since the Amparo Law lists no other exceptions, it must be assumed that all other persons normally subject to such statutory disability are required to seek *amparo* exclusively through the agency of their legal representatives or guardians.

In examining the scope of *amparo*, it has been seen that the Constitution itself prescribes certain exceptions to the general rule of procedural capacity. The most explicit of these are to be found in article 3 and in section XIV of article 27. The first treats the establishment of private schools and the second the expropriation of agricultural and grazing lands. In both instances, persons adversely affected by governmental action are denied all judicial recourse. By necessary inference, similar exclusions can be derived from the terms of articles 33, 60, and 111, dealing, respectively, with the expulsion of undesirable aliens, the elections and qualifications of members of Congress, and the impeachment process. The denial of procedural capacity to persons who claim that their political rights have been violated should probably be included in the list of constitutional exclusions also, although, as previously observed, it has been established by a somewhat questionable process of judicial construction. Lastly, the provisions for the suspension of guarantees contained in article 29 may permit an indefinite number of temporary exceptions.[55]

---

*Federal y Territorios*, p. 19. Also see Suprema Corte, *Bravo Vda. de Bonilla Magdalena, Sucn. de.*, 81 *S. J.* 4865 (1944).

[54] For a detailed classification of persons partially or wholly deprived of procedural capacity, see the Federal Civil Code and Code of Civil Procedures. When not otherwise provided in the Amparo Law, these statutes also govern in amparo. Mainly, those disabled include minors, the mentally incompetent, and convicted felons.

[55] See the detailed discussion of each of these in chapter five.

Article 10 of the Amparo Law prescribes additional disabilities in the following terms:

The victim or persons who, in conformity with the law, are entitled to an indemnity or to exact the civil liability arising when a crime is committed may initiate an *amparo* suit only against acts emanating from the indemnity or civil liability motions. They may also initiate an *amparo* suit against acts performed during the course of a criminal trial that are immediately and directly related to preserving the object of the crime or property that may be subject to having an indemnity or civil liability imposed on it.

Despite its apparent clarity, the Supreme Court has interpreted this article in such different and conflicting ways during recent years that its present significance is uncertain.[56] The more liberal line of decisions has tended to validate *amparo* suits contesting a variety of actions occurring within the course of a criminal proceeding when their legal effect would be to bar a subsequent suit for indemnity or civil liability.

In still another area, the Supreme Court has ruled that foreign corporations, in order to enjoy procedural capacity for purposes of *amparo*, must prove their legal existence within the confines of Mexican territory. To do so, they must "officially register not only their by-laws, contracts, and other documents relating to their foundation, but also a certificate that they have been constituted and empowered in conformity with the laws of their respective countries, the certification in question to be issued by the appropriate Mexican diplomatic or consular representative."[57]

Although the foregoing remarks have been confined to the capacity of the complainant in *amparo*, clarity of exposition requires no more than minimal additional comment about the other parties. For authorities, the usual assumption is that they possess juridical capacity within the limits of their jurisdictional competency. Obviously, however, this rule requires modification in *amparo*, where the act complained of is necessarily contested as *ultra vires*. Consequently, an authority can be said to possess procedural capacity to act as the adversary party in an

---

56 See Burgoa, *El juicio de amparo*, pp. 295–296, and the cases cited therein.
57 Suprema Corte, *Jurisprudencia de la Suprema Corte*, thesis 1031, V, 1864.

*amparo* suit when he has the material ability to perfom any of the acts prohibited in article 103 of the Constitution. In the case of injured third parties, it is presumed that the rules prescribed in the Civil Code and the Code of Civil Procedures apply, since the Amparo Law itself establishes no special exclusions or exceptions. The capacity of the Federal Public Ministry, finally, is sufficiently attested and defined by the terms of its inclusion as a party in article 4, section IV, of the Amparo Law.

Turning from the factor of capacity to that of personality, one finds in article 4 of the Amparo Law explicit provision for the original and derivative forms in which that status may be expressed: "The *amparo* suit may be initiated only by the person injured by the act or law complained of. He may do so personally, through his representative, his defense counsel if the injurious act arises from a criminal proceeding, or through some relative or other person in those cases expressly permitted by this law. The suit may be prosecuted to a conclusion only by the injured party, by his legal representative, or by his defense counsel." In *amparo*, as in any other suit, original personality resides exclusively in real persons. Where the complainant is an artificial person, whether public or private, it must necessarily be derivative, since such entities are classified as persons solely by virtue of a legal fiction. When they appear as complainants, the Amparo Law provides, in articles 8 and 9, respectively, that private artificial persons are to act through their legitimate representatives and public artificial persons through the officials or representatives designated by law.[58] Both real persons and private artificial persons, whether acting as complainants or injured third parties, are permitted to appoint an agent to represent them by means of a written power of attorney, confirmed in the presence of the district judge or other judicial authority having cognizance of the suit.[59] In the event, presumably, that this procedure has not been followed, or should any question arise about the validity of the personality claimed, it is further provided that "in those cases not

[58] Article 8 bis, added to the Amparo Law in 1963, specifies those persons who may represent agrarian communes.

[59] Amparo Law, article 12, paragraph 2. See also paragraphs 3 and 4, added in 1963, describing in detail the manner of establishing personality in agrarian cases.

otherwise provided for in this law, personality in the *amparo* suit will be proved in the manner determined in the law governing the subject matter from which the act complained of arises. In the event that the aforesaid law does not specify, the provisions of the Federal Code of Civil Procedures will rule."[60] Ordinarily, the identity of the person or persons entitled to represent a private artificial person is indicated in an officially registered general power of attorney. Even in the absence of such registration, however, the Supreme Court has held that a person claiming the powers of an agent may initiate an *amparo* suit on behalf of his principal.[61] In this case, the rules concerning proof of personality would be applied prior to any substantive consideration of the suit.

For somewhat more restricted purposes, article 27 of the Amparo Law permits limited or quasi-agents to be appointed. The regulation in question states that "the complainant and the injured third party may authorize any person with procedural capacity to accept the service of legal instruments in their names. The power to accept such service authorizes the person designated to initiate proceedings or interpose motions that may be in order, to offer and submit evidence, and to present allegations during hearings."[62]

The power of the courts to inquire into the validity of derivative personality is restricted by article 13 of the Amparo Law in cases in which this personality has been recognized by the responsible authority. Where this has been done, the personality claimed by the representative of the complainant or the injured third party must be recognized for all legal purposes in the *amparo* suit as well. The Supreme

---

[60] Ibid., paragraph 1.

[61] *Jurisprudencia de la Suprema Corte,* thesis 784, IV, 1426.

[62] Paragraph 2. Also see Burgoa, *El juicio de amparo,* p. 303, where it is argued that the expression "any person with procedural capacity" (*cualquiera persona con capacidad legal*) indicates that the representative in question need not be a qualified attorney. This would be an exception to the rule expressed in article 26 of the *Ley reglamentaria de los artículos 4 y 5 constitucionales, relativos al ejercicio de las profesiones en el Distrito y Territorios Federales* (Law of Professions), which requires this qualification for serving in this capacity. Also see Suprema Corte, *Jurisprudencia de la Suprema Corte*, thesis 184, II, 366, and idem, *The British Benevolent Society of México,* 116 S. J. 98 (1953).

Court has interpreted this to mean that the representative in question must present to the court some written evidence that his personality has been so recognized, a simple affirmation to this effect being legally insufficient.[63]

In those cases in which a general power of attorney has been given, it is not necessary that the person designated as agent be explicitly empowered to initiate an *amparo* suit. Such explicit authorization is required, however, in order to stop the suit once it is in progress.[64]

Contrary to the usual provisions of the Civil Code, should the complainant or the injured third party die during the course of an *amparo* suit and before a final judgment is issued, their representatives are required to continue in that status until replaced by the heirs or their representatives. This assumes that the act complained of is not restricted in its effects to purely personal and nontransferable rights.[65]

When a complaint is submitted by two or more persons, they are required to select a common agent to represent them in *amparo*. If they fail to do so, the judge may grant a period of three additional days in which to comply with this requirement. If, at the end of this period, no common representative has been chosen, the judge himself must designate one of the complainants to act in that capacity.[66] Presumably, when the contested interest is the same, this rule would also apply, by analogy, to injured third parties.

In cases in which proof of personality is not submitted with the complaint, the Supreme Court has held that this fact "does not constitute a manifest cause of inadmissibility, but should be considered as

---

[63] *Jurisprudencia de la Suprema Corte*, thesis 764, IV, 1403–1404. For further details about applying article 13, see Suprema Corte, *Fábrica de Zapatos "Eclipse," S. A.*, 77 *S. J.* 6055 (1943); *Fernández Máximo*, 79 *S. J.* 5031 (1944); *Azarías Huerta José*, 81 *S. J.* 4872 (1944); *Sindicato de Trabajadores de las Fábricas Alcoholeras del Distrito Federal*, 82 *S. J.* 1033 (1944); *Verges y Zea María de la Luz y coags.*, 83 *S. J.* 1235 (1945); *Corbalá Constantino*, 83 *S. J.* 1707 (1945); and *Mutualista de México, Cía. de Seguros, S. A.*, 109 *S. J.* 2203 (1951).

[64] Amparo Law, article 14.

[65] Ibid., article 15. The usual rule, as prescribed in article 2595, section III, of the Federal Civil Code, holds that a power of attorney dies with the person who granted it.

[66] Ibid., article 20, paragraphs 1 and 2.

an obscurity in the complaint itself. Consequently, it is in order to request its clarification, in conformity with the terms of the law, rather than to flatly reject the complaint."[67] Although the Court has ruled otherwise on occasion, this conclusion follows necessarily from the fact that article 73 of the Amparo Law lists no such grounds of inadmissibility. A proven absence of personality, however, because of the peremptory requirements of article 4 of the Amparo Law, must result in dismissal of the suit. Consequently, an initial judicial recognition of the personality of the complainant does not preclude further inquiry into the question if events, the allegation of parties, or evidence seem to require it.[68]

The rules of personality discussed above apply to complainants and injured third parties in *amparo* suits of every type, whether the act complained of be criminal, civil, administrative, or labor in origin. However, because of the special vulnerability of persons accused or convicted of crime, articles 16 and 17 of the Amparo Law provide additional rules intended to simplify and expedite access to *amparo* when the act complained of arises from a criminal trial. Article 16 requires the courts to admit complaints in criminal *amparo* when submitted by any person who claims himself to be the defense counsel of the injured party. After the complaint has been admitted on these terms, the court is directed to request confirmation of the personality claimed by the initiator of the suit from the judicial authority responsible for the contested act. Should this not be forthcoming, the continuation of the action is dependent upon the approval of the injured party, who will be heard in his own person until he is able to appoint a proper legal representative. In the event that the injured party fails to confirm his interest in the complaint, the suit must be dismissed and judicial rulings and orders that may have resulted from it are automatically voided. Article 17 is concerned with acts involving danger to life, deprivation of liberty without judicial process, deportation, exile, or the imposition of punishments prohibited by article 22 of the

---

[67] *Jurisprudencia de la Suprema Corte*, thesis 762, IV, 1392.

[68] See, among others, Suprema Corte, *Sánchez Luz, Suc. de*, 68 S. J. 2570 (1941), and *Lanche de Corrigan María Teresa*, 71 S. J. 2025 (1942).

Constitution. Since such cases are likely to be urgent and the execution of such acts difficult or impossible to correct, any person, even a minor, is permitted to petition for *amparo* in the name of the individual threatened with imminent injury. These persons are, however, only permitted to intervene when the injured party finds it impossible to act in his own behalf. In a case of this kind, the courts are instructed to take all measures necessary to secure the appearance of the injured party, who must, within a period of three days, confirm or deny the complaint. In the absence of such confirmation, the same legal consequences follow as those prescribed in article 16. The supplementary provisions of article 18 indicate that this departure from the usual rules of derivative personality goes considerably further in its effects than that prescribed in article 16. It is not limited merely to submitting the complaint, but extends to considering it and issuing a ruling on the question of the definitive suspension of the act complained of.

The exercise of personality on behalf of the responsible authority is regulated in the following somewhat ambiguous terms by article 19 of the Amparo Law: "Responsible authorities may not be represented in the *amparo* suit, but they may, simply by letter, accredit deputies for the sole purpose of presenting evidence, offering allegations, and effecting procedural motions during hearings." Although it could be argued that the functions exercised by these deputies constitute a form of representation, they are clearly much more limited in scope than those permitted the agents of complainants and injured third parties. The latter, when properly empowered, substitute for their principals in every respect and may prosecute the suit from its initiation to its final disposition. The relation between deputy and responsible authority is more equivalent to that between attorney and client.

Nonetheless, since the responsible authority is more likely to appear in collective than individual guise, representation, within some meaning of the term, may be indispensable. Presumably, therefore, the intention of article 19 is simply to deny to the authority the right to freely choose and empower its own agent. Its "representative," properly speaking, is the official legislatively designated to serve in that capacity. In support of this interpretation, the Supreme Court has ruled that "in the *amparo* suit the responsible authority cannot delegate its representation, but should appear either personally or in the person of its representative organ."[69]

The only exception to the above rule applies to the president, who may be represented by the secretaries and chiefs of departments or, in their absence, by their immediate subordinates when the act complained of falls within the area of their responsibility. In the event that the act originates in the executive office of the president, he may be represented by the attorney general.[70]

The officials empowered to represent the Federal Public Ministry in various types of *amparo* suits are designated in articles 15, 26, and 47–52 of the law establishing that agency.[71]

## Complaint and Answer

The regulations governing the form, content, and evaluation of the complaint differ in various respects in indirect and direct *amparo*. For the sake of clarity, therefore, the two forms of the suit will be considered in order except for those instances in which procedure is identical in both.

As provided in articles 116, 116 bis, and 166, the complaint must be presented in writing. In indirect *amparo*, however, an exception is permitted when the acts complained of involve danger to life, deprivation of liberty without judicial process, deportation, exile, or imposition of any of the punishments prohibited by article 22 of the Constitution. In these cases, the complaint may be presented verbally and with a modified content, restricted to citing the act complained of, the identity of the authority responsible for the original order, if known to the initiator of the suit, the location of the injured party, and the authority or official responsible for the execution of the contested act.[72] In urgent cases, when some obstacle prevents recourse to local courts, it is also permissible to file the complaint by telegraph but with the same requirements of content that apply to written complaints. In any

---

[69] *Jurisprudencia de la Suprema Corte*, thesis 182, II, 364–365.

[70] Amparo Law, article 19, paragraph 2. Also see Suprema Corte, *Jurisprudencia de la Suprema Corte*, thesis 805, IV, 1468.

[71] *Ley orgánica del Ministerio Público Federal.*

[72] Amparo Law, article 117.

event, the petitioner must confirm the complaint in writing within three days.[73] If he fails to do so, the complaint is considered not to have been presented, and any judicial rulings made concerning it are automatically voided.[74]

In both direct and indirect *amparo*, the written complaint must include the name and residence of the complainant and those of his representative, if any, the name and residence of the injured third party, if any, and the identity of the responsible authority or authorities.[75]

The regulations prescribing the further content of the complaint in indirect *amparo* are as follows: (1) It must specify the unconstitutional law or act imputed to each of the authorities that has been cited as responsible. The complainant is also required to state under oath the facts that led to the act complained of being committed or that serve as the basis for his claims of unconstitutionality.[76] Perjury in the latter statement subjects the complainant to a fine of from five hundred to two thousand pesos and a term of imprisonment that may range from six months to three years.[77] (2) If *amparo* is sought in conformity with section I of article 103 of the Constitution, the complaint must list the constitutional guarantees that the plaintiff considers to have been violated and set forth arguments (*conceptos de violación*) demonstrating that these violations necessarily follow from the character of the laws or acts contested.[78] As noted in the earlier discussion of *stricti juris* and the correction of defective complaints, this information and the arguments and conclusions of law based upon it should be set forth in as much detail and with as much precision as

[73] Ibid., article 118.

[74] Ibid., article 119.

[75] Ibid., article 116, sections I, II, and III, and article 166, sections I, II, and III.

[76] Ibid., article 116, section IV.

[77] Ibid., article 211, section I. These penalties, however, are not applicable if the acts complained of include any of those cited in article 17, i.e., danger to life, deprivation of liberty without judicial process, deportation, exile, or imposition of any of the punishments prohibited by article 22 of the Constitution.

[78] Ibid., article 116, section V.

possible. (3) When *amparo* is sought under the terms of sections II or III of article 103 of the Constitution, the complaint must cite the precept or precepts of the federal Constitution allegedly violated by an invasion of sovereignties committed by the federation against a state, or vice versa.[79] Also, although the statutory provision in question contains no such requirement, both logic and practice necessitate the assumption that the complaint must set forth those legal arguments or *conceptos de violación* called for in section V. (4) Lastly, article 146 of the Amparo Law provides that the complaint must set forth with clarity and precision each of the items called for in article 116. If this has not been done, the courts are instructed to grant the complainant a period of three days in which to make the necessary additions or clarifications. However, as noted above, the situation envisaged in article 117 would constitute an exception to this rule.[80]

The complaint, when presented to the court, must be accompanied by one copy each for the responsible authorities, the injured third party or parties, and the Federal Public Ministry, and two for use in ruling on the suspension motion, if the latter is appropriate. A failure to provide these copies has the effect of suspending all judicial action on the suit. If they should not be provided within the statutory term for initiating *amparo*, the complainant's cause is definitively lost.[81] In those cases contemplated in article 117, the court itself is responsible for providing the necessary copies of the complaint as it also is in the cases

[79] Ibid., section VI.

[80] Ibid., article 116 bis, added in 1963, specifies in agrarian *amparos* that all these requirements be met when possible but, if not, demands only that the complaint be in writing and that it contain the name and democile of the complainant and his representative, the act or acts complained of, and the identity of the authority who executes or attempts to execute the act complained of. Article 146 was also amended in 1963 to provide a fifteen-day period for additions and clarifications in agrarian complaints. If these are not forthcoming from the complainant, the judge is to take any steps that may be necessary to secure them.

[81] Ibid., article 120. The terms are fifteen days for suits against acts of application and thirty days for suits against self-executing laws. See articles 21 and 22 of the Amparo Law. A failure to comply with all requirements within the appropriate period leads to the assumption of consent and, consequently, the inadmissibility of the suit.

contemplated in article 116 bis if the complainant fails to provide them.[82] The only additional documentation required consists of proofs of personality in instances in which the complainant is represented by an agent, and even this requirement is waived in the cases covered by the provisions of article 17.[83]

Under certain circumstances, the plaintiff has the privilege, after filing suit, of amplifying the content of the complaint relating to the acts complained of, the authorities cited as responsible, or the legal arguments or *conceptos de violación*. Generally, this must be done before the responsible authorities submit their answers to the complaint, that is, prior to the establishment of the *litis contestatio* and within the statutory term for seeking *amparo*.[84] A further opportunity for augmenting the content of the complaint may occur between the submission of answers and the holding of the principal hearing (*audiencia constitucional*). This is the case even though the *litis contestatio* has been established, when it is evident from the answers that the acts complained of have not been performed by authorities originally cited as responsible or have resulted from other acts not contested in the complaint.[85]

In direct *amparo* the statutory content of the complaint, insofar as it differs from indirect *amparo*, is as follows: (1) The complainant must cite the act complained of and, if this consists of the violation of procedural laws, must explicitly identify that part of the proceeding in which the violation occurred and the manner in which its commission deprived him of defense.[86] (2) The complaint must indicate the date on which the plaintiff was notified of the contested judgment or arbitral award or on which he first had knowledge of the resolution

---

[82] Ibid., article 121, and paragraph 3, article 120, respectively.

[83] This conclusion is implied in Suprema Corte, *Jurisprudencia de la Suprema Corte*, thesis 330, III, 634.

[84] Ibid., thesis 117, II, 259–260.

[85] Ibid., thesis 328, III, 631–632. Also see, thesis 329, III, 633–634, which holds that the provisions of article 120 of the Amparo Law concerning copies apply also to clarifications and additions to the complaint.

[86] Amparo Law, article 166, section IV. Also see, articles 159 and 160.

he wishes to attack.[87] (3) The constitutional precepts whose violation is claimed must be indicated as well as the argument or arguments serving to demonstrate these violations (*conceptos de violación*).[88] (4) When the complaint contests the inexact application of substantive as distinguished from adjective law, it must identify the statute that the plaintiff believes to have been misapplied or that should have been applied but was not. In the event that several statutes are involved, this information is to be provided in separate, numbered paragraphs. The same rules govern when the contested judgment is based on general principles of law rather than upon statutory provisions.[89] (5) The amount of money at issue must be determined when the question of jurisdiction between the Supreme Court and the collegial circuit tribunals depends on this fact.[90]

In direct *amparo*, the complaint may be presented either directly to the president of the Supreme Court or of the appropriate collegial circuit tribunal by the plaintiff himself, or it may be transmitted to them by the responsible authority, or by the district judge within whose jurisdiction the responsible authority resides.[91] When the *amparo* suit has been filed, the responsible authority must submit the original records of the case to the Supreme Court or to a collegial circuit tribunal, as may be appropriate. If for some reason this cannot be done, the injured party, within fifteen days of receiving official notification of this fact, must request and transmit certified copies of the necessary records. In addition, certified copies of records that may

[87] Ibid., section V.

[88] Ibid., section VI. For additional information concerning the content of *conceptos de violación* in direct amparo, see the following: Suprema Corte, *Ruiz Velis y coags.*, 81 S. J. 3591, (1944); *Burns Ellen*, 82 S. J. 902 (1951); *Cravioto Mora María*, 107 S. J. 2047 (1951); *León Villagómez Agustín, Sucn. de*, 107 S. J. 878 (1951); *García Merino Fausto*, 108 S. J. 865 (1951); *Magaña Alberto*, 108 S. J. 345 (1951); *Aleas Rosario y coaga.*, 109 S. J. 2476 (1951); *Pérez Rafael y coags.*, 109 S. J. 1680 (1951); *López Valencia Desiderio*, 109 S. J. 1197 (1951); and *Aldaco Rico Rosaura*, 111 S. J. 403 (1952).

[89] Amparo Law, article 166, section VII.

[90] Ibid., section VIII.

[91] Ibid., article 167. Also see article 13, sections VII and VIII, and article 9 bis, of the Judiciary Law.

be specified by the injured third party and by the responsible authority must accompany the complaint.[92] Prior to the amendments of 1968, article 164 of the Amparo Law provided explicitly that if the responsible authority failed in its duty to issue these certified copies within the statutory period allowed for initiating the *amparo* suit, the plaintiff would be relieved of his responsibility and could submit the complaint without them. The amended version of article 164 states merely that the responsible authority must issue the requested certified copies within a period of fifteen days or suffer the risk of a maximum fine of one thousand pesos. Despite this alteration, equity demands the continued applicability of the earlier rule as well. Finally, in those cases in which the complainant is obliged to submit a certified copy of the judgment or award and, by his own fault, fails to do so, the Court has ruled that *amparo* should be denied.[93]

In conformity with article 168 of the Amparo Law, in instances in which the complaint is submitted directly to the Supreme Court or to the appropriate collegial circuit tribunal and in those in which it is transmitted by a district court, the plaintiff is obliged immediately to inform the responsible authority that he has initiated suit. This notification should be accompanied by copies of the complaint, both for use by the responsible authority and for distribution by him to all other interested parties.[94] Copies for distribution to other interested parties must also accompany complaints transmitted through the responsible authority.

In civil and labor *amparos* in which the complaint is transmitted by the agency of the responsible authority, the latter is directed to refrain from forwarding the complaint to the Supreme Court or appropriate circuit tribunal and from ruling on the suspension of the act complained of unless the proper copies have been presented. If this is not

---

[92] Ibid., article 163.

[93] *Jurisprudencia de la Suprema Corte*, thesis 302, III, 568.

[94] Burgoa observes that in practice complainants frequently neglect to perform this duty by transmitting all copies of the complaint directly to the Supreme Court or the collegial circuit tribunal. In such cases, the courts are accustomed to remit copies to the responsible authority for its information and distribution. *El juicio de amparo*, p. 576.

the case, the responsible authority must direct the complainant to provide them within a period of five days. If, at the expiration of that period, he has not done so, the complaint is transferred to the Supreme Court or to a circuit tribunal, as appropriate, for a ruling that the plaintiff has, by this omission, abandoned the suit.[95] The procedure is essentially the same in criminal *amparo*, except that the responsible authority, in urgent cases, may rule on the suspension of the act complained of, while the grace period for the provision of copies is ten days rather than five.[96]

The answers submitted by responsible authorities in response to *amparo* complaints are of two types, the *informe previo*, or preliminary answer, and the *informe justificado*, an answer embodying a complete rejoinder to the contentions of the complainant. The first of these is in order only in cases in which the complainant seeks the definitive suspension of the act complained of, and is limited to a statement either affirming or denying the existence of that act and setting forth arguments for rejecting the suspension motion.[97] A failure to submit the preliminary answer leads to the presumption, for the purposes of the suspension motion only, that the act complained of has been performed as alleged in the complaint.[98]

As defined in article 149 of the Amparo Law, the *informe justificado* in indirect *amparo*, except as specially regulated in agrarian *amparos*, should consist of the following elements: (1) the legal precepts and arguments that, in the opinion of the responsible authority, demonstrate the constitutionality of the act complained of or the inadmissibility of the complaint, and (2) certified copies of all records required to substantiate these contentions. The *informe justificado* should be submitted to the court within a period of five days following notification of the suit, although the judge may, at his discretion, extend this term for an additional five days.[99] As previously noted, the

---

[95] Amparo Law, article 168, paragraph 3.

[96] Ibid., paragraph 4.

[97] Ibid., article 132, paragraph 1.

[98] Ibid., paragraph 3.

[99] The Supreme Court has ruled that the *informe previo* cannot be substituted for the *informe justificado*. Where only the former has been submitted, its denial of

answer must contain proof of the constitutionality of the acts complained of. An unsubstantiated affirmation of their validity is without juridical effect.[100]

Should the responsible authority fail to submit an answer, the complainant's allegations about the act complained of enjoy the presumption of truth, subject, however, to subsequent disproof. Despite this presumption, if the act does not manifestly violate individual guarantees, the complainant remains obligated to prove its unconstitutionality.[101] In other words, the absence of an answer implies nothing about the constitutionality of the acts complained of.[102] Finally, in the event that the complaint cites as responsible both the executing authority and the authority that ordered the execution of the act, a denial on the part of the latter precludes this presumption concerning the truth of the plaintiff's affirmations about the act, even though the former fails to submit an answer.[103]

As the result of amendment in 1963, paragraph 5, sections I through IV, and paragraphs 6 and 7 of article 149, now impose special obligations on the responsible authority in agrarian *amparos*. In summary, in *amparo* suits initiated by collective agrarian communities, the *in-*

---

the act complained of has no legal bearing when deciding the merits of the case. *Jurisprudencia de la Suprema Corte*, thesis 572, III, 1046. Burgoa, *El juicio de amparo*, p. 545, observes that, in practice, the *informe justificado* is frequently submitted immediately prior to or at the beginning of the hearing on the merits, thus depriving the complainant of an adequate opportunity to respond. In such cases, a postponement is usually ordered. The consequences of less flagrant delays in submitting the answer are left to the discretion of the district judge.

[100] Suprema Corte, *Jurisprudencia de la Suprema Corte*, thesis 566, III, 1034. Compare with thesis 571, which does establish a presumption of truth about the affirmation or denial of the act in the preliminary answer. Attention should also be called to thesis 569, p. 1042, which forbids violations of the "legal basis and motivation" requirement of article 16 of the Constitution to be corrected in the *informe justificado*.

[101] Amparo Law, article 149, paragraph 3.

[102] For a discussion of those cases in which the act complained of can be considered as violating individual guarantees, see Burgoa, *El juicio de amparo*, pp. 542–544. These would mainly be confined to so-called "simple" acts, that is, those not a result of any preceding chain of decisions and orders, and to acts contravening express constitutional prohibitions.

[103] Suprema Corte, *Jurisprudencia de la Suprema Corte*, thesis 177, II, 359.

*forme justificado* must indicate (1) the name and domicile of the injured third party, if there is one; (2) a precise statement about the existence of the acts complained of, or of other similar or different acts if they have or might have the effect of negating or reducing the complainants' agrarian rights; (3) the legal precepts justifying those acts performed or whose performance is threatened; and (4) the date on which the allegedly endangered agrarian rights were legally established and the manner and period within which they were actually vested in the complainant communities, in the event that the responsible authorities are also agrarian authorities. In this latter case, the *informe justificado* should be accompanied by certified copies of all records relevant to ascertaining the existence and content of the agrarian rights claimed by the complainants as well as the nature of the acts complained of.

When the suit is initiated by an *ejidatario*, or individual member of any other rural collective, concerning his personal rights in the collective property, the responsible authorities are required to fulfill all of the conditions established in (1)–(3) above. If they are also agrarian authorities, they must submit certified copies of all records necessary in order to determine the content of the complainant's agrarian rights.

The *informe justificado* in direct *amparo* should set forth briefly and clearly arguments designed to demonstrate the constitutionality of the act complained of.[104] Given the nature of direct *amparo*, this would normally be accomplished by a reasoned exposition of arguments supporting the validity of the selection, interpretation, and application of substantive and adjective law by the responsible tribunal, although, as we have seen, it is possible that the constitutionality of a statute may also be questioned in a suit of this type. Naturally, in view of the character of the injuries protested in direct *amparo*, no question about the existence of the act complained of can arise. In actual practice, as observed in the discussion of parties, the responsible authority customarily confines its response to submitting a certified copy of the contested judgment or arbitral award. As a rule, this is adequate enough when the act complained of is the judgment or award itself,

[104] Amparo Law, article 169, paragraph 1.

but it is clearly insufficient in cases in which the contested act arises from a procedural ruling handed down during the course of the trial and that is neither referred to nor explicitly justified in the judgment or record.

The only consequence established for a failure to submit the *informe justificado* in direct *amparo* is an instruction to the Supreme Court or appropriate collegial circuit tribunal to order its submission within a period of three days.[105]

## Stages in the Trial of Amparo

In brief, the trial stages in an indirect *amparo* suit are as follows: (1) The complaint is examined in order to determine its admissibility and conformity with the rules of form and content. Should any of the causes of inadmissibility appear, the complaint is to be rejected forthwith. Irregularities are to be corrected, pursuant to an order from the court, within a period of three days (fifteen days in agrarian cases).[106] In a limited number of cases, the courts will also determine, ex officio, the question of provisional suspension at this stage.[107] (2) During the second stage of proceedings, the responsible authorities submit preliminary answers when a ruling on definitive suspension has been requested, and a separate hearing is held for the exclusive purpose of passing on this motion. When suspension is not involved, the second stage is reduced to submitting the *informe justificado*, which, as noted above, establishes the *litis contestatio*.[108] (3) The final stage consists of a public hearing, known as the *audiencia constitucional*, for presenting evidence and additional arguments followed by a judgment granting or denying *amparo*, or if appropriate in the light of the evidence, dismissal of the suit.[109]

In appeals (*revisiones*) from indirect *amparo* judgments and from direct *amparo* judgments awarded by the collegial circuit tribunals, the procedure is even simpler.[110] Assuming for descriptive purposes that

[105] Ibid., paragraph 2.
[106] Ibid., articles 145 and 146.
[107] Ibid., article 123.
[108] Ibid., articles 124, 132, 133, and 149.
[109] Ibid., articles 150–157.
[110] Ibid., article 88, paragraph 2, which provides for such appeals when the cir-

the appeal lies with the Supreme Court, the steps involved are as follows: (1) A written bill of appeal is submitted and its admissibility and regularity of form are determined by the president of the Court.[111] (2) Copies of the bill are distributed to the parties who are granted a period of ten days within which to submit briefs. At the end of this period, whether briefs have been submitted or not, the bill is transmitted to the Federal Public Ministry, which is also permitted ten days within which to intervene in or abstain from the proceedings.[112] (3) Should the case be one of those requiring consideration *en banc*, the president of the Supreme Court will assign the record to one of the ministers for preparing a draft decision. If it is not to be discussed *en banc*, the president will assign the case to the appropriate chamber, whose president, in turn, will make the assignment to an individual minister. The ordinary term for preparing a draft decision is thirty days, although this may be extended if the difficulties presented by the case require it.[113] (4) When completed, copies of the draft decision are distributed to members of the chamber or to the entire membership of the Court, as may be appropriate. Within ten days of the day following that on which the copies are distributed, the president of the chamber or of the Court, as the case may be, is required to set a date for a hearing.[114] (5) The hearing itself, interestingly enough, is entirely public. The draft, and any other part of the record requested by the ministers, is read by the secretary of the chamber or of the Court and is then openly debated. When the discussion ends, a vote is taken, and the draft, if accepted without amendment by a majority, serves as a final judgment. If not so approved, a member of the majority is designated to draft a decision expressing the conclusions reached in debate. The statutory period for accomplishing this task is fifteen days. The presentation of dissenting opinions is also permitted.[115]

---

cuit tribunal declares a law unconstitutional or establishes the direct interpretation of a constitutional provision.

[111] Ibid., articles 86–88, and 90, and Judiciary Law, article 13, section VII.

[112] Amparo Law, articles 88–90, 181–183, and 185–191.

[113] Ibid., article 182.

[114] Ibid., article 185.

[115] Ibid., articles 186–188. See also, article 10 of the Judiciary Law. The latter

The procedure followed in direct *amparo* differs very little from that followed in appeals (*revisiones*). Indeed, from the establishment of the *litis contestatio* to the final decree it is identical. Insofar as the preliminary stages are concerned, the discussion of complaints and answers is sufficiently descriptive.[116]

Procedure in the collegial circuit tribunals, both in appeals and direct *amparo*, is essentially similar to that followed by the Supreme Court. In the former, however, the time permitted for preparing the draft decision is reduced to five days and discussions are held in closed session.[117]

It is evident from the brevity of the various time limits described above that the *amparo* suit is intended to be summary in form. In practice, however, the strict enforcement of these terms is usually ignored. Given the complexities of procedure and the inordinate case load imposed on the federal courts, particularly the Supreme Court, it could hardly be otherwise.[118]

## Dismissals

The dismissal (*sobreseimiento*) of the *amparo* suit makes a final disposition of the controversy but does not involve any decision about its merits.[119] A ruling for dismissal is required in the following circumstances: (1) when the complainant has expressly abandoned the suit, or when his acts or omissions, in conformity with the terms of the law,

---

does permit closed sessions when morals or the public interest require it, but this procedure is rare in practice. Attention is again called to article 92 of the Amparo Law for a description of procedure in appeals that involve both a question about the constitutionality of a law and charges of violation of secondary legislation.

[116] For details, consult articles 166–191 of the Amparo Law. Procedure in those limited forms of appeal known as *queja* and *reclamación* is examined at a later point.

[117] Ibid., article 184, sections I and II.

[118] For a discussion of this inconsistency between law and reality, see Mariano Azuela, "Lagunas, errores y anacronismos de la legislación de amparo," *Problemas jurídicos y sociales de México*, p. 24.

[119] Article 75 of the Amparo Law provides explicitly that the dismissal of the suit shall not be construed as prejudging the responsibility incurred by the responsible authority in committing the act complained of. Thus, the dismissal of the amparo suit, for whatever reason, is no bar to a criminal prosecution of the authority if that should be appropriate.

have this effect; (2) when the injured party dies during the course of the trial, provided that the interests affected by the act complained of are exclusively personal; (3) when, during the course of trial, any of the causes of inadmissibility listed in article 73 of the Amparo Law arises or becomes evident; (4) when the nonexistence of the act complained of is clearly demonstrated, or the complainant fails to prove its existence during the principal hearing (*audiencia constitucional*); and (5) when the complainant in civil or administrative *amparo* refrains entirely from presenting or promoting pleadings, and no other procedural act has been performed for a period of three hundred consecutive days, including holidays, providing always that no question about the constitutionality of a law is involved.[120] The primary, if not the only, reason for adding this last basis for dismissal, accomplished in the constitutional and statutory amendments of 1950–1951 and modified in 1968, was the desire to dispose of the Supreme Court's inordinate backlog of undecided cases. Procedural inactivity for the same period of time in *amparo* appeals (*revisiones*) results in discontinuing the appeal (*caducidad de la instancia*) and affirming the decision of the court below. Neither dismissal of the suit nor discontinuance of appeals, however, may be based on these provisions when the complainant or appellant is an agrarian collective or a member of such a collective endeavoring to protect his communal rights.[121]

When the effects of the act complained of have ceased or some evident basis for dismissal arises, both the complainant and the responsible authority are required, on pain of fines ranging from ten to three hundred pesos, to inform the court of this fact.[122]

## Suspension of the Act Complained of

No aspect of *amparo* has been subject to such diversity of interpretation or remains affected by so many uncertainties of doctrine and

---

[120] Amparo Law, article 74, sections I–V. Court rulings hold that any procedural act, regardless of who initiates it, interrupts the process. See, *Jurisprudencia de la Suprema Corte*, theses 1022, 1023, and 1024, V, 1847–1848, 1849–1850, and 1850–1851, respectively.

[121] Ibid., section V, paragraph 3.

[122] Ibid., section IV, paragraph 2, and section V, paragraph 4.

practice as the suspension of the act complained of. Avoiding these difficulties of interpretation, however, it can be said that suspension has the effect of a temporary injunction and, as such, is intended to preserve the rights and interests claimed by the plaintiff until a final judgment can be reached.[123]

The constitutional basis for suspension is contained in sections X and XI of article 107, which read as follows:

X. Contested acts may be subject to suspension in those cases and under those conditions and guarantees specified by law, for which purpose account shall be taken of the nature of the alleged violation, the difficulty of remedying the damages that might be incurred by the aggrieved party should it be executed, and damages that the suspension might cause to third parties and the public interest.

The aforesaid suspension should be granted in final judgments in criminal matters at the time notice is given of the initiation of the *amparo* suit, and in civil matters when bond is posted by the complainant to cover liability for damages occasioned by the suspension. This latter requirement is waived if the other party gives bond (*contrafianza*) to guarantee restoration of matters to their former status if *amparo* is granted and to pay the resulting damages.

XI. The suspension shall be requested from the responsible authority in the case of direct *amparo* before the Supreme Court of Justice or a collegial circuit tribunal; in this case the aggrieved party shall notify the responsible authority of the petition for *amparo* within the period fixed by law and under affirmation to tell the truth. [He must] attach two copies of the complaint, one to be included in the record and the other to be transmitted to the opposing party. In other cases, the district courts shall take cognizance of and rule on suspension.

In indirect *amparo* suspension may be granted either ex officio or in response to a petition submitted by the complainant. In conformity

---

[123] For a variety of views about the juridical nature and effects of suspension, see Ricardo Couto, *Tratado teórico-práctico de la suspensión en el amparo, con un estudio sobre la suspensión con efectos de amparo provisional*, pp. 43, 45–70; Burgoa, *El juicio de amparo*, p. 590; and Romeo León Orantes, *El juicio de amparo*, p. 298. The first two of these are particularly recommended for their detailed description of all aspects of suspension.

with article 123 of the Amparo Law, suspension ex officio is in order in the following cases: (1) when the acts complained of involve danger to life, deportation, exile, or the imposition of any of the punishments prohibited in article 22 of the Constitution[124]; (2) when, in any other situation, the execution of the act would make it physically impossible to restore the complainant to the enjoyment of the right at issue; and (3) when the acts complained of have or may have the effect of totally or partially, temporarily or definitively, depriving an agrarian collective of its property or of removing such property from the *ejido* category. When, from the content of the complaint, it appears that any of these situations is involved, the court should order the suspension of the act complained of in the same decree that authorizes the admission of the complaint. No additional preliminary pleas or other procedural acts may be required of the complainant.

Suspension may be granted on the petition of the complainant in cases meeting the following conditions: (1) when the suspension of the act complained of would neither damage the interests of society nor transgress dispositions intended to preserve public order; and (2) when the damages threatened by the act complained of would be difficult to redress.[125] In granting a suspension of this type, the courts must define the situation that is to be maintained and take measures that may be necessary to preserve the substance of the suit pending its final resolution.[126] Even if suspension, in conformity with the foregoing terms, is in order, the complainant must first post a bond covering all potential damages if its concession would be injurious to a third person. The latter, in turn, may secure the cancellation of the suspension order by posting a counter bond sufficient to cover both possible damages to the complainant and the costs incurred by him in supplying the original bond. The privilege of posting a counter bond is not

---

[124] As observed in discussing capacity, articles 38 and 39 of the Amparo Law authorize state and local courts, and federal courts below the district level, to grant a temporary suspension in cases falling within this rule on occasions when they act as channels of transmission for the complaint.

[125] Amparo Law, article 124, sections I, II, and III.

[126] Ibid., section III, paragraph 2.

available, however, when a grant of suspension is essential to preserving the substance of the suit, nor when the interest defended by the
complainant cannot be expressed in monetary terms.[127]

Under certain circumstances, a suspension petitioned for by the
complainant may involve two procedural stages: the grant of a provisional or temporary suspension based solely on the allegations made
in the complaint, and a special hearing confined to conceding or denying a definitive suspension effective for the duration of the trial.
The former is in order when, at the discretion of the district judge,
the complaint indicates that there is imminent danger that the act complained of will be executed and that this execution would be manifestly injurious to the plaintiff. The effect of a provisional suspension is
limited to maintaining the status quo until the question of definitive
suspension can be resolved.[128]

The concession or denial of a definitive suspension must be determined in a special and autonomous hearing limited exclusively to
considering that question and involving the participation of all the
parties authorized to intervene in the *amparo* suit.[129] The effect of a
definitive suspension varies, depending on the nature of the act complained of and the interests, other than those of the complainant,
which may be involved. Basically, a definitive suspension is designed
to maintain that state of affairs most conducive to the subsequent execution of a judgment granting *amparo*. At the very least, the substantive issues presented in the suit must be preserved and, insofar as
possible, the complainant should be protected from the prejudicial
consequences flowing from the execution of the contested act. Consequently, the suspension order, when granted, may permit the partial
execution of the acts complained of, if this is compatible with the
preservation of the suit itself. When necessary for achieving the latter,
the suspension order may also restore to the complainant the enjoyment
of rights already infringed, that is, it may have the effect of a provisional grant of *amparo*. Nonetheless, the Supreme Court's customary
view of this matter is that "the effects of suspension consist in main-

---

[127] Ibid., articles 125–127.
[128] Ibid., article 130.
[129] Ibid., article 131. Also see article 132.

taining things in the state in which they existed at the time it was granted rather than in restoring the conditions that existed prior to the violation of the Constitution. The latter effect can be achieved only by granting *amparo* with respect to the substantive issues presented in the suit."[130]

Although the petition for suspension would normally be submitted with the complaint, the request may be made at any time before the final judgment is pronounced.[131] In any event, it is within the power of the court at any time during the course of trial to modify or revoke the ruling granting or denying suspension if events justify such action.[132] Both this ruling and that which initially grants or denies suspension may be appealed (*revisado*) to a collegial circuit tribunal by the party or parties adversely affected.[133]

In direct *amparo*, suspension has the effect of temporarily staying the execution of the contested judgment or arbitral award, and is ordered by the court or arbitral commission responsible for the act complained of. The granting of a suspension is normally automatic, however, only in criminal *amparo*.[134] In civil *amparo* all the conditions and limitations prescribed in article 124, in the second paragraph of article 125, and in articles 126 through 128 are applicable.[135] In labor *amparo*, when the award favors the worker, the president of the responsible arbitral commission may suspend its execution only if this would not deprive that party of the means of subsistence. If the award exceeds the amount necessary for this purpose, however, the excess is subject to suspension. Whatever the character of the suspension, in labor as in civil *amparo*, the rules on the posting of bonds and counter bonds are applicable.[136] Furthermore, in all types of direct *amparo* suspension is in order only if considered compatible with the public interest.[137]

130 *Jurisprudencia de la Suprema Corte*, thesis 1053, V, 1897.
131 Amparo Law, article 141.
132 Ibid., article 140.
133 Ibid., article 83, section II, and article 85, section I.
134 Ibid., articles 171 and 172.
135 Ibid., article 173.
136 Ibid., article 174.
137 Ibid., article 175.

Contrary to the situation in indirect *amparo*, suspension in direct *amparo* is subject to the remedy of complaint (*queja*) rather than to that of appeal (*revisión*.)[138]

## Judgments

As we have seen, the *amparo* suit may result in the issuance of a writ of *amparo*, in denial of the writ, or in dismissal. Since the content of the latter two types of judgment is sufficiently obvious, consideration here is limited to the nature and execution of the writ.

When the act complained of is of a positive character, the writ of *amparo* has the form of a prohibitory injunction plus whatever additional elements that may be necessary to repair damages already inflicted. The latter is to be accomplished by reproducing the situation that existed before the Constitution was violated.[139] When the act is negative in character, the writ takes the form of an order directing the responsible authority to actively comply with the provisions of the violated constitutional guarantee. In both cases, the purpose of the judgment is to restore to the complainant the full and unimpaired enjoyment of his constitutional rights. Consistent with this purpose, monetary damages are not appropriate remedies in *amparo*.[140]

The permissible scope of judgments granting *amparo* is governed, in varying degrees, by four general rules. Universally applicable is the requirement that the judgment must be concerned solely with the plaintiff or plaintiffs, that it must be limited exclusively to the special case to which the complaint refers, and that it must refrain from making general declarations about the law or act complained of.[141] The significance of these precepts has been examined at length in chapter

---

[138] Ibid., article 95, section VIII.

[139] Suprema Corte, *Peregrina Vda. de Martínez Soledad, Sucn. de*, 105 S. J. 2631 (1950).

[140] Amparo Law, article 80; Suprema Corte, *Zúñiga Robles Isidora*, 121 S. J. 1152 (1954); and idem, *Jurisprudencia de la Suprema Corte*, thesis 998, V, 1813. It should also be noted that the judgment is obligatory only insofar as its content is confined to the constitutional questions posed and the means essential to its execution. Conclusions on any other subjects are *obiter dicta*.

[141] Article 107, section II, paragraph 1, of the Constitution and article 76, paragraph 1, of the Amparo Law.

VI and need not be elaborated further here. In civil and administrative *amparo*, and in those labor *amparo* suits initiated by the employer, the subject matter that may be considered by the courts and, consequently, the scope of their judgments is limited by the rule of *stricti juris*. In criminal *amparo*, and in labor *amparo* suits initiated by the worker, on the other hand, the scope of what is to be considered and of the judgment is governed by the rule regulating the correction of defective complaints.[142] Lastly, the courts are forbidden to take cognizance of evidence other than that submitted during the course of the proceedings which resulted in the act complained of.[143] This refers not only to the content of the complaint but also to attempts, in the answers submitted by responsible authorities, to correct illegalities committed in the course of such proceedings.[144] Although expressed in the most general terms, this rule is necessarily limited in its application to those cases in which the act complained of does arise from a proceeding, judicial or otherwise, in which the complainant has had opportunity to be heard and to avail himself of such defenses as the law allows. When this is not the case, as, for example, in certain types of criminal *amparo*, in suits contesting isolated administrative acts, and in *amparo* against laws, the complainant may present any evidence tending to demonstrate the existence of the act and its unconstitutionality. Indeed, the rule seems totally irrelevant in criminal *amparo*, because of the unrestricted power to correct defective complaints in these cases, as well as in labor and agrarian *amparos* to which this faculty is applicable.[145] Further exceptions are permitted when the complainant has been deprived of the right to appear in his own defense through failure of proper notification or for any other reason not attributable to his own negligence, when he is a complete stranger to the proceedings wherein he is injured, and when, although a party, his evidence or other de-

---

[142] Ibid., paragraphs 2 and 3, respectively. Note also that defective complaints, as previously discussed, may be corrected in any type of *amparo* suit when the act complained of is based on laws declared unconstitutional in *jurisprudencia*. For detailed discussion of these rules, see chapter seven.

[143] Amparo Law, article 78.

[144] Suprema Corte, *Jurisprudencia de la Suprema Corte*, thesis 569, III, 1042.

[145] Ibid., thesis 454, III, 877, and thesis 726, IV, 1339.

fensive pleadings have been illegally disallowed and do not appear in the final judgment or administrative resolution.[146]

In addition to the statutory prescriptions examined above, the Supreme Court has established the following additional rules concerning the content of the *amparo* judgment: (1) The constitutional question raised must be resolved in its entirety, not in part; (2) The decision should be confined to points that bear upon the constitutionality of the acts complained of;[147] and (3) The courts may not substitute their own judgment for that of other authorities in matters where the law confers discretionary powers on the latter.[148] The last of these limitations is effective, however, only when the discretionary power in question has been properly employed.[149]

In direct *amparo*, the pronouncement of the judgment establishes res judicata since the law normally affords no possibility of reconsideration. The only exception occurs in cases in which collegial circuit tribunals render decisions on the constitutionality of a law or directly interpret provisions of the Constitution. Even in these cases, the judgments of circuit tribunals are final if based on *jurisprudencia*. The status of res judicata also pertains to the decisions of the Supreme Court and the collegial circuit tribunals in appeals from judgments in indirect *amparo*.[150]

The judgments pronounced by district courts in indirect *amparo* establish res judicata in the following instances: (1) when the appeal procedures established in the Amparo Law are not employed within the permissible time limits; (2) when the appellant, or prospective

---

[146] See Suprema Corte, *Milmo Vda. de Radziwill Prudenciana*, 28 *S. J.* 823 (1930); *Ferrocarriles Nacionales de México*, 68 *S. J.* 1453 (1941); *Badit Clemente y coags.*, 69 *S. J.* 2518 (1941); and *Barba Macario*, 73 *S. J.* 3489 (1942). Also, consult Burgoa, *El juicio de amparo*, pp. 433–435.

[147] Asociación, *Comité Ejecutivo Agrario de Ampliación Ejidal del Poblado "El Rincón," Municipio de Ixtlahuaca, Edo. de México*, 131 *BIJ* 409 (July 1958).

[148] *Jurisprudencia de la Suprema Corte*, theses 999, 997, and 1107, V, 1817, 1812, and 1984–1985, respectively.

[149] *Informe, 1956* (Informe de la segunda sala). Also see Asociación, *José María Vázquez Alba*, 132 *BIJ* 461 (August 1958).

[150] Amparo Law, article 83, section V, and article 104. Also, see Eduardo Pallares, *Diccionario de derecho procesal civil*, p. 617, and Burgoa, *El juicio de amparo*, pp. 438–442.

appellant, explicitly waives appeal; and (3) when the parties expressly acquiesce in the judgment. When the judgment is divisible into separate and independently executable rulings, it has been held that only sections actually contested in the appeal may be reexamined and modified.[151] Furthermore, when an appeal taken by one party can be resolved without altering the position of other parties who have failed to appeal in their own right, the initial judgment has the effect of finality with respect to the latter.[152]

When res judicata has been established, the court responsible for the original judgment in indirect *amparo*, or the Supreme Court or appropriate collegial circuit tribunal in direct *amparo*, must immediately and ex officio serve notice of this to the authority or authorities whose compliance is required as well as inform each of the other parties. In urgent cases, this notification may be made by telegraph. The authorities, in turn, are obliged to keep the court informed of the action taken to carry out the judgment.[153] If the judgment has not been executed within a period of twenty-four hours, assuming that this is physically possible, or is not being executed within that period, the court, either ex officio or on the petition of any of the parties, must give notice of this to the immediate superior of the responsible authority. When notified, the former is legally obliged to enforce the compliance of its subordinate. Should the immediate superior also prove recalcitrant, its own hierarchical superior, if any, must be similarly informed and ordered to secure the prompt execution of the judgment. Paragraph 2, article 107 of the Amparo Law provides in these circumstances that the superiors of the responsible authorities incur the same responsibilities for noncompliance that attach to their subordinates. The court order directing compliance must be submitted directly to the responsible authority when the latter has no immediate superior.[154]

If, despite these efforts, the judgment remains unexecuted, the record is transmitted to the Supreme Court, *en banc*, for possible enforcement of the terms of section XVI, article 107 of the Constitution, and

[151] Suprema Corte, *Jurisprudencia de la Suprema Corte*, thesis 1005, V, 1820.
[152] Ibid., thesis 1002, p. 1824.
[153] Amparo Law, articles 104 and 106.
[154] Ibid., article 105.

paragraph 2, article 108 of the Amparo Law, which state that the offending authority may be summarily removed from office and turned over to the Public Ministry for possible criminal prosecution. As written, prior to the amendments of 1968, paragraph 2, article 108 of the Amparo Law explicitly stated that the Supreme Court would consider such questions *en banc*. As amended, this aspect of procedure has been left unclear, but, because of the nature of the sanctions that may be applied, it is probable that previous practice would be continued. Should the responsible authority be among those few officials whose removal can be accomplished only by impeachment (*si . . . gozare de fuero constitucional*), the Court must determine whether this constitutional provision is applicable and, if so, transmit its ruling along with the record of the case to the authority competent to carry out this process.[155] If the tribunal granting the *amparo* judgment rules that its terms have been properly executed, the party injured by this finding may demand, by petition, that the record be submitted to the Supreme Court for review.[156]

As indicated above and further elaborated in articles 107 and 108 of the Amparo Law, noncompliance may take any of the following forms: (1) an outright refusal to execute the judgment; (2) delays produced by evasion or other illegal procedures; and (3) repetition of the act complained of.

Independently of the procedures and sanctions outlined above, article 111 of the Amparo Law authorizes the courts to issue whatever orders are necessary to secure the execution of their judgments. If these orders are not obeyed, the courts must themselves execute the judgments in question, provided that the reparation required is not of such a nature that only the responsible authority is competent to provide it. The court that rendered the judgment may act to execute it either through the instrumentality of its secretary or attached law enforcement officer, if the situation permits, or through the personal intervention of the district judge or of the designated collegial circuit tribunal magistrates, as may be appropriate. If all else fails, the court

[155] Ibid., article 109.
[156] Ibid., article 105, paragraph 3.

may request the assistance of the executive branch. The foregoing dispositions are also applicable, in general, to the unexecuted judgments of Supreme Court chambers in direct *amparo*, although their implementation is confided to the appropriate district judge in each case.[157] Whatever procedures may be required, no *amparo* judgment may be relegated to the files until it has been completely executed or until it becomes evident that there is no longer any material basis for its execution. The Federal Public Ministry is assigned responsibility for supervising compliance with this disposition.[158]

Strictly speaking, the only authorities immediately and directly affected by a grant of *amparo* are those who have appeared in the suit as being responsible for the acts complained of. The same cannot be said, however, about the obligation of executing such judgments. On the contrary, this obligation extends to any and all authorities whose cooperation is physically or organizationally necessary to achieve full compliance. Consequently, if such an authority is guilty of any of the forms of contempt listed above, including the repetition of the act complained of, it becomes liable to the imposition of all appropriate enforcement procedures and sanctions authorized by the Amparo Law.[159]

The most serious equitable problem involved in executing *amparo* judgments arises from the effect they may have on the previously and legitimately acquired rights of third persons not parties to the suit. As the law is presently written, such persons have no remedy other than that of complaint (*queja*) against excesses or defects in the execution of the judgment (*exceso o defecto de ejecución*). Against the substance of the judgment and its exact and proper execution, neither the Amparo Law nor *jurisprudencia* offer any defense whatever.[160] This

---

[157] Ibid., article 112.

[158] Ibid., article 113.

[159] Ibid., article 107, paragraph 1, and Suprema Corte, *Jurisprudencia de la Suprema Corte*, thesis 406, III, 768. Also see Suprema Corte, *Congreso del Estado de Puebla*, 74 *S. J.* 1018 (1942), in which the Supreme Court, on these grounds, confirmed the right of a district court to order a state legislature to pass a law, in this case a salary appropriation, required for the full execution of an *amparo* judgment, even though the legislature in question was not a party to the suit.

[160] Amparo Law, article 95, sections IV and IX, and articles 96, 98, and 99. Also see article 73, section II, which provides that the *amparo* suit is inadmissible

state of affairs, although thoroughly consistent with the intent of article 107 of the Constitution and the enforcement provisions of the Amparo Law, is manifestly incompatible with the rights guaranteed in article 14. In recognition of this, the Supreme Court, in a number of decisions, has subverted the normal meaning of its own *jurisprudencia*. It has held that the cause of inadmissibility established in article 73, section II, of the Amparo Law is operative only in suits attempted by persons who have previously acted as parties in the contested *amparo* action, and that *amparo* judgments should not be executed to the prejudice of third persons whose interests have been acquired in good faith. This good faith is to be demonstrated by evidence proving that the party was ignorant, without contributory negligence, of the existence of the *amparo* suit bearing upon his interests and, consequently, failed to participate in it.[161] Burgoa suggests quite correctly that the only equitable escape from the dilemma presented by these contradictory views would be to establish a clear distinction between the status of those persons whose interests have been acquired either prior to the initiation of prejudicial *amparo* litigation or in demonstrable and legally justifiable ignorance of that fact, and those whose interests have been acquired with the knowledge that they were sub judice. To the former access to *amparo* should be permitted, and to the latter denied.[162] This could best be accomplished by amending the Amparo Law, since the more liberal interpretations adopted by the Supreme Court are of doubtful uniformity in application and comport badly with the express terms and clear intent of the law in its present form.

In addition to the enforcement procedures already examined, the Amparo Law grants to the parties as well as to those third persons mentioned above the remedy of complaint (*queja*) against excesses

---

against *amparo* rulings and judgments or against their execution. For the opinions established by the Supreme Court, consult *Jurisprudencia de la Suprema Corte,* theses 402, 403, 405, and 407, III, 753–754, 757, 767–768, and 770–771, respectively.

[161] See Suprema Corte, *Martínez José D.,* 93 S. J. 2442 (1947); *La Cía. de Fianzas Lotonal, S. A.,* 96 S. J. 2158 (1948); *Sarabia Alvarez Enrique,* 103 S. J. 84 (1950); *Topete Romero Rodolfo,* 103 S. J. 3727 (1950); and *Naneine Emilio I.,* 103 S. J. 814 (1950).

[162] Burgoa, *El juicio de amparo,* pp. 448–451.

or defects in the execution of the judgment.[163] Needless to say, it is frequently very difficult in practice to distinguish between nonexecution, excessive or defective execution, and acts which may be appropriately attacked in new *amparo* suits.

## Forms of Appeal

The forms of appeal permitted in *amparo* are *revisión*, *queja*, and *reclamación*, which may be literally translated as revision, complaint, and claim. Since no exactly equivalent Anglo-American legal terms are available, however, the original Spanish is retained in the following discussion. All are exercised as a matter of right rather than at the discretion of the appellate courts.

*Revisión*, which, of the three, most nearly corresponds to the customary meaning of appeal, is applicable in the following cases: (1) against rulings rejecting the complaint or holding it not to have been submitted; (2) against rulings of a district judge or the superior of the responsible tribunal, as the case may be, that grant or deny definitive suspension or that modify, revoke, or deny revocation of an earlier ruling on suspension; (3) against dismissals and rulings holding that the complainant has abandoned the suit; (4) against *amparo* judgments pronounced by district judges or by the superior of the responsible tribunal in the cases envisaged in article 37 of the Amparo Law; and (5) against direct *amparo* judgments rendered by collegial circuit tribunals when these contain decisions about the constitutionality of a law or direct interpretations of constitutional precepts unless based on the *jurisprudencia* of the Supreme Court. The judgments of the collegial circuit tribunals are never subject to *revisión*, however, when concerned only with the application of procedural norms or the violation of secondary legal dispositions. Even when appropriate, the review of the circuit tribunal judgments must be limited strictly to the constitutional questions involved.[164]

Only those persons who have acted as parties in the suit and whose

---

[163] Amparo Law, article 95, sections II, IV, and IX, and article 98.

[164] Ibid., article 83, sections I–V. For clarification of details consult also Suprema Corte, *Jurisprudencia de la Suprema Corte*, thesis 326, III, 628, and thesis 1063, V, 1918.

interests have been adversely affected by its resolution or by rulings on the suspension motion are entitled to employ the remedy of *revisión*. This must be done, in any case, not later than five days—ten days in agrarian cases—from the day following that on which notification of the contested ruling has been made.[165] However, as previously noted, the Federal Public Ministry, although technically a party in *amparo* suits in which it sees fit to intervene, has been denied this status for the purpose of initiating *revisión*.[166]

The request for *revisión* must be presented in writing and must contain arguments that demonstrate the illegality of the judgment or other rulings to which objection is made ( *el recurrente expresará los agravios que le causa la resolución o sentencia impugnada . . .* ).[167] One effect of this requirement, as determined by *jurisprudencia*, is to exclude the review of questions of fact.[168] Another has been to conclude that the appellant's petition is insufficient and must be rejected if it does nothing more than reproduce arguments advanced in the suit, since these can only demonstrate the constitutionality or unconstitutionality of the acts complained of rather than the legality or illegality of the judgment or other rulings to which objection is taken.[169] Further, the appellant, when he has acted as plaintiff in the suit, may not employ *revisión* as an occasion for introducing new arguments ( *conceptos de violación* ) against the constitutionality of the acts complained of. This conclusion follows not only from the principle of relevancy but also from the requirement that the responsible authority be given opportunity to answer the complaint in full, which clearly could not be

---

[165] Amparo Law, articles 86 and 88, and Suprema Corte, *Jurisprudencia de la Suprema Corte*, thesis 66, II, 139, and thesis 927, V, 1728. Also see thesis 936, V, 1737, from which it can be inferred that a person has no right to initiate *revisión* unless his status as a party to the suit is genuine. The mere recognition of such status by the district court does not suffice as proof.

[166] *Jurisprudencia definida de la Suprema Corte, apéndice al tomo LXXVI* (1944), thesis 626, pp. 986–987.

[167] Amparo Law, article 88.

[168] Suprema Corte, *Jurisprudencia de la Suprema Corte*, theses 62 and 64, II, 133 and 135–136, respectively.

[169] Ibid., theses 60 and 65, II, 129 and 238, respectively.

done if it were permissible to alter the content of the *litis contestatio* at this stage.[170]

Normally, the responsible authority may initiate *revisión* only against parts of the judgment or other rulings that refer directly to his own acts. There is a major exception to this rule, however, when a law has been declared unconstitutional either in *amparo* against laws or against the first act of application. In such cases, the *revisión* may be taken not only by the appropriate legislative authority but also by the authority responsible for promulgating the law. This authorization, added to the Amparo Law in the amendments of 1950–1951, corrects a serious jurisdictional deficiency, since the customary failure of the legislative authority to have recourse to *revisión* has, in practice, resulted in depriving the Supreme Court of the opportunity to review such declarations.[171]

The role of the responsible authority as appellant in *revisión* has been further conditioned by the following jurisprudential rules: (1) In conformity with the provisions of article 19 of the Amparo Law, which prohibits authorities, except the president of the Republic, to be represented in *amparo*, a petition for *revisión* is acceptable only if submitted by the person designated by law to act for the authority in question; (2) when *amparo* has been granted against both acts of execution and against the orders on which these acts were based, and the two are not legally or logically separable, only the authority responsible for the latter is considered competent to initiate the *revisión*; (3) *revisión* may not be sought by the hierarchical superior of the responsible authority when *amparo* has been granted against acts attributable entirely to the latter; and (4) when the act complained of consists of a resolution deciding some controversy between private persons, the authority responsible for the resolution is not qualified, because of lack of personal interest, to initiate the *revisión*.[172]

---

170 Ibid., thesis 63, II, 134. This conclusion also seems to be implicit in the provisions of sections I and II of article 91 of the Amparo Law.

171 Amparo Law, article 87. Also see Suprema Corte, *Jurisprudencia de la Suprema Corte*, thesis 935, V, 1736.

172 Suprema Corte, *Jurisprudencia de la Suprema Corte*, thesis, 928, V, 1730;

In conformity with the provisions of section I, article 91 of the Amparo Law, and by analogy from those of section II, article 107 of the Constitution and article 76 of the Amparo Law, it appears that both the rules of *stricti juris* and the regulations relating to the correction of defective complaints are applicable in *revisión* as well as in the *amparo* suit proper. It should be noted, however, that it would be inappropriate to correct defective petitions for *revisión* submitted by the accused in a criminal proceeding or by the worker in a labor arbitration when these persons have appeared as injured third parties rather than as complainants in the *amparo* suit. This conclusion follows from the manifest incompatibility between the interest pursued by the injured third party as appellant—to revoke the writ of *amparo* or other damaging resolution—and the objective sought through the procedure of correction—to equalize the status of the adversary parties by assisting those who are presumptively inferior in education, wealth, and access to qualified legal advice so that *amparo* may be granted, if justified on the merits, despite technical errors or insufficiencies in the complaint.[173]

The effect of the ruling in *revisión* is determined by the nature of the injuries (*agravios*) claimed. When it is found that fundamental rules of *amparo* procedure have been violated, or that the court of original jurisdiction has been guilty of an omission that has deprived the complainant of his defense or conditioned the content of the judgment, the appellate court is instructed to revoke the contested ruling and return the case for reconsideration. The same procedure applies when a person entitled to appear as a party in the suit has not been heard.[174] In all other cases, the appellate court itself renders a final

---

theses 178 and 937, II and V, 360 and 1737–1738, respectively; theses 939, 938, and 1105, V, 1742, 1738, and 1982–1983.

[173] Amparo Law, article 91, section I, and Suprema Corte, *Jurisprudencia de la Suprema Corte*, theses 927, 932, and 1005, V, 1728, 1734, and 1826, respectively. Note, however, that all of these merely establish the rule of *stricti juris* in *revisión*. Extending the rules on correction of defective complaints is logical but remains to be established with the same degree of clarity. Also, see Burgoa, *El juicio de amparo*, p. 488.

[174] Amparo Law, article 91, section IV.

judgment conceding or denying *amparo*, or, if appropriate, dismisses the suit.[175] If the judgment appealed derives from an *amparo* suit that should have been tried in single rather than double instance, that is, direct rather than indirect *amparo*, the Supreme Court or appropriate collegial circuit tribunal must dismiss it as baseless and retry the suit in conformity with the rules of direct *amparo*.[176]

Recourse to the remedy of *queja* is appropriate in the following cases: (1) against rulings of district judges, or those of the tribunals referred to in article 37 of the Amparo Law, which have admitted notoriously inadmissible complaints; (2) against responsible authorities for excessive or defective execution of the definitive suspension order; (3) against responsible authorities for failure to comply with orders granting freedom on bail; (4) against responsible authorities for excessive or defective execution of the writ of *amparo*; (5) against rulings of district judges, those of the tribunals referred to in article 37, or those of collegial circuit tribunals disposing of *quejas*; (6) against rulings handed down during the course of the trial by district judges or by the tribunals referred to in article 37 that cannot be attacked in *revisión* but that, by virtue of the gravity of their consequences, may result in a final judgment irreparably injurious to one of the parties; and against rulings made after the suit is terminated when their effects cannot be redressed either by the authority responsible for them or by the Supreme Court; (7) against the definitive rulings of district judges in hearings to determine whether damages are due as a result of the concession or denial of suspension under bond, provided that the amount at issue is in excess of three hundred pesos; (8) against responsible authorities in direct *amparo* for failure to grant suspension or to rule on that question within the legal time limit; when they refuse the admission of bonds or counter bonds; when they admit bonds or counter bonds that do not meet legal requirements or may prove insufficient or illusory; when they deny the complainant freedom on bail in appropriate cases; or when their rulings on these matters are manifestly damaging to one of the interested

[175] Ibid., section III.
[176] Ibid., article 94.

parties; and (9) against the responsible authorities in direct *amparo* for excessive or defective execution of the writ of *amparo*.[177]

The effect of a favorable ruling on the *queja* is evident enough from this description of the occasions for the use of that remedy.

The *queja* petition must always be submitted in writing with copies for the authorities against whose actions the complaint is made and, where appropriate, for each of the parties in the *amparo* suit. In the cases referred to in points (2), (3), and (4), above, jurisdiction lies with the court that is in the process of trying or has already adjudged the suit, that is, a district court, one of the tribunals referred to in article 37 of the Amparo Law, or a collegial circuit tribunal. In the cases referred to in (1), (6), and (7), jurisdiction is exercised by the appropriate collegial circuit tribunal and in those referred to in (5), (8), and (9), by either the Supreme Court or a circuit tribunal, each disposing of those complaints arising from the direct *amparo* suits or *revisiónes* tried by itself.[178]

The remedy of *reclamación* is admissible against the procedural rulings of the president of the Supreme Court, against those of the presidents of the Supreme Court chambers, and against those of the presidents of the collegial circuit tribunals. It must be submitted in writing by one of the parties to the suit and with reasonable cause. When directed against rulings of the president of the Supreme Court, the petition will be considered either by the Court *en banc* or by the appropriate chamber. When the rulings of the president of one of the Supreme Court chambers are at issue, jurisdiction lies with the chamber concerned. If the rulings of the president of one of the collegial circuit tribunals are involved, the petition must be considered by the remaining two magistrates of that tribunal. In any of these cases, the petition for *reclamación* must be submitted within three days of the date on which the notification of the contested rulings is handed down.[179]

[177] Ibid., article 95, sections I–IX.

[178] Ibid., articles 98 and 99. For a detailed analysis of the *recurso de queja*, see Burgoa, *El juicio de amparo*, pp. 494–512.

[179] Ibid., article 103, and Judiciary Law, articles 9 bis, 13, section VII, and 28, section III, paragraph 2. Also see articles 11, 12, 24, 25, 26, and 27 of the latter statute.

*Chapter 9*

# *Jurisprudencia*

~~~~~~~~

JURISPRUDENCIA (jurisprudence), in Mexico as elsewhere, is susceptible to a wide variety of definitions. We have seen, however, that in *amparo* the term carries the special, technical meaning of obligatory precedent. Although the Supreme Court has been assigned the power to establish such precedents in all of the *amparo* legislation since 1909, explicit constitutional recognition of this function was lacking until the amendments of 1950–1951 were adopted. As then written, article 107, section XIII, paragraph 1, of the Constitution provided that "the law shall specify the terms and cases in which the *jurisprudencia* of the courts of the federal judicial power is binding, as well as the requirements for modifying it." Despite the general character of this authorization to legislate judicially, subsidiary references to *jurisprudencia* in sections II and IX of article 107 were sufficient to indicate that only certain decisions of the Supreme Court, *en banc* or in chambers, were intended to have such authority. Certainly, the Congress proceeded on this assumption in enacting the relevant provisions of the Amparo Law. As amended in

1968, article 107 no longer provides an explicit statement about the binding character of *jurisprudencia*. Instead, the references to *jurisprudencia* in the present sections IX and XIII of article 107, take this characteristic for granted and extend the power to establish such precedents to the collegial circuit tribunals.[1]

The legal nature and permissible scope of *jurisprudencia* have always been subject to controversy. That this should be so is not surprising, given the rigid doctrinal separation of the legislative and adjudicative functions normally prevailing in civil law systems.[2] Nonetheless, the mere fact that the Constitution, as amended in 1950–1951, declared it to be binding was enough to establish *jurisprudencia* as a true source of law.[3] Even for purposes of doctrinaire argument it is improbable that the less explicit terminology of the present article 107 could raise a new question about this. The legislative characteristics of *jurisprudencia*, however, should not be taken to mean that the lawmaking powers exercised by the Supreme Court, and now by the collegial circuit tribunals as well, are equal in scope to those available to common-law courts through the rule of stare decisis. On the contrary, the majority of the commentators hold, and the Court itself has stated, that *jurisprudencia* should never intrude into the province of the legislative authority. In practical terms, this would mean that *juris-*

[1] It is impossible to say why the above-cited provisions of the former section XIII were deleted, but it appears, from other references to *jurisprudencia* and from the amended provisions of the Amparo Law, that it was the result of sloppy drafting rather than any intent to change the legal character of the institution.

[2] For a variety of views on these questions, consult Ignacio Burgoa, *El juicio de amparo*, pp. 687–688; Ricardo Couto, *Tratado teórico-practico de la suspensión en el amparo, con un estudio sobre la suspensión con efectos de amparo provisional*, pp. 204–212; Felipe Tena Ramírez, *Derecho constitucional mexicano*, pp. 524–525, and his introduction to Juventino Castro, *La suplencia de la queja deficiente en el juicio de amparo*, pp. 13–16; J. Ramón Palacios, *La Suprema Corte y las leyes inconstitucionales*, particularly chapters one, three and six; Romeo León Orantes, *El juicio de amparo*, pp. 415–417; Hector Fix Zamudio, *Estudio sobre la jurisdicción constitucional Mexicana*, p. 234; and Jorge Delgado Bernal, *La jurisprudencia obligatoria*, pp. 40–53.

[3] General agreement on this point was expressed during the course of interviews with Licenciados Antonio Martínez Báez, Ignacio Burgoa, Felipe Tena Ramírez, Arturo Serrano Robles, and F. Jorge Gaxiola, and a similar impression was obtained from discussions with members of the secretarial staff of the Supreme Court.

*prudencia*, to be valid, must be confined to interpreting statutes, *reglamentos*, constitutional precepts, and other rules of law enacted by properly constituted legislative and constituent authorities. Consistent with this view, for the judiciary to enunciate new legal norms, that is, norms not founded directly upon pre-existing legislative enactments or constitutional provisions and limited to the clarification and necessary elaboration of their meaning, would mean an unconstitutional usurpation of power.[4] As generally understood, therefore, *jurisprudencia* can be considered an auxiliary but not an autonomous source of law.[5] That the Supreme Court has, in fact, acted in conformity with this proposition is well documented by the content of its collected *jurisprudencia*. Of the 1122 theses contained in the compilation, published in 1955, almost all are concerned, partially or wholly, with technical points of statutory or constitutional interpretations, the majority of these relating to the Amparo Law itself. Nowhere does one find anything comparable to the dominance of the Constitution, political in its essence, which has marked the history of judicial review in the United States. Thus far, Mexican *jurisprudencia* affords nothing genuinely equivalent to the development by the Supreme Court of the United States of, for example, the commerce clause, the taxing power, or substantive due process.[6] This is not to say that *jurisprudencia* is of no consequence, but that the Supreme Courts of Mexico and the United States are the heirs of substantially different legal and political traditions and, as a result, act within dissimilar environments and on

[4] Suprema Corte de Justicia, *Cantú Vda. de Villagómez Santos*, 75 S. J. 517 (1943), and *Pinto Vda. de Manjarrez Petrona*, 56 S. J. 1351 (1938). Also, see Burgoa, *El juicio de amparo*, p. 688.

[5] The Court has determined that *jurisprudencia*, unlike statutory law, does not create private rights. As a result, it may be applied retroactively without violating the prohibition on ex post facto laws in article 14 of the Constitution. See Palacios, *La Suprema Corte y las leyes*, p. 51.

[6] Some similarity in scope and significance might be claimed for a few isolated decisions insufficient in number to constitute *jurisprudencia*. Of these, perhaps the best example is the famous case of *Cía. Mexicana de Petróleo "El Aguila," S. A., y coags.*, 62 S. J. 3021 (1939) which proclaimed the constitutionality of the petroleum expropriations carried out by President Cárdenas. As previously noted, however, the political pressures and nationalistic sentiments involved in this situation preclude independent judicial consideration.

different conceptions of the judicial role. From the practical point of view, *jurisprudencia* has been indisputably valuable as a device for clarifying the ambiguities and filling the gaps that neither statutory nor constitutional drafting can entirely avoid. In the doctrinal sense, it has defined the effective scope and limits of *amparo* and, consequently, determined the extent to which that institution can function as an effective constitutional defense.[7]

Of course, the rules governing the interpretation of legal texts do not constitute an exact science that produces invariant results. Furthermore, both logically and in practice, the power to interpret preexisting legal norms entails the power to interpret or reinterpret the *jurisprudencia* established about them. This being the case, and since the Mexican Constitution is no less ambiguous in its phrasing than that of the United States, there is no logically necessary or purely legal limit on the potential creativity of the Court in establishing *jurisprudencia*. Consistent with the opinions expressed in the preceding paragraph, however, it must be emphasized that tradition, a conception of the judicial function that excludes the idea of policy making, and the realities of the political process are the controlling factors, and there is no present indication of changes in any of these that would warrant an expectation that the Supreme Court will soon, or ever, embark on a more adventurous and independent course.[8]

Aside from the previously examined rulings extending the constitutional applicability of *amparo*, perhaps the most imaginative of the jurisprudential theses thus far established are those that have created

---

[7] The opinions expressed above are based on impressions derived from a variety of sources including study of the collected *jurisprudencia*, interviews and discussions with the attorneys and Supreme Court staff members previously cited, and observation of the Court's daily activities. For jurisprudential theses directly illustrating these points, consult the discussion of the scope and limits of *amparo* in chapter five.

[8] The Mexican judiciary and legal profession in general do not deny that the establishment of *jurisprudencia* is a necessarily legislative function. Both this fact, and the limited scope and significance assigned to it, are commented upon by Minister Joaquín Ortega, then president of the Civil Chamber, in *Informe rendido, 1932*, (Informe de la tercera sala), pp. 234–242. However, for an argument that this is not a legislative function, see Burgoa, *El juicio de amparo*, pp. 691–692.

the *derecho de audiencia* ("right to a hearing"), from the following provisions of article 14 of the Constitution: "No person shall be deprived of life, liberty, property, possessions, or rights without a trial by a duly created court in which the essential formalities of procedure are observed and according to laws issued prior to the act." On face value, this would mean that none of the acts of deprivation listed could acquire legal validity until examined and approved by a court of law. Such a literal interpretation, however, would have a paralyzing effect on administrative processes. Consequently, the Supreme Court has determined:

Although article 14 of the Constitution states that no one may be deprived of his possessions and rights except by trial, this means that when administrative authorities adopt resolutions that may cause such deprivation, they should do so in a proceeding that possesses the essential characteristics of a suit at law, within which the interested party can be heard in his own defense. This constitutional provision should not be interpreted in the sense that every act of an administrative authority, in order to acquire legal finality, must necessarily be subjected to judicial examination. Such an interpretation would result in subjecting the administrative sphere to the control of the judicial power, a situation not intended by the constituent authority.[9]

The observance of this right is incumbent not only upon administrative and, of course, judicial authorities, but also upon legislative bodies. To be considered constitutional, the laws enacted by the latter, if capable of producing any of the effects anticipated in article 14, must prescribe adequate procedures, administrative or judicial, for hearing the parties injured in their application.[10]

[9] *"Renovación"* S. de R. L., 120 S. J. 858 (1954). Also see *Carlos Arroyo Rojas*, 91 S. J. 3108 (1947); *Carmen Riba de Cervantes y coags.*, 108 S. J. 37 (1951); *Ricart Sabate Luís*, 121 S. J. 1610 (1954); and *Montes de Oca y Obregón Ignacio, Suc. de* S. J. 1956 (1932).

[10] Suprema Corte, *Inmuebles Bertha, S. A.*, 103 S. J. 328 (1950); *María Mercedes Loreto Godoy y coags.*, 107 S. J. 963, (1951); *Portillo Margarita y coags.*, 119 S. J. 3353 (1954); *Asúnsolo de Herrera Emilia*, 120 S. J. 1072 (1954); and *Márquez Anaya Rodolfo*, 121 S. J. 412 (1954). Also see idem, *Jurisprudencia de la Suprema Corte*, thesis 468, III, 901; thesis 294, III, 557; and thesis 600, IV, 1078.

*The Formation of* Jurisprudencia

Within their respective areas of jurisdictional competence, *jurisprudencia* is established by the Supreme Court *en banc*, by its chambers, and by the collegial circuit tribunals. In any case, five consecutive decisions to the same effect, uninterrupted by any incompatible rulings, must be rendered. When established by the full Supreme Court, each of the decisions contributing to the formation of *jurisprudencia* must be approved by a majority of at least fourteen ministers. In the chambers, a majority of four is required in each case. In the collegial circuit tribunals, the unanimous approval of all three magistrates is specified.[11] In form, a jurisprudential thesis consists normally of a brief restatement of a single point of law abstracted and summarized from the conclusions of law (*considerandos*) expressed in the appropriate decisions. Consequently, none of the decisions involved is necessarily binding in its entirety, nor need the cases to which these decisions refer be entirely analogous.

The practical task of determining in each case when the conditions required for establishing *jurisprudencia* have been met is performed primarily by the attorneys employed on the secretarial staffs serving the Supreme Court and its four chambers. Presumably the secretarial staffs of the collegial circuit tribunals will perform the same task for their courts. Although the system used affords numerous opportunities for crosschecking, the volume of material to be handled suggests that errors of omission and addition, both as to the fact of establishment and the content of *jurisprudencia*, are not uncommon. Observation certainly indicates that at least some theses appear to differ substantially in emphasis or even in apparent meaning from the impression conveyed by a perusal of the decisions themselves. Given the ambiguity inherent in even the most technical language, however, it would be strange if this were not the case. In conformity with general principles of jurisprudence it is presumed that the thesis should have been, in each of the judgments establishing it, an integral and necessary part

[11] Amparo Law, articles 192, paragraph 2; 193, paragraph 2; and 193 bis, paragraph 2.

of the reasoning on which the decision was based. It seems probable, however, that *obiter dicta* are sometimes inadvertently incorporated.[12]

Finally, it should be observed that the Supreme Court, basing its opinion on a strict interpretation of articles 192, 193, and 193 bis of the Amparo Law, has consistently held that *jurisprudencia* may only be derived from judgments (*ejecutorias*) in *amparo*. As a result, the conclusions of the Court or of its chambers in other forms of adjudication, although meeting in every other respect the requirements listed above, are without obligatory effect.[13] In practice, this means that *jurisprudencia* may be formed from judgments in direct *amparo*, from appeals (*revisiones*) in indirect *amparo*, and from rulings disposing of *quejas* and *reclamaciones*.

## The Legal Scope of Jurisprudencia

In conformity with the provisions of articles 192, 193, paragraph 1, and 193 bis, paragraph 1, of the Amparo Law prior to the amendments of 1968, *jurisprudencia* could refer only to the Federal Constitution, laws, and treaties. The preferred construction of this limitation was that the Supreme Court might also establish *jurisprudencia* dealing, either favorably or unfavorably, with the constitutionality of state and local law, or with the constitutionality of particular interpretations or applications thereof, but that it might not do so in questions of pure statutory interpretation.[14] This and related problems seem to have been satisfactorily solved by the 1968 amendments to articles 192, 193, and 193 bis. The first two articles now state that *jurisprudencia* may be established in the interpretation of the federal Constitution, federal, state, and local laws and *reglamentos*, and international treaties. Arti-

---

12 The above remarks are based primarily on discussions with various members of the secretarial staff of the Supreme Court, on actual observation of the processes employed, and on interviews with the attorneys cited previously.

13 See, for example, Suprema Corte, *Operadora de Hoteles, S. A.*, 124 S. J. 59 (1955), which held that judgments rendered in *revisiones fiscales*, that is, appeals from the judgments of the Fiscal Tribunal, may not contribute to developing *jurisprudencia*.

14 Suprema Corte, *Walls Ricardo*, 118 S. J. 681 (1953). Also, see Palacios, *La Suprema Corte y las leyes*, p. 41; Burgoa, *El juicio de amparo*, pp. 689–690, and Suprema Corte, *Marín Canalizo Joaquín*, 118 S. J. 679 (1953).

cle 193 bis provides only that the collegial circuit tribunals may establish *jurisprudencia* in matters falling within their exclusive jurisdiction, but, by necessary inference, this grant of authority appears to be as broad as that conferred in articles 192 and 193.

## The Obligations and Application of Jurisprudencia

Internally, each judicial entity authorized to establish *jurisprudencia* is bound by its own rulings but not, in the case of Supreme Court chambers, by the precedents of other chambers, or, in the case of collegial circuit tribunals, by those of other such tribunals. Otherwise articles 192 and 193 provide that the *jurisprudencia* of the Supreme Court shall be binding upon the unitary and collegial circuit tribunals, district courts, military courts, administrative and labor tribunals, both federal and state, state courts, and the courts of the federal district and territories. Article 193 bis provides in turn that the *jurisprudencia* of the collegial circuit tribunals shall be obligatory for district courts, state courts, and administrative and labor tribunals that lie within their geographical jurisdictions.

A practical question arises in the proper interpretation and application of those provisions of articles 192, 193, and 193 bis of the Amparo Law, which direct that *jurisprudencia* shall be obligatory not only for subordinate courts but also for the body that has established it. Since article 194 explicitly authorizes the interruption or modification of *jurisprudencia*, the obligation is evidently not intended to be absolute. Taken in conjunction, the provisions of articles 192, 193, 193 bis, and 194 logically permit the following conclusions: (1) that both the collegial circuit tribunals, the Supreme Court chambers, and the full Court are bound by the *jurisprudencia* established by the latter, the former two invariably so; (2) that the *jurisprudencia* formulated by a given chamber is binding upon that chamber and upon all collegial circuit tribunals, but not upon the other chambers nor upon the Court *en banc*; and (3) that individual ministers and magistrates are legally obliged to conform to *jurisprudencia* in appropriate cases, regardless of their personal opinions about its validity, until the requisite extraordinary majority for interrupting or modifying it can be secured.

The first two of these conclusions are firmly established in practice; the third, however, has not met with much favor in the Court itself.[15]

Despite its obligatory character, *jurisprudencia* produces effects only partially equivalent to those resulting from the rule of stare decisis. In a purely technical sense, to be sure, neither *jurisprudencia* nor precedent, in the Anglo-American usage, is binding upon any governmental agencies except courts of law and quasi-judicial administrative bodies that have been subsumed within this functional category. As a matter of practice, however, precedent in common-law systems tends to determine the behavior of the executive and legislative branches of government in much the same manner as that of the judiciary itself. As a result, if the Supreme Court of the United States determines that a given law is unconstitutional the practical effect is normally indistinguishable from abrogation of the offending statute, although technically it is nothing of the sort. Administrative agencies refrain customarily from any further attempts at enforcement, and legislative bodies, although they may attempt to achieve the same ends by different means, at least endeavor to avoid repeating their earlier constitutional errors. Further litigation on the same point is necessary only in extraordinary cases and, if it occurs, the result is usually predetermined. Somewhat differently expressed, precedent in the Anglo-American sense, whatever the nature of its content, is normally effective *erga omnes* when established by the highest court within the jurisdiction. This result cannot be claimed for *jurisprudencia*, although there is apparently a tendency on the part of administrative agencies and legislative bodies to respect those theses whose content is confined strictly to technical statutory interpretation and that have no bearing on questions of policy. Even in the latter cases, however, no consistent pattern of compliance can be demonstrated.[16] In cases in which the unconstitutionality of laws has been established in *jurisprudencia*, neither the administration nor the appropriate legislative bodies have demon-

[15] See, for example, the argument set forth in *Vázquez López Ernesto*, 106 S. J. 150 (1950), against precisely this latter assumption.

[16] This conclusion has been arrived at by examining a substantial number of cases presenting questions presumably long settled by *jurisprudencia*.

strated any considerable inclination to conform unless such action has seemed advisable on policy grounds. Decisions of the latter type, needless to say, are likely to be based on criteria quite different from those that have guided the judiciary. By way of illustration, the Supreme Court long ago declared unconstitutional those sections of the 1944 Law of Professions (*Ley reglamentaria de los artículos 4 y 5 constitucionales, relativos al ejercicio de las profesiones en el Distrito y Territorios Federales*) that discriminate against aliens. Nonetheless, in practice these provisions of the law remain fully in force and are regularly executed.[17] When the executive branch chooses to ignore *jurisprudencia*, the only recourse available to persons adversely affected by this action is another *amparo* suit. This practice results necessarily in the multiplication of litigation and a decided inequality in applying the laws.

These limitations on the obligatory effect of *jurisprudencia* necessarily deprive judicial review, as practiced in Mexico, of the universality and authoritativeness that characterize the constitutional decisions rendered by the Supreme Court of the United States. It is difficult to see, however, how they could be removed without radical changes in the Constitution, in the Amparo Law, and in traditional civil law principles. To attribute the effect of statutory abrogation to a jurisprudential thesis that declares the unconstitutionality of a law, or an equivalent generality of effect to theses of any content, would clearly violate the fundamental constitutional rule (article 107, section II) that the *amparo* judgment be limited to the special case to which the complaint refers and must refrain from any general declaration about the law or act on which the complaint is based. The *jurisprudencia* provisions of article 107 can be considered as modifying this rule, and consequently, as giving generality to the judgments of the Supreme Court, only insofar as they restrict the free discretion of courts in reinterpreting well-settled points of law. In a more general sense, to attribute to the Mexican Supreme Court powers so indisputably legislative in character as those derived from the constitutional jurisdiction exercised

---

[17] See Suprema Corte, *Jurisprudencia de la Suprema Corte, thesis* 825, IV, 1504. For further illustration, see Palacios, *La Suprema Corte y las leyes*, p. 82.

by courts in the United States would be incompatible with civil law concepts of the proper, and distinct, roles of the legislative and judicial branches, and with the strict concept of separation of powers prevailing in Mexican constitutional theory.[18] As *amparo* is presently constituted, it must be concluded that the Supreme Court's ability to defend the Constitution is far more dependent upon the timeliness and persuasive force of its arguments than upon any powers derived from devices such as *jurisprudencia*.

The application of *jurisprudencia* in specific cases is governed by article 196 of the Amparo Law which states: "When the parties in the *amparo* suit invoke the *jurisprudencia* of the Court, or of the collegial circuit tribunals, they shall do so in writing, expressing the sense of the theses cited, and designating precisely the judgments that support them." This rule, on the surface, seems to be incompatible with the provisions of articles 192, 193, and 193 bis, since it suggests that *jurisprudencia* is binding upon the courts only in the event that the parties to litigation make proper reference to it. This ambiguity largely disappears, however, if the rules relating to *stricti juris* and the correction of defective complaints are applied. In cases governed by the former rule, it would be inappropriate for a court to apply *jurisprudencia* ex officio when to do so would amount to correcting a defect in the complaint. A hypothetical illustration may clarify the point. Let us assume that the Supreme Court has established *jurisprudencia* to the effect that orders appropriating property under the power of eminent domain may validly be executed only if the property owner has been given thirty days notice of intent, but that a governmental agency proceeds to take property with only fifteen days notice. An *amparo* suit contesting this action would fall within the administrative category and would be subject to the rule of *stricti juris*. If an injured party should base his case exclusively on the contention that the appropriation was illegal since it served no public purpose, the courts would have no alternative but to decide the issue on that ground. Our hypo-

---

[18] The stress in the final clause, above, should undoubtedly be placed on the word "theory," since domination by the executive effectively nullifies this principle in practice. It is of considerable utility to the courts, nonetheless, as a guide in avoiding policy clashes with the president.

thetical *jurisprudencia* is clearly relevant to the factual situation, and its violation would suffice to justify the grant of *amparo*, but it is totally irrelevant to the legal arguments (*conceptos de violación*) actually presented by the complainant. Should a court, under these circumstances, apply this *jurisprudencia* ex officio, its act would constitute an alteration of the *litis contestatio* to the prejudice of the other parties. On the other hand, when the correction of defective complaints is expressly permitted, including, it will be recalled, all instances in which the act complained of is based on laws declared unconstitutional in *jurisprudencia*, it seems proper to conclude that the courts not only may but should apply any *jurisprudencia* relevant to the complainant's case. This conclusion is admittedly somewhat speculative. It is based on the fact that the obligation expressed in articles 192, 193, and 193 bis of the Amparo Law is stated in flatly mandatory terms. Nonetheless, if the conclusion is true, it would constitute an exception to the usual rule that the correction of defective complaints, where appropriate, is a discretionary act. Paragraph 2, section II, article 107 of the Constitution provides additional evidence against the assumption made here. It states that the courts "may" correct defective complaints when the act complained of is based on laws declared unconstitutional in *jurisprudencia*. Thus far no fixed rule appears to have been formulated to govern practice on this point. Since it is never permissible to correct defects in pleadings other than those of the complainant, it must be concluded further that *jurisprudencia* should never be applied ex officio to the briefs presented by responsible authorities, injured third parties, and the Federal Public Ministry when the consequence of doing so would be to alter the *litis contestatio*. It is perfectly proper, however, for the courts to apply *jurisprudencia* ex officio whenever appropriate in evaluating the validity of the arguments presented by any of the parties to the suit.

These remarks indicate that, despite years of experience with the institution, both the Mexican bar and judiciary are in some confusion about precisely how the obligatory character of *jurisprudencia* can be made to conform with the consequences of *stricti juris*. The suggestions advanced here are, however, reasonably consistent both with practice and with the implications of the relevant provisions of the Constitution and of the Amparo Law.[19]

## The Interruption and Modification of Jurisprudencia

The interruption of a jurisprudential thesis, to employ the terminology of the Amparo Law, is analogous to repealing a statute, that is, the thesis is totally divested of its obligatory effect. *Jurisprudencia* established by the full Court is interrupted whenever that body pronounces a contradictory judgment supported by a majority of at least fourteen ministers. The requisite majority for overruling *jurisprudencia* established by the chambers is four, while in the collegial circuit tribunals unanimity is required. In conformity with the 1968 amendments, the reasons justifying the interruption of *jurisprudencia* should be stated and should be relevant to the justifications originally cited in support of the precedent in question. In any event, the overruling judgment itself does not acquire the status of *jurisprudencia* unless repeated five times in conformity with the dispositions of articles 192, 193, and 193 bis.[20]

The modification of a jurisprudential thesis, on the other hand, does not deprive it of its obligatory character but amends certain provisions of the thesis. Until these amendments take effect, the original text of the thesis remains in force. The procedures for modifying *jurisprudencia* are the same as those for establishing it originally.[21]

## The Resolution of Contradictions in Jurisprudencia

Since the Supreme Court chambers and the various collegial circuit tribunals are authorized to establish *jurisprudencia*, both in the proc-

[19] For an interesting discussion, essentially along the lines suggested here of the limitations imposed by the rule of stricti juris on applying *jurisprudencia*, see the introduction contributed by Minister Felipe Tena Ramírez to Castro, *La suplencia de la queja*, pp. 13–16.

[20] Amparo Law, article 194. The verb used here—*deber*—indicates that an incompatible judgment would interrupt *jurisprudencia* even if appropriate justifications are not given. *Jurisprudencia* may also be revoked by incompatible legislation, or, if it contains a direct interpretation of the Constitution, by constitutional amendment.

[21] Ibid., see articles 192, 193, and 193 bis.

ess of decreeing judgments that cannot be appealed, it is inevitable that they occasionally formulate theses containing contradictory interpretations of the same point of law. Indeed, because of the expanded jurisdictional competence of the collegial circuit tribunals as of the 1968 amendments, such contradictions can be expected to occur with considerable frequency. To resolve this problem, in the event that the contradiction arises within the Supreme Court itself, article 195 of the Amparo Law provides:

> When the chambers of the Supreme Court of Justice sustain contradictory theses in the *amparo* suits falling within their jurisdiction, this fact may be denounced before the Court by any of the chambers, by the attorney general, or by any of the parties to the suits in which the theses were established. The Supreme Court, *en banc*, will then decide which thesis should prevail. When the denunciation has been made by someone other than the attorney general, the opinion of the latter, either directly or through his authorized representative, should be secured.
>
> The resolution of such contradictions shall not affect the concrete juridical situations deriving from judgments in the suits in which the theses were established.

Similarly, article 195 bis directs that contradictory theses sustained by the collegial circuit tribunals may be denounced before the appropriate chamber by any minister of the Supreme Court, by the attorney general, by a collegial tribunal, or by the parties to the cases in which the theses were established. As in the case of contradictions arising within the chambers of the Supreme Court, when the denunciation has been made by someone other than the attorney general, his opinion on the matter must nonetheless be secured. The decisions in these cases are limited to establishing *jurisprudencia* and cannot in any way modify the content of the original judgments. Article 195 bis provides further that the decision of a Supreme Court chamber may be submitted for further consideration by the same chamber in the event that a collegial circuit tribunal concludes, in a concrete case, that there are overwhelming reasons for abrogating the *jurisprudencia* in question.

The texts of articles 195 and 195 bis, as amended in 1968, contain ambiguities of considerable importance. Neither article contains any directive about the majorities required in the full Court or in its chambers for resolving jurisprudential contradictions nor provides any indication of the status of the contested *jurisprudencia* in the event that no majority can be obtained. Unfortunately, the previous text of article 195 also casts no light on these questions. Given the rules about the initial establishment and subsequent modification of *jurisprudencia*, the probable intent of the law is to require the same majorities for resolving contradictions. If so, however, it remains unclear whether the absence of the requisite majority should have the effect of abrogating the contradictory theses or leaving them in equal force. On practical grounds, a simple majority in these cases would seem in every way preferable, but the authoritative resolution of these questions must wait until the amended statute is judicially implemented. Past practice indicates the simple majority interpretation will be selected.

The phrasing of section XIII, article 107 of the Constitution and of the corresponding provisions of articles 195 and 195 bis of the Amparo Law, also raises these further questions: (1) may the full Court resolve contradictory opinions expressed by its chambers and, hence, establish *jurisprudencia*, when these opinions represent simple precedents, or is it authorized to act only when two or more of its chambers have actually established contradictory *jurisprudencia*; and (2) may the full Court, or the appropriate chamber, modify or combine elements of the contradictory opinions presented for resolution, or must they confine themselves to selecting, verbatim, one of these opinions? Concerning the first, it may be noted that section XIII, and the corresponding provisions of the statute, refer to contradictory *tésis*, translated here as thesis or opinion. The term *tésis* need not refer to *jurisprudencia* and, as employed in the virtually identical phrasing used in the 1950–1951 amendments, could not do so in the paragraph authorizing the Supreme Court chambers to resolve the contradictory *tésis* of the collegial circuit tribunals, since these courts were not then authorized to formulate obligatory precedents. In the absence of clarification in the present text, there is a strong implication that the Supreme Court *en banc* may convert the opinions expressed by its chambers into *jurisprudencia*, whether or not these have previously achieved that status. Furthermore, the chambers were authorized under the previous terms of the Constitution and of the Amparo Law to transform the opinions of the collegial circuit tribunals into *jurisprudencia*, which suggests that they retain this power under the unmodified terms of the present statute and that the powers of the full Court with respect to its own constituent parts should be at least as extensive. The same conclusion is suggested by the basic motivation for creating this procedure, namely, to secure uniformity in interpreting and applying the laws.

On the second question, article 195 and 195 bis of the 1950–1951 version of the Amparo Law provided expressly that the *jurisprudencia* established in this process by the chambers and by the full Court might be modified. However, neither article stated whether this could be done in the act of resolving contradictory opinions or only subsequently, in conformity with the terms of article 194, that is, in the same manner as normally required for initially establishing *jurisprudencia*. Since the modification of *jurisprudencia* by the latter process is always permissible, it seems unreasonably restrictive of the discretion of the full Court and of its chambers to hold that they should be bound initially to a simple selection between fixed alternatives. Insofar as it has been possible to ascertain, this has been the view generally entertained in the Court. The present text of articles 195 and 195 bis deletes the former reference to modifying *jurisprudencia*, but the meaning, if any, of this deletion is impossible to determine from the statute itself. Consequently, until the Court determines otherwise, this interpretation retains its validity.

The continued existence of such ambiguities in the field of *jurisprudencia* should be attributed not so much to the problems of statutory drafting as to the inherent difficulty of grafting even a modified version of stare decisis upon the body of a civil law system.

*Chapter 10*

# Summary And Conclusions

⌒⌒⌒⌒⌒

$A$SIDE FROM THE rarely employed and dubiously established jurisdictional powers conferred by articles 105 and 133 of the present Constitution, whereby the Supreme Court has occasionally heard cases in which the Federation and a state have directly contested a constitutional question, the practice of judicial review in Mexico is entirely dependent upon the possibilities afforded by the *amparo* suit. During the 113 years which have elapsed since it was incorporated in article 102 of the Constitution of 1857, *amparo* has evolved into a highly complex and, in some respects, peculiarly Mexican institution performing three distinct functions: (1) the defense of the civil liberties enumerated in the first twenty-nine articles of the Constitution; (2) the determination of the constitutionality of federal and state legislation; and (3) cassation. From the procedural point of view the first of these is fundamental, since no *amparo* suit is admissible unless the complainant, a real or artificial private person or a governmental agency acting as the subject of private law, alleges that individual rights have been violated by some act of a public authority. The range of constitutional issues subject to judicial determination is dependent, consequently, upon the manner in which these rights are interpreted. It is true that sections II and III of article 103 of the Constitution also direct that the federal courts shall decide controversies arising from laws or acts of the federal government which violate States' rights and vice versa. These provisions suggest that *amparo* should also be available to these governmental entities, in their own right, in cases involving the federal distribution of powers. The Supreme Court, however, has held consistently that suits alleging the violation of sections II and III may only be initiated by private persons who can demonstrate that the act complained of has also resulted in the violation of an individual guarantee.

In a purely legal sense, the adequacy of *amparo* as an instrument of general constitutional defense has been determined by the interpretation of the due process clause in article 14 and the "competent authority" and "legal basis and justification" provisions of article 16 of the Constitution. These guarantees have been construed by the Supreme Court as protecting individual complainants from the injurious consequences of unconstitutional laws and arbitrary or legally unfounded actions of administrative and judicial authorities. In this way it has been possible to extend the protective benefits of *amparo* to all those constitutional provisions whose violation is capable of producing an individual injury, legally recognized as such, excepting, of course, cases in which the Constitution explicitly or tacitly prohibits recourse to that remedy. As a result, the constitutional jurisdiction potentially available to the Mexican Supreme Court is similar in scope to that exercised by the Supreme Court of the United States.

The most explicitly stated, although not necessarily the most important, constitutional prohibitions on the use of *amparo* are to be found in articles 3, 27, 33, 60, and 111, dealing, respectively, with private education, the expropriation of land for the creation of *ejidos*, the expulsion of undesirable aliens, the elections and qualifications of members of Congress, and the impeachment process.

More far-reaching in their restrictive potentialities are the provisions of articles 29 and 135. The first of these, which provides for the suspension of individual guarantees during periods of national emergency, could, for the duration of any such emergency, completely nullify the *amparo* jurisdiction. Fortunately, article 29 has been invoked only once, and on that occasion, the period of Mexico's participation in World War II, the limitations imposed were relatively minor. Barring war or major political disorder, it is not probable that any administration would find it either necessary or politically feasible to exploit the full range of restrictive possibilities inherent in this article.

The amending clause in article 135 has been used both to reverse particular constitutional interpretations adopted by the Supreme Court and to limit indirectly the effective scope of judicial independence by manipulating the provisions on tenure and removals. Recourse to this expedient for checking the judiciary, however, has thus far been very infrequent. This is surprising, perhaps, when it is remembered that the dominant position of the executive in the Mexican political system makes it extraordinarily easy to amend the Constitution. Examination of the collected *jurisprudencia* indicates that this restraint must be attributed more to the fact that the Supreme Court has consistently refrained from decisions contradicting the position taken by the administration on questions of major policy significance than to any inclination on the part of the latter to be guided by judicial wisdom. As long as it continues to pursue this policy, it is improbable that the Court's jurisdiction or essential independence will be significantly limited by constitutional amendment. At the same time, the ready availability of this check assists in preventing judicial excursions into the field of policy formation.

The Supreme Court has itself further reduced the constitutional scope of its jurisdiction by denying the admissibility of *amparo* suits that contest the violation of political rights. Such rights are those which relate to the exercise of the suffrage and to the holding of elective or appointive public office. The reasoning employed in reaching this conclusion is extremely ambiguous and is logically incompatible with interpretations of articles 14 and 16 which hold that these guarantees incorporate constitutional provisions not included in the first twenty-nine articles. Because of the political monopoly enjoyed by the governing Party of the Institutional Revolution (PRI), it must be conceded, however, that the Court's position is not only expedient but, from a practical point of view, unavoidable. Intervention in this area would immediately involve the judiciary in a contest it could not possibly win and from which it would necessarily retire with diminished prestige.

Another, and legally distinct, limitation on the effective performance of the constitutional defense function derives from the nature of the *amparo* judgment. When the Supreme Court of the United States determines that a given law is unconstitutional, as a result of custom and the operation of the rule of stare decisis, the practical effect is normally indistinguishable from the abrogation of the offending statute. In Mexico, however, it is generally assumed, both on the basis of constitutional theory and postulates common to civil law systems, that the enactment and repeal of laws is an exclusively legislative function. This assumption is clearly reflected in section II of article 107 of the Constitution, which directs that "the judgment [in *amparo*] shall always be such that it affects only private individuals, being limited to affording them redress and protection in the special case to which the complaint refers, without making any general declaration about the law or act on which the complaint is based." As a result, the *amparo* judgment can never have the effect of abrogating a law. To secure the benefits deriving from a declaration of unconstitutionality, each and every person adversely affected by the law must individually seek the protection of a separate *amparo* judgment. The fact that the Supreme Court can establish obligatory precedents (*jurisprudencia*) by five consecutive repetitions of the same opinion modifies this situation only insofar as such precedents restrict the free discretion of the courts in reinterpreting the points of law thus settled. Since *jurisprudencia* is legally binding only upon courts of law and military, administrative, and labor tribunals, it may be, and very frequently is, ignored by administrative agencies and legislative bodies. Indeed, given Mexican assumptions about the nature of separation of powers—and because of the usual insistence upon ritual compliance—it is necessary to conclude that administrative agencies could not validly refrain from executing laws on the basis of *jurisprudencia* alone. Within the Mexican context, the proper procedure, assuming that the legislature does not act on its own initiative, would be a presidential request for repeal of statutes declared unconstitutional in *jurisprudencia*. In practice, this form of compliance is sometimes forthcoming, but not on any consistent basis. The inevitable result is the multiplication of litigation and inequality in applying the laws.

The scope and consistency of the *amparo* judgment is further limited by applying the rule of *stricti juris* in civil and administrative *amparo* suits, and in those labor *amparos* in which the complainant is the employer. Where applicable, this rule requires the courts to confine themselves strictly to the legal arguments (*conceptos de violación*) presented by the complainant and has the effect of nullifying the usual procedural rule that "the judge knows the law." The effects of *stricti juris* are somewhat modified by constitutional provisions authorizing defective complaints in any type of *amparo* suit to be corrected when the act complained of is based on a law declared unconstitutional in *jurisprudencia*. This, however, is of no benefit to litigants in those cases in which *jurisprudencia* has not yet been established or in which the content of relevant *jurisprudencia* is concerned with subjects other than declarations of statutory unconstitutionality.

In a much more general sense, the Supreme Court's willingness to decide constitutional questions of broad policy significance is restricted by the civil law tradition within which it operates. The strict distinction between the legislative and judicial functions postulated by the civil law necessarily entails a conception of the judicial role that would exclude decisions of a manifestly legislative character.

These technical and theoretical limitations on the effectiveness of *amparo* as an instrument of constitutional defense cannot entirely account for the failure of the Mexican Supreme Court to contribute significantly to resolving such fundamental constitutional issues as the organization, distribution, and exercise of governmental power. For an explanation of this, it is necessary to include political factors, although it should be noted that nothing so crude as direct attempts to influence the judgment in particular cases is meant. The federal judiciary, at least, seems to have been happily free of this sort of pressure. In the United States, the pluralistic organization of power virtually guarantees that any position taken by the Supreme Court will receive support from a public sufficiently possessed of political influence to command the respect of its opponents. As a result, the Court can rarely be suppressed without arousing politically unprofitable opposition, and its opinions must usually be attacked, if at all, indirectly. In Mexico, on the other hand, the politically conscious and active population is small and is mainly organized within a single political party, the PRI, and various quasi-official pressure groups. Judicial decisions conspicuously incompatible with the policy positions supported by the PRI and its allied major interest groups would have no independent power base to sustain them and could not maintain themselves. The Amparo and Judiciary laws amendments promulgated in 1958 are a pertinent illustration. Although, technically speaking, the Court's jurisdiction was left unimpaired by transferring appeals that contested the constitutionality of a law from the chambers to the full Court, the Administrative Chamber's growing tendency to subject fiscal legislation to a strict constitutional scrutiny was effectively reversed. Finally, the possibility of judicial disaffection is certainly diminished by the fact that no one is likely to be elevated to the bench who is not a member in good standing of the PRI organization or considered by it to be reliable. If, despite this, a maverick should nonetheless appear, the president's domination of the Congress would assure easy removal by impeachment or, much more likely, a timely decision to resign.

In conformity with the considerations advanced above, it is necessary to conclude (1) that the *amparo* suit, as an instrument for the defense of the constitution, is technically inferior to the system of judicial review evolved in the United States, both in its constitutional scope and the practical effect of its judgments; and (2) that under current and foreseeable future conditions, political rather than judicial agencies will continue to control the interpretation of the Constitution whenever significant issues of policy are involved. At present, as in the past, *amparo* is most valuable and effective as a defense of individual liberty and in the performance of the cassation function.

Even if considered desirable, it would not be politically practicable to propose modifications in *amparo* that would convert that institution into an equivalent of judicial review as practiced in the United States. Within the existing sphere of judicial competence, however, it is possible to suggest amendments that, if carried into effect, would increase the efficiency of the Supreme Court's operations and the equity of *amparo* judgments generally. These may be briefly summarized as follows: (1) Because of the general opposition to creating a separate court of cassation, it seems advisable to transfer this function entirely to the collegial circuit tribunals. This would reduce substantially the work load of the Supreme Court and permit it to devote a more adequate amount of time to considering cases contesting the constitutionality of laws. However, in order to preserve the principle of judicial hierarchy, assure reasonable uniformity in statutory interpretation, and provide for occasional cases that may present important constitutional issues, the Supreme Court should be granted a discretionary review jurisdiction comparable to that provided in the United States by the writ of certiorari. (2). For the same reasons, the Supreme Court should be granted a similar discretionary power to review cases now exclusively within the jurisdiction of the collegial circuit tribunals. (3). If the foregoing prove impracticable or are insufficient to reduce the Court's work load to manageable proportions, the 1958 amendments to the Amparo and Judiciary laws, insofar as still applicable, should be repealed and jurisdiction to hear cases contesting the constitutionality of laws returned entirely to the chambers. (4). The effects of the *stricti juris* rule should be mitigated both in the interests of equity and uniform statutory interpretation. In the performance of the cassation function there is reason for confining the attention of the courts to the strict terms of the relevant law but to restrict them, as is done in *amparo*, to evaluating the arguments presented by the parties serves no useful, equitable, or reasonable purpose. In administrative *amparo*, where few if any of the arguments usually cited in favor of the rule seem genuinely relevant, it would be desirable to dispense with it altogether and permit the correction of defective complaints.

# BIBLIOGRAPHY

*Public Documents*

Asociación Nacional de Funcionarios Judiciales. *Boletín de información judicial.* Monthly Mexico City, 1946–.

Cámara de Diputados. *Constitución política de los Estados Unidos Mexicanos con sus adiciones y reformas y reglamento del Congreso general. Texto vigente.* Mexico City: Imprenta de la Cámara de Diputados, 1933.

———. *Constitución política de los Estados Unidos Mexicanos con sus adiciones y reformas.* Mexico City: Imprenta de la Cámara de Diputados, 1957.

———. *Decreto constitucional para la libertad de la América Mexicana sancionado en Apatzingán a 22 de octubre de 1814.* Mexico City: Imprenta de la Cámara Diputados, 1912.

———. *Diario de los debates de la Cámara de Diputados del Congreso de los Estados Unidos Mexicanos.* XXXII Legislatura, Año II, vol. II, Período Ordinario, 1928. XXXVI Legislatura, vol. I, no. 11; vol. II, no. 16; and no. 23, 1934. XLI Legislatura, vol. I, no. 18, 1950. Mexico City.

———. *Diario de los debates del Congreso Constituyente.* Edited by Fernando Romero García. 2 vols. Mexico City: Cámara de Diputados, 1917.

———. *Iniciativas, dictámenes de comisiones del Senado de la república, discusiones y opiniones relativos a reformas a la constitución política de los Estados Unidos Mexicanos en la organización del poder judicial federal y en materia de amparo. Material reunido y editado por la comisión de estudios legislativos de la XLIV legislatura.* Mexico City: 1960.

Cámara de Senadores. *Diario de los debates de la Cámara de Senadores del Congreso de los Estados Unidos Mexicanos.* XXVII Legislatura, Año I, Período Extraordinario, vol. 1. Mexico City: 1917.

Comisión sobre Organización de un Supremo Poder Conservador. *Proyecto de la segunda ley constitucional presentado al Congreso general en la sesión de 4 de diciembre de 1835 por la Comisión respectiva sobre organización de un supremo poder conservador.* Mexico City: Impreso por J. M. Fernández de Lara, 1835.

Congreso Constituyente, 1842. *Proyecto de constitución que presenta al soberano Congreso constituyente la mayoría de su Comisión especial, y voto particular de minoría.* Mexico City: I. Cumplido, 1842.

Congreso Constituyente, 1846–1847. *Dictámen de la mayoría de la Comisión de Constitución, y voto particular de uno de sus individuos. Presentados al Congreso constituyente en la sesión de 5 de abril de 1847.* Mexico City: I. Cumplido, 1847.

Dublán, Manuel, et al. *Legislación mexicana o colección completa de las disposiciones legislativas expedidas desde la independencia de la república. Edición oficial.* 50 vols. Mexico City: 1876–1912.

Estados Unidos Mexicanos. *Acta constitutiva de la federación mexicana.* Mexico City: Imprenta del Supremo Gobierno, 1824.

——. *Constitución federal de los Estados Unidos Mexicanos, sancionada y jurada por el Congreso general constituyente el día 5 de febrero de 1857, adicionada por el 7° Congreso constitucional el 25 de septiembre y 4 de octubre de 1873 y el 6 de noviembre de 1874, juntamente con las leyes orgánicas expedidas hasta hoy.* Mexico City: Imprenta del Gobierno, 1875.

——. *Constitución de los Estados Unidos Mexicanos expedida por el Congreso general constituyente el día 5 de febrero de 1857, con sus adiciones y reformas, leyes orgánicas y reglamentarias, texto vigente de la constitución.* Mexico City: Imprenta del Gobierno Federal, 1905.

——. *Constitución federal de los Estados Unidos Mexicanos sancionada por el Congreso general constituyente de 4 de octubre de 1824.* Mexico City: Imprenta del Supremo Gobierno, 1824.

——. *Diario oficial, órgano del gobierno constitucional de los Estados Unidos Mexicanos.* Vol. 13, nos. 44, 46, 47. Mexico City: 1919.

——. *Ley reglamentaria de los artículos 103 y 104 de la Constitución federal.* Mexico City: Imprenta del Diario Oficial, 1922.

Junta de Administración y Vigilancia de la Propiedad Extranjera. *Legislación de emergencia relativa a propiedades y negocios del enemigo.* Mexico City, 1943.

Junta Nacional Legislativa. *Proyecto de bases de organización para la República Mexicana, presentado a la h. junta nacional legislativa por la Comisión nombrada al efecto.* Mexico City: Imprenta del Aguila, 1843.

Ministerio de Gobernación. *Informes y manifiestos de los poderes ejecu-*

*tivos y legislativos de 1821 a 1904.* Mexico City: Imprenta del Gobierno Federal, 1905.

Ministerio de Justicia. *Exposición de motivos de las reformas hechas al código federal de procedimientos civiles.* Mexico City: Imprenta de A. Enríquez, 1909.

Ministerio de Relaciones Exteriores y Gobernación. *Bases de organización política de la República Mexicana.* Mexico City, 1843.

Montiel y Duarte, Isidro Antonio. *Derecho público mexicano, compilación que contiene importantes documentos relativos a la independencia, la Constitución de Apatzingán, el Plan de Iguala, Tratados de Córdoba, la Acta de Independencia, cuestiones constitucionales tratadas por el primer Congreso Constituyente, la Acta Constitutiva de los Estados Unidos Mexicanos, la Constitución de 1824, las Leyes Constitucionales de 1836, las Bases Orgánicas, la Acta de Reformas, la Constitución de 1857, y la dicusión de estas constituciones.* 4 vols. Mexico City: Imprenta del Gobierno Federal, en Palacio, 1871–1882.

Pan American Union. *Constitution of the United Mexican States, 1917.* Washington, D.C.: Legal Division, Department of International Law, 1957.

Secretaría de Estado y del Despacho de Justicia e Instrucción Pública. *Código de procedimientos federales, expedido en uso de la autorización que concedió al ejecutivo de ley de 2 de junio de 1892.* Mexico City: Tiprografía de la Oficina Impresora del Timbre, 1898.

Secretaría de Gobernación. *Informe leido por el C. Primer Jefe del Ejercito Constitucionalista encargado del poder ejecutivo de la unión, ante el Congreso Constituyente de Querétaro el 1 de diciembre de 1916, y proyecto de reformas a la Constitución Política de 1857.* Mexico City: Imprenta de la Secretaría de Gobernación, 1916.

―――. Manuel Avila Camacho. *Informe que rinde al h. Congreso de la Unión, para pedir la declaración del estado de guerra con los paises del Eje, la suspensión de algunas de las garantías individuales y el otorgamiento de facultades extraordinarios.* Mexico City: Secretaría de Gobernación, Dirección General de Información, 1942.

Secretaría de Hacienda. *Proyecto de ley de amparo que presente el ejecutivo, para su estudio, a la h. Cámara de Senadores, por conducta del subsecretario de estado, encargado del Despacho del Interior: Dictámen acerca del mismo asunto que presentan las comisiones unidas 1 de puntos constitucionales y 2 de justicia, con algunas modificaciones a la ley reglamentaria de los artículos 103 y 104 de la Constitución federal.*

Mexico City: Tipografía de la Oficina Impresora de la Secretaría de Hacienda, 1917.

Secretaría de Justicia. *Iniciativa que por la Secretaría de Justicia e Instrucción Pública dirige el ejecutivo al Congreso de la Unión sobre la reforma de la ley de 20 de enero de 1869 orgánica de los artículos 101 y 102 de la Constitución federal.* Mexico City: Imprenta del Gobierno, 1877.

Soberana Junta Provisional Gubernativa. *Colección de órdenes y decretos de la Soberana Junta Provisional Gubernativa, y soberanos Congresos generales de la nación mexicana. 1821–1837.* Vols. 7, 8. Mexico City: Imprenta de Galvan a cargo de M. Arévalo, 1829–1840.

Suprema Corte de Justicia. *Jurisprudencia definida de la Suprema Corte de Justicia en sus fallos pronunciados del 1 de junio de 1917 al 3 de septiembre de 1948: Apéndice al tomo XCVII del semanario judicial.* Mexico City: Imprenta de Murgía, 1949.

———. *Homenaje de la Suprema Corte de Justicia de la Nación, en nombre del poder judicial de la federación al Código de 1857 y a sus autores, los ilustres constituyentes.* Mexico City: Imprenta de Murguía, 1957.

———. *Informe rendido a la Suprema Corte de Justicia de la Nación por su presidente.* Published annually. Mexico City: Imprenta de Murguía, 1918–.

———. *Jurisprudencia definida de la Suprema Corte, apéndice al tomo LXXVI.* Mexico City, 1944.

———. *Jurisprudencia de la Suprema Corte de Justicia en los fallos pronunciados en los años de 1917 a 1954, apéndice al semanario judicial de la federación.* 4 vols. Mexico City: Imprenta de Murguía, 1955.

———. *El problema del rezago de juicios de amparo en materia civil.* Mexico City: 1946.

———. *Semanario Judicial de la Federación, fundado por la ley de 8 de diciembre de 1870.* Fifth Series. Mexico City: 1918–1956.

———. *Semanario judicial de la federación, fundado por la ley de 8 de diciembre de 1870.* Sixth Series. Mexico City: 1957–.

*Books*

Aguilar y Maya, José. *Breve reseña de la legislación de emergencia.* Mexico City, 1944.

Andrade, Manuel, ed. *Constitución política Mexicana, con reformas y adiciones al día.* Loose-leaf. Mexico City: Editorial Información Aduanera de México, 1956.

Azuela, Mariano. "Lagunas, errores y anacronismos, de la legislación de amparo." *Problemas jurídicos y sociales de México, anuario 1953*, pp. 13–26. Mexico City: Editorial Jus, 1955.

Black, Henry Campbell. *Black's Law Dictionary*. 4th ed. St. Paul: West Publishing Co., 1951.

Bolaños Cacho, Miguel. *Estudios jurídicos*. Mexico City: Imprenta "Benito Juárez," 1907.

———. *Los derechos del hombre: Integridad personal y real*. Mexico City: A. Carranza e hijos, 1909.

Botella Asensi, Juan. *La expropriación en el derecho mexicano: El Caso del petróleo*. Mexico City: Editorial Moderna, 1941.

Bremauntz, Alberto. *Por una justicia al servicio del pueblo*. Mexico City: Editorial "Casa de Michoacán," 1955.

Buenrostro, Felipe. *Historia del segundo congreso constitucional de la República Mexicana, que funcionó en los años 1861, 62 y 63*. Mexico City: Imprenta Políglota, 1874.

Burgoa, Ignacio. *El amparo en materia agraria*. Mexico City: Editorial Porrua, S.A., 1964.

———. *Dos estudios jurídicos, algunas consideraciones sobre el artículo 28 constitucional. Las normas de órden público y el intéres social*. Mexico City: Editorial Porrua, S.A., 1953.

———. *Las garantías individuales*. 2nd ed. Mexico City: Editorial Porrua, S.A., 1954.

———. *El juicio de amparo*. 4th ed. Mexico City: Editorial Porrua, S.A., 1957.

———. *La legislación de emergencia y el juicio de amparo*. Mexico City: Editorial Hispano-Mexicana, 1945.

———. "Las normas de órden público y el interés social. Su referencia especial a la suspensión del acto reclamado en el juicio de amparo." *Problemas jurídicos de México*, pp. 19–46. Mexico City: Editorial Jus, 1953.

———. *Reformas a la ordenación positiva vigente del amparo, proyecto de modificaciones a la Constitución federal, a la ley de amparo y a la ley orgánica del poder judicial de la federación*. Mexico City: Unión Gráfica, 1958.

Campillo Camarillo, Aurelio. *Tratado elemental de derecho constitucional mexicano: Compilación de la novísima jurisprudencia de la Suprema Corte de Justicia de la Nación, adicionada con los estudios que, acerca de nuestras dos últimas constituciones federales, han escrito ilustres jurisconsultos mexicanos. También contiene la doctrina de autores extranjeros, con especialidad americanos.* Jalapa, Veracruz: Tipografía "La Económica," 1928.

Carrillo, Antonio, and Ezequiel Burguete, eds. *Ley orgánica del poder judicial de la federación. Ley reglamentaria del artículo 102 constitucional.* Mexico City: Editorial Porrua, S.A., 1934.

Carrillo Flores, Antonio. *La defensa jurídica de los particulares frente a la administración en México.* Mexico City: Editorial Porrua, S.A., 1939.

Caso, Angel. *Derecho agrario.* Mexico City: Editorial Porrua, S.A., 1950.

Castillo Negrete, Gustavo A. del. "Disquisiciones sobre el interés jurídico en el juicio de amparo." *Problemas jurídicos de México,* pp. 63–75. Mexico City: Asociación Nacional de Funcionarios Judiciales, Editorial Jus, 1953.

Castillo Velasco, José María del. *Apuntamientos para el estudio del derecho constitucional mexicano.* Mexico City: Imprenta del Gobierno, 1871.

Castro, Juventino A. *La suplencia de la queja deficiente en el juicio de amparo.* Mexico City: Editorial Jus, 1953.

Chávez Hoyhoe, Salvador. *Prontuario de ejecutorias de la Suprema Corte de Justicia de la Nación.* 12 vols. Mexico City: 1935–1956.

Clagett, Helen L. *The Administration of Justice in Latin America.* New York: Oceana Publications, 1952.

*Código agrario.* 4th ed. Mexico City: Editorial Porrua, S.A., 1959.

*Código de procedimientos civiles para el Distrito Federal y Territorios.* 2nd ed. Mexico City: Editorial Porrua, S.A., 1956.

Couto, Ricardo. *Tratado teórico-práctico de la suspensión en el amparo, con un estudio sobre la suspensión con efectos de amparo provisional.* 2nd ed. Mexico City: Editorial Porrua, S.A., 1957.

Cueva, Mario de la. "El constitucionalismo mexicano." In *El constitucionalismo a mediados del siglo XIX.* 2 vols. Mexico City: Facultad de Derecho, 1957.

Eder, Phanor J. *A Comparative Study of Anglo-American and Latin American Law.* New York: New York University Press, 1950.

Esquivel Obregón, Toríbio. *Apúntes para la historia del derecho en México.* Mexico City: Publicidad y Ediciones, 1943.

———. *La constitución de Nueva España y la primera del México independiente.* Mexico City: Imprenta M. León Sánchez, 1925.

*Evolución del derecho mexicano, 1912–1942.* Series B, vol. 6. Mexico City: Editorial Jus, Escuela Libre de Derecho. n.d.

Fabila Montes de Oca, Manuel. *Cinco siglos de legislación agraria, 1493–1940.* Mexico City: Banco Nacional de Crédito Agrícola, 1941.

Farrera, Agustín. *Jurisprudencia de la Suprema Corte de Justicia.* Mexico City: Publicaciones Farrera, 1946.

Fix Zamudio, Héctor. *Estudio sobre la jurisdicción constitucional mexicana.* Mexico City: Imprenta Universitaria, 1961. (Part of double volume including Mauro Cappelletti, *La jurisdicción constitucional de la libertad.* Héctor Fix Zamudio, trans.).

Fraga, Gabino. *Derecho administrativo.* 6th ed. Mexico City: Editorial Porrua, S.A., 1955.

Gaither, Roscoe Bradley. *Expropriation in Mexico: The Facts and the Law.* New York: W. Morrow & Co., 1940.

Gamboa, José María. *Cuestiones constitucionales: Prescripción de la acción de queja en juicios de garantías, Libertad y soberanía de los tribunales locales.* Mexico City: 1893.

Garza, Servando J. *Las garantías constitucionales en el derecho tributario mexicano.* Mexico City: Editorial Cultura, 1949.

Gaxiola, F. Jorge. *Mariano Otero: Creador del juicio de amparo.* Mexico City: Editorial Cultura, 1937.

Gumpel, Henry J., and Hugo B. Margain. *Taxation in Mexico.* Boston: Little Brown & Co., 1957.

Iglesias, José María. *Estudio constitucional sobre facultades de la Corte de Justicia.* Mexico City: Imprenta de Díaz de León y White, 1874.

Información Aduanera de México. *Nueva ley de amparo orgánica de los artículos 103 y 107 de la Constitución Federal,* and *Ley orgánica del poder judicial de la Federación.* Mexico City, 1956.

Kelsen, Hans. *General Theory of Law and State.* Translated by Anders Wedberg. Cambridge: Harvard University Press, 1945.

Kunz, Josef L. *Latin American Philosophy of Law in the Twentieth Century.* New York: Inter-American Law Institute, 1950.

Lanz Duret, Miguel. *Derecho constitucional mexicano y consideraciones sobre la realidad política de nuestro régimen.* 4th ed. Mexico City: Imprentas L. D., S.A., 1947.

León Orantes, Romeo. *El juicio de amparo.* 3rd ed. Mexico City: Editorial José M. Cajica, 1957.

*Ley orgánica de los artículos 101 y 102 de la Constitución federal de 5 de febrero de 1857.* Orizaba: Tipografía del Hospicio, 1883.

López Rosado, Felipe, ed. *El régimen constitucional mexicano*. Mexico City: Editorial Porrua, S.A., 1955.

Lozano, José María. *Tratado de los derechos del hombre: Estudio del derecho constitucional patrio en lo relativo a los derechos del hombre, conforme a la Constitución de 1857 y a la ley orgánica de amparo de garantías de 20 de enero de 1869*. Mexico City: Imprenta de Dublan y Cía, 1876.

Martínez Báez, Antonio, et al. *La constitución de 1917 y la economía mexicana: Cursos de invierno, 1957*. Mexico City: Universidad Nacional Autónoma de México, 1958.

Mejía, Miguel. *Errores constitucionales: Las arbitrariedades judiciales y los juicios de amparo*. Mexico City: Tipografía de "La Epoca," 1886.

Minguijón y Adrián, Salvador. *Historia del derecho español*. 4th ed. Barcelona: Editorial Labor, 1953.

Montiel y Duarte, Isidro Antonio. *Compilación de apreciaciones, opiniones y doctrinas de publicistas mexicanas tomadas de iniciativas, dictámenes, proyectos de constitución de 1840 y 1842 y de constituciones anteriores a la de 1857*. Mexico City: Imprenta de I. Paz, 1891.

———. *Estudio constitucional sobre la soberanía de los juicios de amparo*. Mexico City: Imprenta de Díaz de León y White, 1874.

———. *Estudio sobre garantías individuales*. Mexico City: Imprenta del Gobierno, 1873.

Moreno Cora, Silvestre. *Tratado del juicio de amparo conforme a las sentencias de los tribunales federales*. Mexico City: Tipografía de J. Aguilar Vera y Cía., 1902.

Muñoz, Luis. *Comentarios a la ley de amparo: Antecedentes, derecho comparado, concordancias, legis-conexa, jurisprudencia, índice y prontuario*. Mexico City: Ediciones Lex, 1952.

Olea y Leyva, Teófilo. "Genealogía jurídica de la casación y el amparo mexicana en materia penal." In *Problemas jurídicos y sociales de México; Anuario 1953*, pp. 41–90. Mexico City: Editorial Jus, 1955.

Palacios, J. Ramón. "Caducidad y sobreseimiento." In *Problemas jurídicos de México*, pp. 77–90. Mexico City: Editorial Jus, 1953.

———. *La Suprema Corte y las leyes inconstitucionales*. Mexico City: Ediciones Botas, 1962.

Pallares, Eduardo. *Diccionario de derecho procesal civil*. 2nd ed. Mexico City: Editorial Porrua, S.A., 1956.

Pérez Gallardo, Basilio. *Opiniones de los constituyentes y del Sr. Lic. D. José María Iglesias, redactor del Siglo XIX en 1856 sobre los artículos*

*16 y 101 de la constitución.* Mexico City: Imprenta de Díaz de León y White, 1874.

Pina, Rafael de, and José Castillo Larrañaga, eds. *Instituciones de derecho procesal civil.* 3rd ed. Mexico City: Editorial Porrua, S.A., 1954.

*Problemas jurídicos y sociales de Mexico.* Mexico City: Editorial Jus, 1955.

Rabasa, Emilio. *El artículo 14,* and *El juicio constitucional: orígenes, teoría, y extensión.* 2nd ed. Mexico City: Editorial Porrua, S.A., 1955. [Double volume.]

————. *La constitución y la dictadura; Estudio sobre la organización política de México.* Mexico City: Tipografía de Revista de Revistas, 1912.

Rabasa, Oscar. *El derecho angloamericano; Estudio expositivo y comparado del "Common Law."* Mexico City: Fondo de Cultura Económica, 1944.

Reyes, Rodolfo. *La defensa constitucional; Recursos de inconstitucionalidad y amparo.* Madrid: Espasa-Calpe, S.A., 1934.

Ripa, Juan Francisco la. *Segunda ilustración a los quatro procesos forales de Aragón: Orden de proceder en ellos según el estilo moderno, y reglas para decidir conforme a la naturaleza de cada uno.* Zaragoza, 1772.

Rojas, Isidro, and Francisco Pascual García. *El amparo y sus reformas.* Mexico City: Tipografía de la Cía. Editorial Católica, 1907.

Ruíz Sandoval, Manuel. *Manual de procedimientos en el juicio de amparo.* 2nd ed. Mexico City: Oficina tipografía de la secretaría de fomento, 1896.

Scott, Robert E. *Mexican Government in Transition.* Urbana: University of Illinois Press, 1959.

Serrano Robles, Arturo. "La suplencia de la deficiencia de la queja cuando el acto reclamado se funda en leyes declaradas inconstitucionales." In *Problemas jurídicos de México,* pp. 47–61. Mexico City: Editorial Jus, 1953.

Simpson, Eyler N. *The* Ejido; *Mexico's Way Out.* Chapel Hill: University of North Carolina Press, 1937.

Somohano Flores, Mario. *Monografía sobre la suspensión del acto reclamado en el juicio de amparo.* Mexico City: Imprenta de Murguía, 1928.

Tannenbaum, Frank. *Mexico: The Struggle for Peace and Bread.* New York: Alfred A. Knopf, 1954.

Tena Ramírez, Felipe. *Derecho constitucional mexicano.* 3rd ed. Mexico City: Editorial Porrua, S.A., 1955.

————, ed. *Leyes fundamentales de México, 1808–1957.* Mexico City: Editorial Porrua, S. A., 1957.

Tocqueville, Alexis de. *Democracy in America.* Translated by Henry Reeve, rev. Francis Bowen, ed. Phillips Bradley. New York, Alfred A. Knopf, 1948.

Toro, Alfonso. *Historia de la Suprema Corte de Justicia de la Nación.* Mexico City, 1934.

Torre, Juan de la. *La Constitución federal de 1857; sus ediciones, reformas y leyes orgánicas, anotadas, concordadas y explicadas.* 2nd ed. Mexico City: Imprenta "El Fénix," 1896.

Trigo, Gaspar. *La suspensión en los juicios de amparo en materia obrera.* Mexico City: Ediciones Botas, 1940.

Trueba Urbina, Alberto, ed. *Ley de amparo reformada: Doctrina, legislación y jurisprudencia.* Mexico City: Editorial Porrua, S. A., 1950.

Trueba Urbina, Alberto. *Nueva jurisprudencia sobre suspensión del acto reclamado en el amparo; Administrativa, civil, penal y de trabajo.* Mexico City. Editorial Porrua, S. A., 1937.

————, and Jorge Trueba Barrera, eds. *Nueva legislación de amparo: Doctrina, textos y jurisprudencia. Código federal de procedimientos civiles. Ley orgánica del poder judicial federal.* 12th ed. Mexico City: Editorial Porrua, S.A., 1968.

Tucker, William P. *The Mexican Government Today.* Minneapolis: University of Minnesota Press, 1957.

Vallarta, Ignacio L. *Cuestiones constitucionales. Votos del C. Ignacio L. Vallarta, presidente de la Suprema Corte de Justicia en los negocios más notables.* 4 vols. Mexico City. Imprenta de Francisco Díaz de León, 1879–1883.

————. *El juicio de amparo y el Writ of Habeas Corpus: ensayo crítico-comparativo sobre esos recursos constitucionales.* Mexico City: Imprenta de Francisco Díaz de León, 1881.

Vance, John T. *The Background of Hispanic American Law: Legal Sources and Juridical Literature of Spain.* New York: Central Book Co., 1943.

————, and Helen L. Clagett. *A Guide to the Law and Legal Literature of Mexico.* Washington, D.C.: The Library of Congress, 1945.

Villers, M. G. *El sobreseimiento en los amparos administrativos de carácter fiscal: Estudio sobre la constitucionalidad y legalidad de la jurisprudencia de la segunda sala de la Suprema Corte de Justicia y de las disposiciones legales relativas.* Mexico City: Editorial Polis, 1935.

Zarco, Francisco. *Historia del congreso extraordinario constituyente, 1856–1857.* Mexico City: Fondo de Cultura Económica, 1956.

*Licentiate Theses*: Privately Printed.

Abarca Quintero, José. *El amparo contra laudos.* Universidad Nacional Autónoma de México. Mexico City, 1945.

Adame Cuevara, Luís. *La reforma de la constitución federal y la obligatoriedad de la jurisprudencia.* Universidad Nacional Autónoma de México. Mexico City: 1951.

Aguilar Arriaga, Manuel. *El amparo de México y sus antecedentes nacionales y extranjeros.* Universidad Nacional Autónoma de Mexico. Mexico City, 1942.

Aguilar y Maya, Marcelo. *Garantías constitucionales de la aplicación del derecho.* Universidad Nacional Autónoma de México. Mexico City, 1953.

Aguirre y Arguelles, Eugenio. *El sistema probatorio en materia de amparo.* Universidad Nacional Autónoma de México. Mexico City, 1943.

Alcaraz Verduzco, Marín. *La autoridad de cosa juzgada y la procedencia del recurso de queja en materia de amparo.* Universidad Nacional Autónoma de México. Mexico City, 1950.

Alcazar A., José. *De la acción establecida por la fracción I del artículo 103 de la constitución federal: Su naturaleza jurídica.* Universidad Nacional Autónoma de México. Mexico City: 1932.

Alfaro González, Lamberto. *La reparación constitucional.* Universidad Nacional Autónoma de México. Mexico City, 1950.

Alvarez del Castillo L., Enrique. *La legitimación para defender la constitucionalidad de las leyes: Interpretación del artículo 86 de la ley de amparo.* Universidad Nacional Autónoma de México. Mexico City, 1947.

Aranda Serrano, René. *La suplencia de la queja deficiente cuando el acto reclamado se funda en ley declarada inconstitucional por la jurisprudencia de la H. Suprema Corte de Justicia de la Nación.* Universidad Nacional Autónoma de México. Mexico City, 1954.

Aranda y Arana, Gustavo N. *El juicio de amparo y la suspensión del acto reclamado.* Universidad Nacional Autónoma de México. Mexico City, 1939.

Arceo Cortés, Manuel. *Lo que se resuelve en el amparo a través de sus sentencias.* Universidad Nacional Autónoma de México. Mexico City, 1933.

Arellano García, Carlos. *La queja por exceso o defecto en la ejecución de las resoluciones de amparo.* Universidad Nacional Autónoma de México. Mexico City, 1954.

Athie Gutiérrez, Amado. *El amparo en México y su repercución internacional.* Universidad Nacional Autónoma de México. Mexico City, 1949.

Aviña López, Eduardo. *La suspensión del acto reclamado en el juicio de amparo.* Universidad Nacional Autónoma de México. Mexico City, 1949.

Ayala Garza, Fernando. *El juicio de amparo y los derechos políticos.* Universidad Nacional Autónoma de México. Mexico City, 1943.

Beltrán Martínez, Antonio. *Comentarios a los antecedentes extranjeros y nacionales del juicio de amparo.* Universidad Nacional Autónoma de México. Mexico City, 1934.

Beltrán Rodríguez, Humberto H. *El fuero militar en relación con el amparo.* Universidad Nacional Autónoma de México. Mexico City, 1935.

Bolado Salinas, Lindorfo. *Los recursos en el juicio de amparo.* Universidad Nacional Autónoma de México. Mexico City, 1944.

Bonilla, Luis D. *Estudio crítico sobre el amparo indirecto.* Universidad Nacional Autónoma de México. Mexico City, 1937.

Brauer T., Max. *El amparo ante la ciencia procesal.* Universidad Nacional Autónoma de México. Mexico City, 1937.

Burgoa, Ignacio. *La supremacía jurídica del poder judicial de la federación en México.* Universidad Nacional Autónoma de México. Mexico City, 1939.

Bustamante, Luis Pablo. *La sentencia de amparo.* Escuela Libre de Derecho. Mexico City, 1949.

Cabrera Muñoz, Carlos. *Nuestro juicio de amparo y la Suprema Corte de Justicia de la Nación.* Universidad Nacional Autónoma de México. Mexico City, 1944.

Cáceres Losa, Joaquín. *La reparación constitucional, en juicios del órden civil, como medio preparatorio del juicio de garantías.* Universidad de Yucatán. Mérida, 1942.

Candiani Bodian, Jorge. *La reparación constitucional.* Universidad Nacional Autónoma de México. Mexico City, 1943.

Cano Angeles, Cecilio. *La suspensión del acto reclamado en el juicio de amparo.* Universidad Nacional Autónoma de México. Mexico City, 1945.

Cano Angeles, Luis. *El juez ante la ley inconstitucional.* Universidad Nacional Autónoma de México. Mexico City, 1953.

Canseco Fortis, Antonio. *El amparo y el artículo 27 constitucional.* Universidad Nacional Autónoma de México. Mexico City, 1950.

Canseco Noriega, Emilio. *El juicio de amparo en relación con la pequeña propiedad rural.* Universidad Nacional Autónoma de México. Mexico City, 1940.

Cantú Nuño, Guillermo. *La queja en el amparo.* Universidad Nacional Autónoma de México. Mexico City, 1946.

Caraza Escobedo, Rafael. *Los sistemas de defensa de la constitucionalidad en el derecho mexicano.* Universidad Nacional Autónoma de México. Mexico City, 1945.

Carsolio Pacheco, Juan Carlos. *Los sistemas de defensa constitucional.* Universidad Nacional Autónoma de México. Mexico City, 1949.

Castañeda del Villar, Salvador. *Ensayo sobre la suspensión del acto reclamado y de los efectos que produce como parte integrante del juicio de amparo.* Universidad Nacional Autónoma de México. Mexico City, 1937.

Castellanos Everardo, Milton. *La suspensión del acto reclamado: Insuficiente garantía de los derechos públicos individuales.* Universidad Nacional Autónoma de México. Mexico City, 1943.

Ceballos y Nápoles, Armando. *El órden público en el juicio de amparo.* Universidad Nacional Autónoma de México. Mexico City, 1951.

Clemente Arce, Homero. *El incidente de suspensión del acto reclamado en el amparo.* Universidad Nacional Autónoma de México. Mexico City, 1953.

Corona Blake, Sergio. *La degeneración del juicio de amparo: Causas, consecuencias y remedios.* Universidad Nacional Autónoma de México. Mexico City, 1941.

Cortes Macías, Daniel. *Algunas consideraciones procesales sobre la reparación constitucional.* Universidad Nacional Autónoma de México. Mexico City, 1955.

Cosio Díaz, Mario. *La queja en el amparo.* Universidad Nacional Autónoma de México. Mexico City, 1945.

Coss y Castillo, Alfredo. *Breves comentarios al incidente de suspensión en el amparo y en especial la suspensión previa fianza.* Universidad Nacional Autónoma de México. Mexico City, 1935.

Cuéllar, Francisco J. *La competencia en el juicio de amparo.* Universidad Nacional Autónoma de México. Mexico City, 1944.

Dávia González, Melchor. *Situación jurídica del quejoso en el juicio constitucional de amparo.* Universidad Nacional Autónoma de México. Mexico City, 1944.

Delgado Bernal, Jorge. *La jurisprudencia obligatoria.* Universidad Nacional Autónoma de México. Mexico City, 1952.

Delgado Flores, Melita. *Orígen y evolución del juicio de amparo.* Universidad Nacional Autónoma de México. Mexico City, 1936.

Deschamps Blanco, Rafael. *El juicio de amparo, como medio indirecto del control del sistema federal.* Escuela Libre de Derecho. Mexico City, 1958.

Díaz Rojo, Arturo. *La reparación constitucional como protectora de la garantía de la aplicación de la ley.* Universidad Nacional Autónoma de México. Mexico City, 1942.

Díaz Sautto, José. *De las improcedencias y causas de sobreseimiento en el juicio de amparo.* Universidad Nacional Autónoma de México. Mexico City, 1935.

Echeverría y Barrutia, Salvador. *El amparo contra leyes.* Universidad Nacional Autónoma de México. Mexico City, 1943.

Espínola Samperio, José. *La fianza y el juicio de amparo.* Universidad Nacional Autónoma de México. Mexico City, 1938.

Farías, Luis M. *Las reformas constitucionales de 1950 en materia de amparo.* Universidad Nacional Autónoma de México. Mexico City, 1952.

Fix Zamudio, Héctor. *La garantía jurisdiccional de la Constitución mexicana: Ensayo de una estructuración procesal del amparo.* Universidad Nacional Autónoma de México. Mexico City, 1955.

Gamas Colorado, Hilario. *Procedencia del amparo en materia de derechos políticos.* Universidad Nacional Autónoma de México. Mexico City, 1934.

García Avalos, Pablo. *Procedencia del juicio de amparo en materia agraria cuando se afecte la pequeña propiedad agrícola en explotación para dotar ejidos.* Universidad Nacional Autónoma de México. Mexico City, 1943.

Garduño Ballesteros, Luís. *El juicio constitucional de amparo en materia obrera.* Universidad Nacional Autónoma de México. Mexico City, 1941.

Garza García, Cecilio. *La improcedencia y el sobreseimiento en el amparo: Breves consideraciones.* Universidad Nacional Autónoma de México. Mexico City, 1943.

Gavaldon S., Ignacio. *El juicio de amparo y los writs americanos.* Universidad Nacional Autónoma de México. Mexico City, 1937.

Gómez del Castillo, Fernando. *Algunas consideraciones sobre la suspen-*

*sion del acto reclamado en el juicio de amparo.* Escuela Libre de Derecho. Mexico City, 1955.

Gómez Guerra Morales, Miguel. *Naturaleza y efectos jurídicos de la sentencia de amparo.* Universidad Nacional Autónoma de México. Mexico City, 1950.

González Múzquiz, José G. *El Ministerio Público Federal como parte en el juicio de amparo.* Universidad Nacional Autónoma de México. Mexico City, 1948.

González Navarro, Moisés. *Vallarta y su ambiente político-jurídico.* Universidad Nacional Autónoma de México. Mexico City, 1949.

González Treviño, Evelio H. *El amparo contra leyes.* Universidad Nacional Autónoma de México. Mexico City, 1932.

Guerra Polledo, José Antonio. *La extensión del amparo por la violación de las garantías individuales en relación con las fracciones II y III del artículo 103 constitucional: Breve estudio.* Universidad Nacional Autónoma de México. Mexico City, 1950.

Guilbot Serros, Alberto. *Reinstitución del juicio de amparo en materia agraria.* Universidad Nacional Autónoma de México. Mexico City, 1956.

Hernández García, Armando. *Suspensión en el amparo de actos que se consuman en plazo perentorio.* Universidad Nacional Autónoma de México. Mexico City, 1947.

Hernández Duque, Jorge. *La interposición del amparo por las personas morales.* Universidad Nacional Autónoma de México. Mexico City, 1936.

Hernández Ramírez, María del Carmen. *Amparo contra leyes.* Universidad Nacional Autónoma de México. Mexico City, 1954.

Herrera Bañuelos, Fernando. *Consideraciones sobre la representación de la autoridad administrativa federal como responsable en el juicio de amparo.* Universidad Nacional Autónoma de México. Mexico City, 1956.

Hoyos Espinosa, Enrique de. *El problema del rezago en la Suprema Corte de Justicia de la Nación.* Universidad Nacional Autónoma de México. Mexico City, 1946.

Irueste German, Antonio. *La reparación constitucional y el juicio de amparo directo.* Universidad Nacional Autónoma de México. Mexico City, 1938.

Islas Vázquez, Gabriel. *El estado como promovente del juicio de amparo.* Universidad Nacional Autónoma de México. Mexico City, 1940.

Jaime Palacios, Rubén. *El estado como quejoso en el juicio de amparo.* Universidad Nacional Autónoma de México. Mexico City, 1950.

León Espinosa, Octavio. *El amparo como protección a la pequeña propiedad inafectable.* Universidad Nacional Autónoma de México. Mexico City, 1946.

Lievana Palma, Gilberto. *La suspensión provisional en el juicio de amparo.* Universidad Nacional Autónoma de México. Mexico City, 1948.

Lima Loera, Juan de. *De la ejecución de las sentencias de amparo.* Universidad Nacional Autónoma de México. Mexico City, 1938.

Lorandi Aguilar, Héctor. *La pequeña propiedad agrícola y el amparo.* Universidad Nacional Autónoma de México. Mexico City, 1944.

Loria Pérez, Felipe. *El amparo es una imitación que tuvo como fuente "La democracia en América" por Alexis de Tocqueville: Reforma que es necesaria para los casos de suspensión de oficio.* Universidad Nacional Autónoma de México. Mexico City, 1942.

Luna Vizueto, Jesús. *Comentarios sobre la suspensión del acto reclamado en el juicio de amparo y el procedimiento para hacer efectivas las garantías y contragarantías, otorgadas con motivo de esa suspensión.* Universidad Nacional Autónoma de México. Mexico City, 1940.

Marrón Viveros, Federico. *Alcance de las sentencias dictadas en los juicios de amparo en relación con terceros.* Universidad Nacional Autónoma de México. Mexico City, 1956.

Medina Ibarra, Gustavo. *El amparo como recurso de casación en el sistema jurisdiccional mexicano.* Universidad Nacional Autónoma de México. Mexico City, 1942.

Medina y Aguilar, Víctor Manuel. *El amparo en materia agraria.* Universidad Nacional Autónoma de México. Mexico City, 1946.

Mejía Moscoso, Mariano. *Interposición del amparo por la Secretaría de Hacienda.* Universidad Nacional Autónoma de México. Mexico City, 1940.

Méndez Mansilla, Miguel Angel. *La garantía de la exacta aplicación de la ley.* Universidad Nacional Autónoma de México. Mexico City, 1934.

Morales Rodríguez, Victoria. *El amparo contra leyes a la luz de las reformas de 1951.* Universidad Nacional Autónoma de México. Mexico City, 1951.

Namihira Heredin, Andrés. *Procedencia del amparo contra leyes inconstitucionales.* Universidad Nacional Autónoma de México. Mexico City, 1950.

Novaro, Octavio. *El amparo político.* Universidad Nacional Autónoma de México. Mexico City, 1934.

Núñez Olmos, Hortensia. *El amparo y la realidad social mexicana.* Universidad Nacional Autónoma de México. Mexico City, 1953.

Olivares Vite, Augusto. *Estado actual del problema del amparo contra leyes, en la doctrina y en la jurisprudencia.* Universidad Nacional Autónoma de México. Mexico City, 1936.

Osorno Castro, Fernando. *Violaciones de fondo y del procedimiento en el juicio de amparo.* Universdad Nacional Autónoma de México. Mexico City, 1941.

Otero Gama, Carmen. *El amparo como un juicio de garantías colectivas.* Universidad Nacional Autónoma de México. Mexico City, 1937.

Pablo y García, Víctor de. *La suspensión del acto reclamado en el juicio de amparo, su origen y diversos aspectos.* Universidad Nacional Autónoma de México. Mexico City, 1943.

Padilla Acevedo, Arturo. *Los efectos del amparo en las sentencias civiles.* Universidad Nacional Autónoma de México. Mexico City, n.d.

Paez Stille, Carlos. *La pequeña propiedad y el ejido: Su protección mediante el amparo.* Universidad Nacional Autónoma de México. Mexico City, 1952.

Patiño Escalante, Alfredo. *Nuestro juicio de amparo: Antecedentes y proyecciones.* Universidad Nacional Autónoma de México. Mexico City, 1953.

Pellicer Cámara, Juan. *Algunas consideraciones acerca de la procedencia del amparo contra leyes.* Universidad Nacional Autónoma de México. Mexico City, 1936.

Peniche López, Efraín. *El amparo de México y su doctrina.* Universidad Nacional Autónoma de México. Mexico City, 1939.

Pérez Gavilán Villegas, Héctor. *Intervención del Congreso en el amparo contra leyes.* Universidad Nacional Autónoma de México. Mexico City, 1944.

Pirrón León, Alejandro A. *Los recursos en materia de amparo.* Universidad Nacional Autónoma de México. Mexico City, n.d.

Portillo Salvador, Rosendi. *¿Puede el estado pedir amparo?* Universidad Nacional Autónoma de México. Mexico City, 1940.

Preciat Segura, Jesús Armando. *El amparo directo en materia de trabajo.* Universidad Nacional Autónoma de México. Mexico City, 1950.

Ramírez Romo, Agustín. *El amparo a la pequeña propiedad y diversos aspectos agrarios.* Universidad Nacional Autónoma de México. Mexico City, 1947.

Rangel y Vásquez, Manuel. *El control de la constitucionalidad de las leyes y el juicio de amparo de garantías en el estado federal: La defensa integral de la constitución.* Universidad Nacional Autónoma de México. Mexico City: Editorial Cultura, 1952.

Rodríguez Real, Adolfo. *Conflicto entre la federación y los estados, en los que no procede el juicio de amparo.* Universidad Nacional Autónoma de México. Mexico City, 1937.

Sandoval, Jesús R. *El amparo contra leyes.* Universidad Nacional Autónoma de México. Mexico City, 1939.

Santillán Ortiz, Lamberto. *El sistema de control constitucional en México y en los Estados Unidos del Norte.* Universidad Nacional Autónoma de México. Mexico City, 1944.

Siller García, Humberto. *La suspensión del acto reclamado en los amparos directos.* Universidad Nacional Autónoma de México. Mexico City, 1945.

Sosa Cervantes, Mario. *Las partes en el juicio de amparo.* Universidad Nacional Autónoma de México. Mexico City, 1943.

Tamborrell, José G. *Procedencia del amparo por violación de derechos políticos.* Universidad Nacional Autónoma de México. Mexico City, 1943.

Tellez Cruces, Agustín. *El amparo indirecto en materia civil: Actos en el juicio cuya ejecución sea de imposible reparación.* Universidad Nacional Autónoma de México. Mexico City, 1944.

Torres Torija, Angel. *El hecho superveniente en la suspensión del acto reclamado.* Universidad Nacional Autónoma de México. Mexico City, 1942.

Valdes Flores, Enrique. *Ensayo jurídico sobre la sentencia de amparo.* Universidad Nacional Autónoma de México. Mexico City, 1942.

Valdes Villarreal, Miguel. *Amparo contra leyes.* Universidad Nacional Autónoma de México. Mexico City, 1951.

Vergara Garza, Manuel. *El amparo político.* Universidad Nacional Autónoma de México. Mexico City, 1936.

Villar, Rafael R. *El amparo contra leyes y breve apreciación de las ejecutorias de la Suprema Corte de Justicia de la Nación dictadas sobre esta materia.* Universidad Nacional Autónoma de México. Mexico City, 1935.

Villarreal Garza, Juan Ernesto. *El juicio de amparo y la suspensión del acto reclamado en materia de trabajo.* Universidad Nacional Autónoma de México. Mexico City, 1941.

Zavala de la Garza, Gerardo. *La condena en costas en el juicio de amparo.* Universidad Nacional Autónoma de México. Mexico City, 1949.

*Articles, Periodicals, Pamphlets*

Azuela, Mariano. "Trayectoria y destino del juicio de amparo." *El foro: Órgano de la barra mexicana* 4th series, nos. 4–6 (April–December 1954), pp. 125–149.

Burgoa, Ignacio. "La eficacia del juicio de amparo. El recurso de queja por defecto o exceso de ejecución y el incidente de incumplimiento de las resoluciones de amparo de fondo suspensionales." *Nuevas generaciones de abogados* no. 74 (July 1953), pp. 10–22.

―――. "El incidente de incumplimiento o desobediencia de las ejecutorias de amparo." *Nuevas generaciones de abogados* no. 75 (August 1953), pp. 18–24.

―――. "La suspensión en los juicios de amparo contra actos de autoridad judicial que afecten la libertad personal." *Revista de la facultad de derecho de México* 20 (October–December 1955): 167.

Cabrera A., Lucio. "History of the Mexican Judiciary." 11 *Miami Law Quarterly* 439 (Summer 1957).

Carreño, Franco. "Homenaje a Rejón." *La justicia* 24 (March 1952): 11292–11294.

Carrillo Flores, Antonio. "Algunas reflexiones sobre el juicio de amparo." *La justicia* 18 (March 1951): 10930–10937.

Cortés Figueroa, Carlos. "Sobre la administración de justicia federal." *Revista de la facultad de derecho de México* 7 (October–December 1957): 178.

Díaz Soto y Gama, Antonio. *Indicación motivada de las reformas que convendría hacer al código de procedimientos federales en el capítulo destinado al juicio de amparo*. Mexico City: Imprenta "El Arte Moderno," 1906.

Echánove Trujillo, Carlos A. "El juicio de amparo mexicano." *Revista de la facultad de derecho de México* 1 (January–June 1951): 91–116.

―――. *La obra jurídica de Manuel C. Rejón, padre del amparo*. Mexico City, 1937.

―――. *Rejón, jurista y constituyente. La Constitución nacional de 1824. El amparo yucateco de 1841. El amparo nacional de 1847* [*Revista de derecho y ciencias sociales*]. Mexico City: Jus, 1940.

Fernández del Castillo, Germán. "El amparo como derecho del hombre en la Declaración Universal." *Revista de derecho y ciencias sociales* 37 (January–March 1957): 61–69.

————. *Los efectos restitutorios del amparo con relación a tercero* [Revista de derecho y ciencias sociales]. Mexico City: Jus, 1942.

————. *La sentencia de amparo y sus extralimitaciones* [Revista de derecho y ciencias sociales]. Mexico City: Jus, 1944.

Fraga, Gabino. "Carta del Licenciado Gabino Fraga." In "Sorpresivas reformas a las leyes de amparo y orgánica del poder judicial y debate al respecto." *El foro: Órgano de la barra mexicana* 4th series, nos. 20–21 (January–June 1958): 184–187.

García, Trinidad. "¿Es el amparo defensa constitucional extraordinaria?" *Revista general de derecho y jurisprudencia* 2 (1931): 145–176.

García Figueroa, Sofía. "El juicio de amparo ante las leyes de emergencia." *Boletín jurídico-militar* 2nd series, nos. 9–10 (July–August 1953) 326–332.

Gaxiola, F. Jorge. *León Guzman y la Constitución de 57.* Mexico City: El Foro, 1957.

————. *Orígenes del sistema presidencial, génesis del Acta Constitutiva de 1824.* Mexico City: Imprenta Universitaria, 1952.

————. "Ponencia del Licenciado F. Jorge Gaxiola relativa a las recientes reformas en materia de amparo." In "Sorpresivas reformas a las leyes de amparo y orgánica del poder judicial y debate al respecto." *El foro: Órgano de la barra mexicana* 4th series, nos. 20-21 (January–June 1958), pp. 161–170, 172–177.

————. *¿Una estátua para Rejón? Tres artículos sobre un mismo tema.* Mexico City, 1955.

Herrera y Lasso, Manuel. "Los constructores del amparo." *Foro: Revista de derecho y ciencias sociales, órgano del colegio de abogados de la Laguna* no. 4 (October 1947), pp. 45–51.

Herrerias Telleria, Armando. "Orígenes externos del juicio de amparo." *Revista de la facultad de derecho de México* 5 (July–September 1955): 35–63.

Landerreche Obregón, Juan. "Sobre el amparo político." *Jus: Revista de derecho y ciencias sociales* 26 (January–March 1952): 15–42.

León Orantes, Romeo. "La caducidad en materia de amparo." *La justicia* 18 (April 1951): 10992–10993.

Martínez Báez, Antonio. "Versión relativa a las diversas intervenciones en la reunión de estudio de las leyes de amparo y orgánica del poder judicial federal." In "Sorpresivas reformas a las leyes de amparo y orgánica del poder judicial y debate al respecto." *El foro: Órgano de la barra mexicana* 4th series, nos. 20–21 (January–June 1958), pp. 195–198.

Medina, Hilario. "El amparo de Rejón." *La justicia* 24 (April 1952): 11334–11339.

Medina, Ignacio. "La sentencia civil impugnada en amparo en el derecho mexicano." *Foro de México: Órgano del centro de investigaciones y trabajos jurídicos* no. 54 (September 1957), pp. 20–33.

Murillo, Guilebaldo. "La ejecución de las ejecutorias de amparo en perjuicio de tercero." *El foro: Órgano de la barra mexicana* 4th series, nos. 4–6 (April–December 1954), pp. 151–180.

Olea y Leyva, Teófilo. "Jurisprudencia obligatoria y suplencia de la queja deficiente en materia penal, administrativa y civil." *La justicia* 18 (April 1951): 10980–10989.

Palacios, J. Ramón. "La jurisprudencia obligatoria." *La justicia* 24 (March 1952): 11295–11297.

———. "El mito del amparo." *Foro de México: Órgano del centro de investigaciones y trabajos jurídicos* no. 48 (March 1957), pp. 92–101, and no. 49 (April 1957), pp. 46–62.

Pallares, Eduardo. "Jurisprudencia errónea de la H. Suprema Corte de Justicia." *Foro de México: Órgano del centro de investigaciones y trabajos jurídicos* no. 26 (May 1955), pp. 3–8.

Peniche López, Vicente. "Alrededor del concepto de autoridad en el amparo." *La justicia* 18 (April 1951): 10990–10991.

Rabasa, Oscar. "Diferencias entre el juicio de amparo y los recursos constitucionales norteamericanos." *El foro: Órgano de la barra mexicana* no. 3 (September 1947), 253–274.

"Reformas al amparo contra leyes." *Revista de la facultad de derecho de México* 7 (October–December 1957): 159–162.

Rodríguez Adamo, Julian. "El problema agrario: Bases constitucionales, realizaciones, estado actual." In *La constitucion de 1917 y la economía mexicana: Cursos de invierno 1917*, edited by Antonio Martínez Báez et al. Mexico City: Universidad Nacional Autónoma de México, 1958.

Rodríguez Gómez, Jesús. "Sorpresivas deformas a las leyes de amparo y orgánica del poder judicial federal y debate al respecto." *El foro: Órgano de la barra mexicana* 4th series, nos. 20–21 (January–June 1958), pp. 157–161.

Tena Ramírez, Felipe. "El amparo de estricto derecho, orígenes, expansión, inconvenientes." *El foro: Órgano de la barra mexicana* 4th series, no. 2 (October–December 1953), pp. 21–41.

————. "El control de la constitucionalidad bajo la vigencia de la constitución de 1824." *Revista de la barra mexicana* 12 (April–June 1950): 31–38.

Yllanes Ramos, Fernando. "El amparo. El mejor instrumento de defensa de los derechos individuales. Antecedentes, experiencias y análisis comparativos del amparo mexicano." *El foro: Órgano de la barra mexicana* 4th series, nos. 8–10 (April–December 1955), pp. 63–90.

————. "Reformas inconstitucionales al amparo." *Revista de la facultad de derecho de México* 7 (October–December 1957): 186–196.

*Interviews*

Licenciado Ignacio Burgoa, 6 December 1958 and December 1958, Mexico City.

Licenciado Raúl Carrancá y Trujillo, 14 October 1958, Mexico City.

Licenciado F. Jorge Gaxiola, 13 December 1958, Mexico City.

Licenciado Antonio Martínez Báez, 14 October 1958, and 23 October 1958, Mexico City.

Ministro Agapito Pozo, 5 November 1958, Mexico City.

Licenciado Arturo Serrano Robles, 11 December 1958, Mexico City.

Secretarial staff of the Suprema Corte de Justicia during October, November, and December 1958, Mexico City.

Ministro Felipe Tena Ramírez, 29 October 1958, Mexico City.

# INDEX

Acosta Romo, Fausto: opposition of, to 1957 *amparo* amendments, 71
*Acta Constitutiva de la Federación Mexicana*: 6
*Acta de Reformas*: *amparo* in, 22, 26; mentioned, 12
administrative regulations: constitutionality of, 199–200
Agrarian Code: provision for presidential authority in, 132–133; rights of landowners under, 135; admissibility of *amparo* in, 136–137
agrarian reform: in Constitution of 1917, 48, 93
*agraviado*. SEE injured party
Alamán, Lucas: 34
Alemán, Miguel: proposals of, for reorganization of judiciary, 66; mentioned, 149
Alemán amendments: 64
amendment proposals of 1944: delegation of jurisdiction under, 61–62; criticism of, 62; withdrawal of, 63
*amicus curiae*: in Amparo Law, 190, 207
*amparo*: origins of, 12, 27–31, 32, 33; first appearance of, 13; characteristics of, 17, 37; in *Acta de Reformas*, 21–25; scope of, 23, 79, 93, 94, 112, 117, 119, 123–124, 129, 155, 254, 271; in Constitution of 1857, 36, 41, 48; and regulation of federal-state relations, 36, 50–51, 104; trial by jury in, 37–38; jurisdiction in, 37, 49, 60, 91–92, 132, 138–140, 162–163, 184–185, 201; admissibility of, 37, 94–95, 97, 101, 103, 104–105, 107, 108, 109, 111, 129, 132, 161, 162, 182, 217, 269; implementation of, 42; legislative regulation of, 42–44; amendment

of constitutional provisions relating to, 45; in Constitution of 1917, 46, 47, 48–49; and principle of division into direct and indirect, 50; and individual guarantees, 50, 93, 107, 272; and cassation, 50, 272; limitations on, 51, 104, 124, 131, 140, 146, 271; in *Ley Reglamentaria* . . ., 52; compared to *súplica*, 52, 53; inadmissibility of, 52, 95, 96–97, 99, 100, 108–109, 122, 135, 153–154, 155–156, 160, 161; parties to, 52, 108, 207; inadequacy of, 53; establishment of *jurisprudencia* for, 54; and judicial amendments of 1928, 54–56; and landowners, 56, 132, 134, 136; as constitutional defense, 61, 89, 111, 130, 268, 272; procedural inactivity in, 66; applicability of, 94, 111; exclusions from, 96, 132, 136, 152–156; res judicata in, 99; initiation of, 104, 106; beneficiaries of, 107; traditional theory of, 110; concordance theory of, 116; expansion of, 120–121, 126–127; and political rights, 130, 152–156, 161; restrictive amendments to, 131; in *Ley de Prevenciones*, 143–144, 146; in national emergencies, 146; and foreign relations, 162–163; rule of *stricti juris* in, 185; Federal Public Ministry in, 211–212, 221; summary form of, 232; forms of appeal in, 245; functions of, 267; and judicial review, 267; prohibitions on use of, 268–269
—administrative: injured third parties in, 210–211; judgments in, 239; *stricti juris* in, 271
—against laws: described, 164, 165; *jurisprudencia* in, 165; inadmissibility